JUSTICE AS MISSION:
AN AGENDA FOR
THE CHURCH

JUSTICE AS MISSION: AN AGENDA FOR THE CHURCH

Essays in Appreciation of Marjorie and Cyril Powles

EDITED BY

Christopher Lind   Terry Brown

TRINITY PRESS
Burlington, Ontario, Canada

Testimony
for Marjorie & Cyril

that once on water walked
on water still
walks He
in atmosphere
so dense in miracle
they here found fins
for flying

Joy Kogawa

The publication of this volume is sponsored by the Ecumenical Forum of Canada.

The Ecumenical Forum is a Canadian centre for dialogue, education and training on contemporary approaches to mission and ecumenism. Through its publications program, the Forum seeks to encourage ecumenical dialogue, in Canada and internationally, on current issues of mission, world development and social justice.

The books published, however, reflect the opinions of their authors and are not meant to represent the official position of the Forum.

Editorial Board:

Pauline Bradbook
Willard G. Oxtoby
Virginia A. Peacock
Rhea M. Whitehead

ISBN 0 920413 12 9

© 1985 by Trinity Press

Trinity Press
960 Gateway
Burlington, Ontario
L7L 5K7   Canada

Printed in Canada

Contents

VI War and Peace

Appendix

Introduction

This book is about the future of the church — the Canadian church, the church in the world, the church of God. It is a hopeful book. It believes in the Christian message and its relevance for our time. It lives in the spirit of the Resurrection, hoping, praying and working for the realization of God's justice on earth. But it is a critical book. The writers here are not content with the performance of our churches to date. We have sinned and are in need of repentance. We have been unfaithful to our calling. Faced with the cries of the poor and the oppressed, we have turned away and crossed to the other side of the road.

In part our sins are cultural, for our own culture conditions our reaction to the world. The first section deals with some of the many sides of this reality. Ray Whitehead's paper, based on his Asian experience, shows how our cultural assumptions conceal from us the way we use our power, and reveals the damage this can do. Arturo Chacón's paper, in turn, gives us a glimpse of what is being damaged and how that finds its own expression in the life of the people. Terry Brown's paper shows us how this damage continues in the life of independent churches even after the colonizers have gone. John Rowe's paper describes cultures that are defined by class and calls us to account for our unwillingness to take seriously the cleavages that exist within our own communities.

One of the cultural sins of First World Christians is the persistent assumption that God's truth exists in some exclusive way in First World society and that it is therefore the responsibility of those Christians to spread this truth to those less fortunate (namely, the peoples of the Third World). In this volume we have tried to let Third World Christians speak for themselves. One result is that the papers here assembled include the voices of four continents. Another result is that we have an entire chapter devoted to the experience of a Third World church. Some may be puzzled by our designation of the church in Japan as a Third World church. To that we can only respond that we are following the lead of Cyril Powles who has often remarked that, while Japan may have emerged as a Second World nation, the experience of Japanese Christians is the experience of a Third World church. In keeping with this Third World experience, John Takeda and John Howes write as Christians reflecting on the Japanese experience, while Yuzo Ota writes as a Japanese outside the church.

If we have sinned in the past and yet find hope for the future, we surely must be clear as to the foundations for the mission of the church. The next section has this concern in mind. Don Thompson and Virginia Peacock review recent changes in theological education and theological thinking. They suggest changes necessary to maintain continuity with the church's historical task of witnessing to justice in the world. Roger Hutchinson considers the changing strategies and emphases in the mission of the Canadian church. His question is how we determine priorities in mission at a time of shrinking financial resources. Gregory Baum renews the ecumenical debate by asking whether the emphasis on justice as mission doesn't cut across the older denominational lines, making new forms of cooperation possible.

The fourth section of the book deals with one of the most urgent and contentious issues facing Christians today — the place of women in the church. It is at one and the same time a question of justice, as women demand equality, and a question of mission, as women experience God in their struggles and call the church to be with them. Mary Rose D'Angelo deals with the question of language and whether faithful witness can be identified with traditional or more contemporary forms of speech. Christopher Lind describes the other problems that are revealed when the Church resists experimentation with inclusive liturgical forms. Pauline Bradbrook points to the need for women to know their own history. Perhaps the dismantling of older organizations for women such as Anglican Church Women have not served the interests of women at all. A continuous question throughout this section is whether women as a group have an identifiable culture. Do women do things differently than men? Jeanne Rowles suggests that in her experience they do and that national church headquarters are organized along male lines — to the detriment of the church as a whole. At a time of growing acceptance of the ordination of women, at least in the non-Roman Catholic world, Donna Hunter and Elizabeth Wensley ask what is happening to the ministry of the laity. Do we not need to rethink the mission of the church in terms of the mission of the whole church?

The fifth chapter deals with the role of the church in issues of economic justice. The first paper in this chapter is a challenge issued by four experienced workers from a skid row mission. Reflecting on their experience in a traditional social ministry of the church, they challenge the basis of this work as an act of charity. By contrast, they suggest that the mission of the church is to call society to account for those economic patterns that produce an embarrassment of riches for some, while others are sent hungry away. While the first paper calls us to account for our economy, the second calls us to account for our history. In this case Janet Silman points to a role for the churches in calling Canadian society to account for the way in which its laws have systematically discriminated against Indian women. Brian Ruttan identifies some new ways in which the Canadian churches have begun to identify their mission with regard to the formation and critique of public policy. Lee Cormie identifies some of the resources in the history of the Canadian church and society that are supporting the Canadian Catholic bishops in their evangelical attempt to raise up the justice issue in the current economic debate. In a similar vein, but writing from the English experience, Ronald Preston calls for and gives an example of the kind of critique the church is in a position to deliver on current free market debates.

The sixth and final chapter deals with war and peace. Many Christians are already convinced that the churches have a role to play in this debate, but there is little agreement about what that role should be. Ernie Best has some suggestions based on his review of the role of the churches in this century. Jim Endicott also has some suggestions based on his own experience of some of the most significant wars of the same period — namely, World War I, World War II, the Chinese Revolution and the Korean War. Reiko Shimada also reflects on experience, but this time it is the Japanese experience of nuclear war. Her descriptions of how the Japanese YWCA works at the issue of war and peace is a challenge to us all. Finally, Don Grayston brings the issue close to home by linking our tolerance of violence as a way to solve domestic disputes and our tolerance for violence as a way to solve international disputes.

This book was first conceived as a way of honouring two outstanding Canadian Christians, Marjorie and Cyril Powles. As we began to plan the volume, though, it rapidly became clear that to write a book about them would be unfaithful to the goals they have set for themselves. Rather, the greatest way to honour them would be to continue to work in the direction in which they have pointed us. In order that you might understand something of their lives, though, Terry Brown has written a short biography, which is included in the appendix.

All their lives Marjorie and Cyril have pushed and prodded the church to be open, attentive, and responsive to the Gospel call for justice in our mutual relationships. They have constantly worked to revise the church's agenda in this direction. It is for this reason that each of the papers in this volume has taken up the question: What is the agenda for the church?

Some readers may be looking for a more direct consideration of the traditional understanding of mission as evangelism, or conversion to the faith. For this we would refer them to an article written by Cyril Powles himself, entitled "Towards a Theology of Mission for Today." It is available from the World Mission Office of the Anglican Church of Canada, 600 Jarvis Street, Toronto, Ont. M4Y 2J6. In many ways the articles printed here follow the lead of that paper. After a lifetime of missionary endeavour the Powles have concluded that justice is the mission of the church and that faithfulness to that vision will create its own disciples.

As editors we are in debt to many people. First of all, we are indebted to the writers whose willingness to contribute original material of such high quality has made the project possible. Secondly, we are indebted to the editorial committee who laboured for two years designing a process to facilitate matters and doing more work at the editorial stage than was proper. We are also indebted to the staff of the office of the provost of Trinity College, Toronto. Mrs. Maggie Grisdale, Ms. Kartini Rivers and Ms. Ella Fox all worked with energy, grace and efficiency, correcting our errors and making voluminous correspondence possible. We also wish to thank the provost of Trinity College, Dr. Kenneth Hare, and the Corporation of Trinity College. Through the encouragement of the provost, the Corporation made a generous and early contribution that has helped make the publication of this book possible.

It is appropriate to close by expressing our gratitude to the Ecumenical Forum of Canada and particularly to its Co-Director, Michael Cooke. The Ecumenical Forum has helped provide funds to enable publication, but what is especially gratifying to us is that the Ecumenical Forum has been willing to act as literary agent and co-publisher. Taking on this burden has saved the editors from a task for which we have little patience and less skill.

Christopher Lind,\
Terry Brown,\
Editors.\
July 1, 1984.

I
Christianity Across Cultures

Neocolonialism in the Third World Church

Terry Brown

Two Brief Sketches:

An indigenous Third World bishop comes to Canada, England, or the United States on a deputation tour. He speaks at a variety of church gatherings, both on the parish and ecumenical levels. The theme of his talks is the autonomy, creativity, and self-sacrifice of the Third World church. Now that the missionaries have all gone home, the church there is no longer European, but has become genuinely indigenous in its worship, ministry, and organization. The local church is learning to depend on itself and its own resources rather than on handouts from overseas. Things are looking very good. The child that the missionaries so carefully tutored has grown into an adult. The church is alive, filled with the Holy Spirit. Indeed, it will soon be ready to send out missionaries of its own.

Two months later:

The same bishop has returned home to his Third World diocese. It is time to make a parish visit to a village church some ten miles down the road. The bishop climbs into his late model chauffeur-driven English sedan and, episcopal flag fluttering in the breeze, drives to the village. He is met at the village by a choir of children who greet him with a song. All go to the church for the service. Although few in the village understand the language, the service is in English, since the bishop is from a different language area and cannot understand the local language. The servers (a thurifer, crucifer, and several others, all male and dressed in red cassocks and white cottas) are very nervous; one of them smiles — the bishop loses his temper and cuffs him on the ear. The bishop preaches about self-sacrifice.

After the service, there is a village meeting. One of the village elders points out that the village is very poor, lacks good drinking water and that its youth are all leaving for town. Can the church do something? Would it be possible to have a development project? The bishop explains that since independence, development has become the responsibility of the government, not the church. The church has no money to give away; besides that, the concern of the church is spiritual life. Jesus teaches us that we have to sacrifice in life. This is what the cross is all about. You will have to learn to support yourselves. He reminds the elder that he has heard that people in the village have not been attending church every day and that there is a problem with drunkenness. He reminds the people how important prayer is and that drunkenness is a sin. He reminds them that the village has not yet paid all of its apportionment to the diocesan budget. He ends the meeting with his blessing, all kneeling.

He then goes to dinner at the priest's house. One of the priest's small flock of chickens (kept especially for events such as this one) has been killed and the meal is a good one. It is the first fresh meat that the priest and his family have eaten in several weeks, though by the time the bishop and the priest are finished, there is little left for the women and children. The priest complains that he has received no pay from either the people or the diocese for four months and that he has no money to buy soap, tea, clothes or to pay school fees. The bishop tells him that the policy of the diocese is self-support and that the people are supposed to pay him. What is wrong with his ministry that the people do not pay him? The priest says he wants to move to town to take a government job to support his family. The bishop reminds him of his ordination vows; he cannot become a "worker priest" without the bishop's permission. He reminds him that sacrifice is a part of the Christian life.

The bishop returns to town in the freshly polished car, which the chauffeur has washed during the visit, to his large house, the last expatriate bishop's episcopal palace. He sits down to another meal, prepared for him and his family by their four houseboys. After dinner, he retires to his study. He sits down at his new word processor, purchased on his last trip overseas, to jot down a few things to say tomorrow on his annual visit to the theological college. There is trouble there. The students have gone on strike over their rations of rice and tinned fish. If they are going to be priests in this diocese, they will have to learn obedience.

Telling these two stories immediately makes one vulnerable to the charge of having a colonialist attitude. I, a First World white male, presume to criticize the Third World indigenous church. Yet, I believe that the criticism falls flat. I have told the above two stories not simply from my own First World perspective, but from the perspective of large numbers of powerless Third World Christians who are oppressed by their own neocolonial churches. The above sketches are not taken from my experience in one part of the Third World only, but from talking with powerless and voiceless Christians from many parts of the Third World, including Asia, Africa, and the Pacific.[1] The internal struggles in many churches in Latin America make it clear that neocolonialism is also a problem there.[2] So this essay seeks to express not just my own frustration with neocolonialism in the Third World church, but also the frustration that very many Third World peoples themselves feel. However, it must be emphasized that not all (nor even the majority) of the leadership of the church in the Third World is neocolonial — indeed, in some parts of the church, particularly where hierarchies have been conscientized by a struggle against oppressive governments (for example, the Roman Catholic hierarchy in Brazil), ecclesiastical neocolonialism is virtually non-existent. In such situations, the hierarchy is positively liberating.

The link between western European missionary expansion and colonial economic, political and cultural expansion has been well-documented and almost accepted as commonplace.[3] Most missionaries of that time consciously or unconsciously believed in the link although there were always a few prophetic ones who rejected the alliance. These proclaimed the Gospel's condemnation of exploitation, racism and dependency. Eventually their vision of the "younger churches" came to include the development of self-government, indigenous leadership, creative use of the local culture and, ultimately, full autonomy in the body of Christ. Today this view of Third World churches has become very widely accepted, both in the First and Third Worlds, though not without a continuing struggle. (It is ironic that while Protestant ecumenical missionary organizations put forward this view of the "younger churches" very strongly in the early twentieth century, their heir, the World Council of Churches, found it difficult to fully appreciate the support Chinese Christians gave to the Chinese Revolution in the late forties and early fifties.) The Roman Catholic Church, of course, is limited in its acceptance of the autonomy of the Third World church by its worldwide authoritarian structure. (Again, the Vatican's current conflict with the Catholic church in China is an instructive example.)

While the theory of the autonomy of the Third World church is generally accepted, the actual transition from colonial churches with expatriate leadership and western European church structures and models of worship, to autonomous churches with indigenous leadership (including leadership style), church structures and worship has been slow. For churches that have only recently become "independent," much of the blame must rest on the last few generations of expatriates in the colonial churches (that is, those working in the first half of the twentieth century). Much of the enthusiasm for indigenous "younger churches" in the late nineteenth and early twentieth centuries (for example, the consecration of the first African Anglican bishop, Samuel Crowther, in 1864, and the enthusiastic endorse-

ment of indigenous churches at the Edinburgh Missionary Conference of 1910) vanished in the period after World War I.

Some expatriate leaders in the colonial churches never really
accepted the idea of completely indigenous churches but thought
that some expatriate leadership would always be necessary to keep
the administration in order. Failures of indigenous Christians put in
positions of authority strengthened this view. In situations where
power and leadership were concentrated in the hands of one expatriate leader (the bishop or moderator, for example), it seemed
unthinkable to expatriate and local Christians alike that an indigenous Christian could take on such responsibility. So in many colonial
churches, while numbers of indigenous clergy and lay workers
increased dramatically, the hierarchy remained expatriate. One has
only to look at a photograph of the West Indian Anglican bishops
from the 1950s to see an example. Not until the post-World War II
period of nationalism and decolonization were most colonial
churches forced to shed their expatriate hierarchies.[4] Colonial
churches, including indigenous clergy, frequently opposed these
movements of nationalism and decolonization.

As a result, the first generation of indigenous hierarchy stepped
into a colonial church structure with little guidance other than the
behaviour of the previous expatriate leaders. Sometimes the process
was much slower. The outgoing expatriate leader, seeing the writing
on the wall, chose his successor and trained him how to lead within
the still very colonial structure, perhaps even sending him overseas,
which in many cases increased the alienation from indigenous culture. Or, if the church was moving from colonial to independent
status (ceasing to be, for example, the diocese of a First World
church), the outgoing expatriate wrote the constitution of the new
church, incorporating traditional western views of how the church
should operate, in an attempt to save the church from the imagined
incompetence of future indigenous hierarchy.[5]

A neocolonial Third World church resulted. Though the church is
legally independent of its First World parent and the leadership
indigenous, its structures, leadership, worship and often even its
relation to society and culture continue to be colonial, that is,
dependent on earlier colonial models.[6] Such churches, like the
neocolonial political regimes which they often support, frequently
continue to be economically dependent on the First World churches.
The use of that money is, of course, as with neocolonial political
regimes, in the hands of the neocolonial elite — the Third World
head of his church. (The use of the male pronoun here and above is
deliberate. The continued oppression of Third World women within
the Third World church is a part of the neocolonial enterprise.
Women are usually excluded from positions of genuine leadership,
even where the indigenous culture provided for it.) He is free to

spend that money on his word processor, limousine, house or diocesan administration, rather than on the genuine needs of the people.

Because the First World churches quite legitimately seek to encourage indigenous churches in the Third World, there is usually some discomfort in publicly recognizing neocolonialism as a problem of the Third World church, lest this criticism be used to reintroduce, justify or support a colonialist stance towards the Third World. ("You see, they *can't* govern themselves.") There is much to be said for such ill ease, since the neocolonial indigenous Christian is more the victim of colonialism than its perpetrator.[7] On the other hand, to pretend that such neocolonialism does not exist is not helpful. The First World church supports ecclesiastical regimes that cause much harm and suffering.

Third World Christians are not so shy in condemning neocolonialism. Shouting matches at synods and other church meetings, clergy and student strikes, parish and diocese rebellions, caustic comments about the neocolonial hierarchy and theological critiques of neocolonialism are all common in the Third World church. Often, however, such actions do little good, for the neocolonial elite controls the church structure, constitution, choice of new leaders and funds, much of which come from overseas. Powerless Third World Christians see the First World church as supporting the neocolonial hierarchy rather than themselves. Indeed, this analysis is often correct. For example, the Anglican Communion has for the last ten years undertaken a series of "Partners in Mission" consultations between First and Third World churches. Yet, such consultations are often dominated by the Third World neocolonial elite who choose their church's delegates. The real needs and concerns of the Third World church do not necessarily surface and such consultations often do not touch the life of the poor and suffering in the Third World.

What does one do about ecclesiastical neocolonialism? It seems to me that there are two very separate agenda: one for each Third World church and one for the First World church. The two agenda are related, for neocolonialism derives much of its strength from continued support (even if unwitting) by the First World church. As a First World person, I can legitimately put forward an agenda only for the First World church. However, to do this, I must look at how the Third World church responds to the problem of neocolonialism. Our efforts in this struggle must be coordinated.

From speaking and working with Third World Christians engaged in the struggle against colonialism and neocolonialism, I am able to point out some ways that parts of the Third World church are responding to these forms of oppression. First, the problem of neocolonialism and colonialism, where it continues, must be recognized. This in itself can be difficult, especially where a theology,

typically one of suffering, has developed to support the
neocolonialist position, or where people who would normally
oppose it have been co-opted into the structure. Here the Third
World Christian prophet has his or her place, pointing out such
situations of injustice.

My experience of the struggle against neocolonialism suggests
that another need is for those opposed to neocolonialism to take on
the positions of highest leadership and resolutely develop liberating
styles of leadership. For those opposed to neocolonialism to gain
such power is not easy, for often the ecclesiastical regime in power
has the right of veto over such appointments. In many places,
however, those opposed to neocolonialism have been moving into
higher positions of leadership. This is a cause for hope. Ultimately
church structures will have to be altered to prevent neocolonial
leadership from re-emerging. Very much depends on the leadership
of the Third World church. The church leader opposed to
neocolonialism does not just have to voice his or her opposition but
must *live* that opposition, in accessibility to and in support of the
poor and suffering. Third World women and laity have a special role
to play in this struggle as they have been particular victims of
neocolonialism.[8]

Understanding the economic realities that sustain ecclesiastical
and political neocolonialism and possible solutions is also a part of
the agenda. For example, helping people to develop enterprises that
produce enough wealth to make self-support genuinely possible may
be better than simply advocating "self-support." Individual First
World Christians living in the Third World may have a role to play
in the supplanting of ecclesiastical neocolonialism if they work in
solidarity with and ultimately under the authority of those in the
Third World church opposing neocolonialism.

Most First World Christians do not spend much time in the Third
World church, so that working directly against neocolonialism is not
an option. However, insofar as First World churches continue to
have relationships with Third World churches through national
church structures, missionary societies, and relief and development
organizations, dealing with neocolonialism in the Third World
church becomes a problem. While national church structures in the
First World are often aware of the problem of neocolonialism, some
missionary societies and relief and development organizations have
not yet come to terms with colonialism, let alone neocolonialism.[9]
Some First World missionaries continue to regard their converts as
incapable of exercising self-government and regard themselves as
necessary for the continued life of the church. Such an attitude is not
uncommon, for example, among white Canadians planning to work
among Canada's native peoples. It is still very common among
evangelical and adventist groups. Christians do well to distance

themselves from such groups, despite their emotional appeals and dramatic, but ultimately false, success stories.

For those working in First World church structures and organizations that deal directly with the Third World church, there must always be the awareness that the Third World church is not the Third World hierarchy, that what the Third World hierarchy wants is not always what is best for the Third World church. First World mission, development and relief policies must reflect this understanding. In many cases there is already much awareness of this. The bishop of a poor Third World diocese will usually not get much support from First World national church offices when he asks for $100,000 to build his new house or cathedral. For the First World church to make decisions about what is right or wrong for a Third World church (for example, that funding a water supply is more important than buying the bishop a new set of vestments) of course leaves the First World church open to the charge of still being colonialist in mentality, not really letting the Third World church decide how it spends its money. This is a false argument. In a neocolonial church, the Third World church decides nothing, only its hierarchy decides, often against the people. In refusing to support neocolonial hierarchies, the First World church sides with Third World people. It does not simply, in a colonialist fashion, try to impose its will on the Third World church.

For First World church structures to support the Third World church rather than the neocolonial hierarchy requires that those in the First World concerned with mission, relief and development become very familiar with the experiences of ordinary Third World Christians. Often Third World hierarchies are not enthusiastic about this prospect. Often the First World official visitor to the Third World church finds that he or she is required to spend most of the time with the bishop and is not really free to venture out, except to those places selected by the bishop.

A greater problem is the structures that are developing between First and Third World churches to facilitate relations between them. Typically, the problem of neocolonialism is ignored in such structures. For example, at consultations between First and Third World churches, a group representing the First World national church meets with a similar Third World group. Selection of delegates is usually in the hands of the respective churches. While First World churches, increasingly sensitive to the oppressed in their own midst, may be inclined to send youth, laity and women to such consultations, Third World neocolonial churches are apt to send bishops, male clergy, and a few laity who are supporters of the bishops. The voice of the genuine Third World church is never heard. (Needless to say, the Lambeth Conference, the international conference of all Anglican bishops held in England once every ten years, contributes more to encouraging neocolonialism than to critiquing it.)

However, even if ordinary parish priests or laity are sent to such conferences, the culture shock is considerable; language is often a problem and they may say little. Culturally, the prospect of causing one's bishop embarrassment by criticizing him in front of strangers may produce only silence, even in one who at home is an outspoken critic of the bishop. I increasingly question the value of such consultations when one is dealing with deeply neocolonial churches. However, First World participants can question situations of injustice in the Third World church and ensure that any money that is given is earmarked and actually used for causes that benefit the people of the Third World, not given as open grants to bishops, dioceses, or other church structures.

Visits between First and Third World churches are also problematic. First World Christians visiting the Third World church are easily co-opted by the neocolonial structure if they are not careful. Such visitors are not appreciated by the Third World church as they only increase its oppression. Visits by Third World neocolonial (not to mention colonial) leaders to the First World are equally problematic. Often such visitors solicit money for private and personal projects that are not helpful to the people. Such visitors often paint a very romantic picture of the life of Third World people so that First World Christians do not really have to face the suffering of the Third World. Neocolonial leaders are encouraged in their neocolonialism by such visits; they become even more "de-contextualized," that is, even more uncritically accepting of western values and society. Through such visits the strong get stronger and the weak, the people of the Third World, get weaker.

Rather than solely supporting deputation visits by Third World bishops and other members of the hierarchy to the First World, though there are many outstanding exceptions, I would favour a broader range of visits including ordinary clergy, laity, women, and youth. These people have much more to contribute to the First World than the neocolonial hierarchy since they come out of an experience of popular Christianity and human struggle. Such people would benefit from the experience of getting out of the isolation of the Third World more than bishops and others in the neocolonial hierarchy. Communication may be difficult and culture shock great, but in the end such visits would be worthwhile for both the First World and Third World churches.

Some might argue that Third World Christians should not be exposed to the evils of the First World — they might want to stay, they might become corrupted. Ultimately, I think this argument is paternalistic. The evils of First World capitalism are already familiar to the Third World. The "noble savage" is a myth that serves only to oppress the Third World. It suggests that Third World people cannot control their own destiny but must be protected. By spending time in the First World, Third World Christians are helped to understand the difficulty of the struggle they face. We in the First World can learn about that struggle from these Christians. But because of the way visits from the Third World are often structured, we do not hear of that struggle. Instead we listen to a romantic myth from those who have "made it" and do not need to struggle any longer.

NOTES

1   More specifically, I am writing out of recently having spent six years teaching theology in an Anglican theological college in the Solomon Islands, from having visited with clergy and grassroots Christians in the Pacific, Asia, and Africa, and from discussions with First World specialists on the Third World. The bishop portrayed in the sketches is not based on one actual person, but is a composite of many of the worst features of a neocolonial bishop. He is not meant to reflect negatively on the many Third World church leaders (including bishops, moderators, etc.) who are struggling against neocolonialism. One such opponent of ecclesiastical neocolonialism is Dom Helder Camara, Roman Catholic archbishop of Recife, Brazil. His condemnation of neocolonial styles of episcopal leadership at Vatican II is outstanding. It is reprinted in *Race Against Time* (London: Sheed and Ward, 1971).

2   For a discussion of neocolonial Christianity in Latin America today, see Jose Miguez Bonino, "Beyond Colonial and Neocolonial Christianity," Chapter 2 of *Doing Theology in a Revolutionary Situation* (Philadelphia: Fortress Press, 1975).

3   See, for example, the discussion of missions in J.H. Parry, *The Age of Reconnaissance* (Berkeley: University of California Press, 1981).

4   One might argue that the Anglican Church of Canada is still undergoing this process of decolonization and has a ways to go. The absence of a native person on the episcopal bench is the most glaring example of the continuing colonial character of the Anglican Church of Canada.

5   While this paragraph is written in the past tense, it should be pointed out that some major First World churches have not even gone this far in the process of decolonization. For example, the Episcopal Church in the U.S.A. includes dioceses in Taiwan, the Philippines, and ten Latin American and Caribbean countries. These dioceses have become so economically dependent on the Episcopal Church in the U.S.A. that autonomy has become very painful.

6   The relationship between neocolonialism and the indigenous culture is a difficult question and obviously varies from culture to culture. One must look at the character of the Christianity that was introduced, the character of the indigenous culture(s), and the character (including class structure) of the resulting church. An uncontextualized Christianity would, of course, encourage the development of a neocolonial Christianity. However, whether a contextualized Christianity is ulti-

mately liberating or neocolonial depends both on the character of the Christianity that is introduced and the character of the indigenous culture. A liberating Christianity that is contextualized (related positively to liberating elements in the indigenous culture) is liberating. An oppressive Christianity that is contextualized (relating positively to oppressive elements in the indigenous culture) is oppressive. Particularly where Christianity, western culture, and the indigenous culture have become fused through centuries of contact (such as in Latin America or the Philippines), one finds a mixture of the above possibilities. I am using the term "neocolonial" to describe those oppressive elements of western Christianity that have been taken into and retained by the Third World church, whether these elements are opposed or supported by the indigenous culture.

7   Classical discussions of the psychological effects of colonialism on the oppressed (and the oppressor) and the resultant neocolonialism are Franz Fanon, *Peau noir, masques Blancs* (Paris: Éditions du Seuil, 1952; English translation, *Black Skin, White Masks*, New York: Grove Press, 1967) and Albert Memmi, *Portrait du colonisé précédé du portrait du colonisateur* (Paris: Buchet Chastel, 1957; English translation, *The Colonizer and the Colonized*, Boston: Beacon Press, 1967).

8   However, the neocolonial ecclesiastical elite is not necessarily all clerical and all male. Women's organizations and the administrative structure offer a chance for a few lay women and men to become part of the neocolonial elite.

9   World Vision is one such group that immediately comes to mind.

Popular Religiosity and the Church in Latin America

Arturo Chacón

The study of popular religiosity is becoming one of the central elements in our understanding of the mission of the church in Latin America today. The extension and persistence of religiosity at the popular level runs counter to interpretations of secularization of Latin American society.[1]

Without exaggeration it can be said that the vital popular religiosity we see in this society today is the result of the first wave of missionary movement from Europe which began in the sixteenth century. Spain and Portugal colonized and Christianized the continent with a persistent effort which lasted over three centuries until the beginning of the nineteenth century, when the wars of independence put an end to it. Other influences came after, including the Protestant missions and the Pentecostal movement.

Because the popular religiosity which we are witnessing today is largely the result of three centuries of missionary effort by Roman Catholic orders,[2] "popular religiosity" has for a long time been equivalent to "popular Catholicism" in the minds of many observers.[3] Today this is not the case since we are witnessing pluralistic developments of both a Christian and non-Christian nature. It is precisely at the popular level that the religious monopoly of the Roman Catholic Church has been broken. The emerging religious pluralism has implications for the present and future practice of mission on this continent. New articulations of the work of the church and its relationship with society at large are posing a challenge which deserves examination. This challenges springs mostly from the presence of an active popular religiosity in the midst of society. This essay is about this challenge and the issues it poses for the mission of the church today.

Two examples of popular religiosity in this part of the world will help to clarify the issues at stake. The first one, which appears with different names all over the continent, is the role played by the figure of the Virgin Mary in popular worship. Two aspects of this role should be mentioned. One, still to be studied from a socio-religious perspective, is the formation of national identity and how the figure of the Virgin Mary has been a central feature in it — for example, the relationship between the people of Mexico and the Virgin of Guada-lupe (even though Mexico appears as a highly secularized state in its organization). The other is the relationship between the figure of the Virgin Mary and Mother Earth, as in the High Andes where the Pachamama (Mother Earth) is behind the figure of the Virgin Mary in special occasions related to the agricultural cycle. Both the sense of being a people and of being in relation to the earth are expressed in popular religiosity through the figure of the Virgin Mary. In this way, the common people have retained and re-created a space for themselves, even though these expressions may appear anachronis-tic and even pagan.

Another example is the role played by Christians, both Roman Catholic and Protestant, in the revolutionary process in Nicaragua in recent years. The highly publicized role of priests in the current government obscures the more decisive and lasting participation of Christians *as Christians* in a revolutionary process. The liturgical and biblical symbols are part of a long struggle, as Solentiname and Father Ernesto Cardenal have shown. The developments in Nicara-gua are becoming a new articulation of popular religiosity, maybe more political and theological than the old expressions, but still linked to the sense of being a people and of being in relation to the earth.

Because of the lack of clear definitions in this area, a brief defini-tion of the terms used is necessary. The terms have come mostly out of discussions in the area of pastoral concern.[4] Popular religiosity is the presence of beliefs, practices, and values, related in a coherent fashion to the sacred in the culture of the majority of the people.[5] The religiosity is popular because, although it is found at all levels of society as an extended practice, only at the level of the lower strata is it found as a coherent practice. Hence the term popular has a double connotation: the practice of the common people, and the extension of that practice to all levels of society. However, at the higher levels, it is found in a fragmented fashion.[6]

It is clear by the amount of literature on the subject that the Roman Catholic Church has seen the presence of this type of religiosity as a challenge. This challenge was articulated as the presence of a religiosity which was not cultivated or permeated by the faith of the church. During the time of Medellin (1968) and Vatican II (1965), the years of ferment and renewal in the Roman Catholic Church, this challenge was perceived as the need to evange-lize the masses who were seen as practising a superficial type of

Catholicism. In Latin America this challenge was expressed in a renewed concern for the poor of the continent, although only in the 1970s did it find a more articulated form in the movement of theological reflection known as the theology of liberation.

This first stage of the challenge had a paternalistic outlook. However, there were those who knew the difference between a mere evangelistic effort aimed at the culture of the common people and the recognition that popular religiosity had a vitality of its own as one expression of a people coming into its own in history. The expressions of popular religiosity were not the manifestation of a decadent Christianity, although many Protestants and secular observers saw it this way, but rather the affirmation of a people in a historical process of emancipation. This affirmation was using the only element of culture available to the people — the religious one. Hence, the evangelizing process which took place with the help of missionaries from abroad found a new dimension present among the people, a desire for liberation and for transformation of their situation. Therefore, a traditional effort at evangelism, aimed at bringing the true faith to the people, especially the lower strata, was met with a new challenge: Is the church on the side of the poor?

Here we enter into the second stage, still in process, in which the church is trying to answer this question. At this point, the challenge is presented to the Christian church, not just to the Roman Catholic Church.[7] The formation of the basic ecclesiastical communities and the congregational organization of the Pentecostal movement facilitate the encounter with the people and their needs in a more intimate way, because of the local emphasis of the work. Roman Catholics in Latin America are discovering the Protestant ecclesial principle of the congregation and its local reality. No doubt this discovery provides for a more incarnational approach and a more vital encounter with the historical reality, but it can also bring about isolation, self-perpetuation, and sectarianism.[8] These bring about the loss of historical continuity and perspective which are most necessary to a process of liberation. But before we examine the people's mode of participation and its political limits, we need to see the challenge which is posed to society.

Society is here defined as the sector which defines, controls and benefits from current arrangements. It comprises segments of the population at all levels, but mostly at the higher levels. Society here is not perceived in terms of social conflict, and therefore it would be misleading to apply categories related to it in this presentation.[9]

Popular religiosity represents the relatively autonomous organization of common people in relation to a society which is becoming more alien in the cultural and material satisfaction of people's needs. It is the expression of and the protest against people's real misery.[10] In this respect, popular religiosity becomes a challenge to society. In current terms, the common people are in the process of creating space for themselves in the midst of an alien society. This space is created in religious terms because religion is the only reality available to the people; thus religion establishes a shared ground for organization, discussion, study, learning, and the promotion of solutions to their plight. The search for the satisfaction of material and cultural needs then becomes a powerful combination in the face of society. It is for this reason that we have difficulties in applying the terminology of secularization to the religious developments taking place in Latin America — not only because religious expression is very much alive, but also because what is taking place is more akin to a religious mutation.[11] Urbanization, industrialization, and scientific knowledge, instead of creating the religious indifference characteristic of secularized societies, has challenged the reservoir of religiosity to look for new expressions. However, these new expressions are coming from the common people and not from an enlightened leadership. The latter are barely able to articulate the challenge posed by the powerful mixture that the people have created: the search for solutions to their material and cultural needs in the context of a new arrangement of society.

It can be said that the relatively autonomous organization of the people through their religiosity is what becomes a challenge to society. Social movements deriving from political ones are relatively easier to understand and to be co-opted by society. But an autonomy based on religion challenges the legitimacy of the society at its very foundation, especially if the religious symbols are shared by all. A persistent, even if slow, withdrawal of religious legitimacy from the current order could become an insurmountable problem for society. Let us examine the implications below.

Some aspects of popular religiosity have already been advanced. Now I shall examine how people participate in this relatively autonomous organized religious expression. This participation has two points of reference, the faith of the Gospel and the social reality.[12] From what has been said, the people have shown the ability to appropriate the religious symbols needed to affirm their own culture and ethos in what has become an increasingly alien society. This is the starting point. But the ambivalence, if we want to call it that, starts at the point of relationship with the social reality: Are local congregations going to be a "samaritan" or a "prophetic" church?[13] The mode of participation will decide how we search for an answer to this question. Insofar as the local congregation allows real participation and includes the surrounding community, the tendency is to move from a samaritan to a prophetic stance. By identifying itself with the surrounding community, the congregation gets away from the temptation to use or instrumentalize the people. If the local congregation allows participation, but with the exclusion of the community around it, the result is the opposite one. The key element is the inclusion or exclusion of the surrounding community in the participation of the local congregation. Both types of congregation include popular participation; both intervene in the social reality; both make an option for the poor; both appeal to the faith of the Gospel as the starting point — they only differ in whether they include the surrounding community in their preoccupations.

The consequences of the non-inclusion of the local community by the local congregation are manifold, but for our purposes I shall mention only the strengthening of authoritarian or vertical forms of power, an individualistic outlook on the ills of society, a spiritualistic understanding of the Gospel, and a non-critical attitude towards society.

This brings us to the point of discussing the political limits of popular religiosity. The manifestation of popular religiosity in Latin America has been interpreted as an expression of disguised political action. However, this is a misreading of the situation, since the starting point has been the faith according to the Gospel as it relates to social reality. Hence, the only possible outcome is the construction of a new religious vision for society and not a political utopia. What is at stake in this endeavour is whether the common people involved in the religious task, alongside those of other sectors of society, will be able to provide a new religious vision which will be an element in the transformation of the current situation. The task is to construct this religious vision in a coherent fashion, not to build a political utopia. This point needs to be made, especially today, since many people in Latin America and abroad, including Christians and non-Christians, are supportive of the struggle for human rights in which the Christians of this continent have been engaging as part of their witness to the Gospel. Many have understood this struggle to mean that the Christian church has almost become the party of opposition to the oppressive regimes reigning in the continent. This wishful thinking has been encouraged by the incapacity of the political forces to build a feasible alternative at the political level.

Popular religiosity in Latin America is trying to build a new religious vision which will provide support for a new kind of society more akin to the understanding of the Gospel in these lands. The struggle for human rights goes hand in hand with a participatory model more closely related to democratic forms of organization, a more inclusive understanding of society in which solidarity can overshadow individualistic forms of relationships, and the development of a more critical consciousness in order to eliminate the dualisms ingrained in current religiosity. All of these developments and others will contribute to a new kind of society which will come from the political utopias under discussion in Latin America. This is a far cry from being involved in politics, as the accusation goes.

In the construction of this religious vision, popular religiosity is rediscovering the original gospel of the kingdom of God. Working towards this kingdom permeates the seemingly "horizontal" preoccupation of popular religiosity. The transcendent element is given by the kingdom proclaimed by Jesus of Nazareth, the Christ. This is the motivating and guiding force which springs from the hermeneutical work throughout the church. Further elaboration will no doubt contribute to a better understanding of the Gospel and its relation to social reality.

I started by saying that the study of popular religiosity is becoming one of the central elements in our understanding of the mission of the church in Latin America today. Some of the implications of this development have been put forth in this paper, many others have been omitted but there is one which I think particularly requires further exploration: pluralism. I mentioned the existence of non-Christian forms of popular religiosity but I did not develop them, because by experience and knowledge I am more qualified to examine the Christian church. However, this popular, non-Christian religiosity places Latin American Christians together with Christians from other parts of the world in our need to examine the implications of a pluralistic society for our understanding of the Gospel. Much is at stake here, because we have not been sensitive to the small but significant presence of non-Christians in our midst. The new type of society will have to include this dimension, since our vision is that it will be a pluralistic one. However, this is one aspect which is noted for a future agenda.

NOTES

1   From a Protestant and ecumenical viewpoint the publications of the Church and Society movement in Latin America, 1965–69, show this emphasis. See *Christianismo y Sociedad* volumes of those years.

    The process of urbanization in this continent did not go hand in hand with secularization. The persistence and growth of spiritualistic and African-related religions, among others, and the growth of the Pentecostal movement showed the vitality of popular religiosity in the urban and rural areas.

2   See Segundo Galilea, *Religiosidad popular y pastoral* (Madrid: Ediciones Cristianadad, 1979), chapter 4; also Gabriel Guarda, "Raíces de la religiosidad popular de América espanola" in *Religiosidad y fe en América Latina* (Santiago, Chile: Ediciones Mundo, 1973).

3   See introduction by Jaime Moreno in *Religiosidad y fe en América Latina*.

4   The reader will notice that most of the titles dealing with the subject include the term *pastoral*. This has led to a redefinition of the scope of this term, including some aspects related to the mission of the church.

5   The concept of the sacred related to religion is discussed by Emile

Durkheim in *Elementary Forms of the Religious Life* (Glencoe, Illinois: Free Press, 1947), pp. 37-42.

6 Cf. Antonio Cruz Pacheco, *La religiosidad popular chilena, estudio sicosociológico* (Santiago, Chile: Centro de Investigaciones Socioculturales, 1970).

7 The growth of the Protestant church in Latin America has been spectacular. For example, in Chile the Protestant population in 1960 comprised only five or six percent of the total population, less than half a million; today it makes up over eleven percent, more than a million and a quarter (1982 figures projected from a survey in the metropolitan area, always below the national average in this respect). División General de Estadísticas y Censos, Santiago, 1962; PRESOR (Programa Evangélico de Estudios Socio-religiosos, Theological Community of Chile), Santiago, 1983. Among the marginal population, Pentecostals and other Protestants account for over twenty percent, according to the same sources.

8 For a comparison of Basic Ecclesiastic Communities (BEC) and Pentecostal congregations see Jether Pereira Ramalho, "Algunas notas sobre dos perspectivas de pastoral popular: la de las comunidades eclesiásticas de base (CEB) y la de los grupos evangélicos pentecostales" in *Christianismo y Sociedad*, 1a. entrega, año XV, segunda época, no. 51 (Buenos Aires, 1977), pp. 3-14; also José Míguez Bonino, "Cuestiones eclesiológicas fundamentales," *Pastoral Popular*, XXXIV, nos. 1-2 (1983), pp. 34-38.

9 Cf. Otto Maduro, *Religion and Social Conflicts* (Maryknoll, N.Y.: Orbis Books, 1982). In terms of his categories the situation lies between a religion as a relatively autonomous terrain of social conflicts and one as an active factor in them, parts III and IV.

10 This according to the dictum of K. Marx in his "Contribution to the Critique of Hegel's Philosophy of Law" in K. Marx and F. Engels, *On Religion* (Moscow: Progress Publishers, 1975).

11 I take the term from Cruz Pacheco although I do not share his application of it. See note 6 above.

12 See Jether Pereira Ramalho, note 8 above.

13 Ronaldo Muñoz, "Ubicasrse hoy y comprometerse," *Pastoral Popular*, XXXIV, no. 4 (1983), pp. 6-18.

Christ and Cultural Imperialism

Raymond L. Whitehead

The charge of cultural imperialism leveled against the missionary movement in the twentieth century was bitter medicine for Christians. Missionaries, not unreasonably, had an image of themselves as sacrificial and self-giving. The very people for whom they made these sacrifices, however, turned against the missionaries, blaming the Christian movement for undermining their cultural dignity. These charges were not unreasonable either. The Chinese People's Revolution of 1949, for example, evidenced an outpouring of animosity toward European and North American missionary structures. Missionaries were condemned by name, and mission organizations were branded as the cultural arm of western imperialism.

This Chinese condemnation of the cultural attitudes of Christians was one of the most dramatic in a series of such critiques. In the 1950s, while the Chinese blast against Christian imperialism and cultural invasion was still loud and strong, a young man by the name of Martin Luther King took leadership of a movement which eventually exposed the heart of Christian racism in the United States. This had repercussions throughout the world. As that battle continued into the 1960s and 1970s yet another cultural critique began to dominate the picture — the feminist challenge to Christian patriarchy, the system of male domination. Native peoples and other ethnic groups added their voices to the cultural counteroffensive. There was a cultural rebellion afoot.

Even bitter medicine can be therapeutic. We should be grateful to those who have criticized the cultural imperialism of the churches and missions. They have exposed the unethical dimensions of the church's cultural policies and Christologies. In liberating themselves they have also given the western churches an opportunity for liberation.

Relating Christ and Culture

The Chinese reaction to western cultural imperialism was part of the world response to the European invasion of the Americas, Africa and Asia in the colonial period and to the accompanying missionary movements. These events raised, in a new way, questions of faith and culture which go back to the Christian communities of the first century. The New Testament texts themselves reflect the struggle to relate Christian faith to Jewish, Greek and Roman thought and to the various cults and world views of the day. In the modern colonial period a firmly established faith and theology had to deal with "new" concepts, "new" world views and "new" cultures from which they had previously been isolated, but the underlying problems were similar to those faced by the first Christians.

One of the most influential studies of these problems was H. Richard Niebuhr's *Christ and Culture*, published in 1951.[1] It quickly became a "classic" among theologians, ethicists and sociologists because it brought order and sense to nearly 2000 years of Christian thought about faith and culture. The study was completed before the impact of the Chinese critique and subsequent movements mentioned above. It provides a useful summary of the "pre-liberation" views on Christ and culture and reflects earlier attempts to deal with cultural challenges within the Mediterranean and Euramerican cultural context.

Niebuhr's Christ and Culture Typology

Niebuhr divides responses to the Christ-and-culture question into five types. "Types" and "typologies" are terms borrowed from the field of sociology of religion. A "type" was meant to describe not any actual person, but a set of traits and characteristics, which, taken together, "typified" a certain approach. For example, a description of the hippie movement might include length of hair, style of clothes, mode of thought, community associations, music and literature, morals, and so forth. It may be that no one person would fit every aspect of the description. The sociologist attempts to construct a "type" for the purpose of understanding a certain movement or mentality, not to describe actual persons.

The five types which Niebuhr describes include two extremes and three median types. The first extreme he calls the Christ-against-culture type. It is an approach to Christianity which places faith in opposition to the world of culture. Niebuhr considers this to be the most radical response. Salvation is the process of rescuing people out of an impure world into a pure Christian fellowship. The monastic movement and groups like the Mennonites are examples of those who lean in the Christ-against-culture direction.

The second extreme type simply merges Christ and culture and reduces all tension between them. Christ is accommodated to a particular culture with no radical challenge to that culture. Niebuhr calls this the Christ-of-culture type. The Culture-Christianity of nineteenth-century Germany, where theologians sometimes simply identified Christ with the best values of their culture, is cited as an example of this type.

These two types may seem to be very far apart, but they can sometimes coalesce quickly. For example, United States fundamentalism may be seen as a Christ-against-culture mind set, seeing the church as opposed to the evils of modern society. Yet this same stance has been able to ally itself with superpatriotic Americanism and militarism, sliding easily into a Christ-of-American-culture mentality.

The third, fourth and fifth of Niebuhr's types all try to achieve a balance between commitment to Christ and the demands of culture. The third in Niebuhr's typology is the Christ-above-culture type. This approach has a high view of culture, finding much to be praised in art and poetry and philosophy, aside from Christianity. Yet above even the highest cultural attainments is the spiritual realm, accessible only through Christian revelation. Medieval Catholicism, especially the thought of Thomas Aquinas, provides an example of this type.

Luther is the archetype of the fourth approach. This one is called the Christ-and-culture-in-paradox type. In this view there is a dynamic, never-ceasing interaction between Christ and culture. The church has its own realm and the secular society its own. Yet the two cannot be isolated from each other. The Christian ruler must be both a good ruler by secular standards and a good Christian by church standards.

The fifth type is that of Christ transforming culture. Christ is seen as the power which is constantly at work within culture to purge it of what is evil and to lift it to its true human possibilities.

Niebuhr does not claim that these five types are exhaustive. He leaves open the possibility that other types could be added. Within his analytic structure, however, the only possibility would be to add further median types, since the extremes are already covered. The five types provide us with a useful conceptual framework. The movements of the past three decades, however, raise some serious problems not covered by Niebuhr.

Christ and Cultural Power

Niebuhr's typology neglects the question of power. He does not deal with patriarchy, or racism, or economic stratification, or imperialism. For colonized people in the Third World, for blacks and native people, for women, what does it mean to talk about

Christ-against-culture? Which culture? Male-dominated culture? White European culture?

Niebuhr defined culture as that which human beings have added to the natural world — tools, language, government, art, literature, commerce — all that sets human life off from other forms of life. It is a useful understanding of culture, but it tries to maintain intellectual neutrality on the question of who has power over language and tools in a particular human society.

Niebuhr uses the term "culture" to include both cultural thought forms and structures of political and economic power. Others distinguish these two aspects of society. Even though such a distinction is made, cultural forms are nevertheless intimately related to structures of power and control. Elisabeth Schüssler Fiorenza gives us a useful clue on this distinction when she contrasts androcentric thought and patriarchy:

> While androcentrism characterizes a mind-set, patriarchy represents a social-cultural system in which a few men have power over other men, women, children, slaves, and colonized people.[2]

For our analysis, the androcentric mind-set would be related to cultural forms, and patriarchy to power structures. Aside from this terminological difference, Schüssler Fiorenza seems to be distinguishing between male-centred cultural thought forms and actual male-controlled political, economic and religious structures.

Very simply, what is being suggested here is that people are controlled both by direct political structures and, more subtly, by mind-sets or cultural thought forms. If we are to strive for freedom and liberation, both the systems of direct power and the cultural forms which exercise indirect power must be uncovered. These dual forms of control exist everywhere, but for the self-critical view of this essay we need to look at the "Euramerican male, white, upper or middle class person."

Western or Euramerican imperialism has been carried out through the use of military and economic power. At the same time western cultural values have been and continue to be imposed on the world in a variety of ways, including control of news media, entertainment and films, and education. Some people in the struggle against western imperialism are still trapped, because of their education and experience, in the web of cultural imperialism.

In a similar way, feminists who are actively working against the structures of male domination may nevertheless still function subconsciously with androcentric or male-centred cultural thought forms. A black person may also assume the cultural forms of the dominant white society, and persons who are the victims of class exploitation may often adopt the cultural values of those who are oppressing them.

These distinctions, in terms of western Christian societies, may be listed as follows:

Grouping	Cultural Form	Political Structure
nation-states	Euramerican cultural centrism	imperialism
gender	androcentrism	patriarchy
race	white ethnocentrism	racist system
class	bourgeois cultural centrism	economic system

How does Niebuhr's Christ-and-culture typology relate to this scheme? If we remove Niebuhr's attempt to assume a neutrality in relation to systems of power, then a fifth line could be added to the chart:

religion	"Christ"	ecclesiastical system

In this line "Christ" is in quotation marks because it is possible to argue that the object of Christian faith has been misused in support of cultural control. The ecclesiastical system has often functioned as a part of the oppressive structures in the right-hand column.

Even though Niebuhr's definition of culture includes the content of both columns, discussion in this paper will deal only with the cultural forms of the centre column, and primarily with Euramerican cultural centrism.

Christ and Euramerican Cultural Centrism

In Asia missionaries encountered ancient civilizations, each with its own literature, technology, social structure and religion. Riding on the rising tide of western power, however, missionaries considered these cultures "heathen," "sub-Christian" or "pre-Christian." A personal experience illustrates how this mentality has continued into recent decades. Not long after arriving in Hong Kong in the early 1960s, I went hiking on one of the outlying islands with some new missionary acquaintances. We lost the trail and had to work our way through the brush up a steep hillside, under the hot tropical sun. We finally arrived exhausted at a small stream and stopped to cool our feet in the water. A Buddhist monk came by and we learned we were not far from a Buddhist monastery from which there was a clear road back. He cordially gave us directions and was about to continue on his way. One of our party, whose missionary zeal overcame his exhaustion, jumped up pulling Christian tracts from his pocket and began preaching at the hapless monk.

This missionary and many other colleagues in Hong Kong considered conversion of "non-Christians" a responsibility which outweighed any considerations of courtesy or propriety or respect. Several missionary doctors argued strongly that the primary purpose of a "Christian" hospital or clinic was the opportunity for "evangelism" (proselytizing), and the conversion of "non-Christians." They were unmoved by the argument that such tactics took advantage of people in their illness.

An Asian Christian, T.K. Thomas, writes persuasively that the term "non-Christian" should not be used at all. He writes:

> ... [It] is a discourteous expression. We are what we are, not what we-are-not. We are not non-apes but human beings. Our Buddhist and Hindu friends are Buddhists and Hindus, not non-Christians.[3]

C.S. Song adds that the term "non-Christian" is an expression of "Christian centrism."[4] It was precisely this attitude which led liberated Asian people to accuse the western church of cultural imperialism. Christian centrism is the process of using Euramerican cultural forms to support an approach which is essentially imperialist.

This oppressive use of "Christ" is a problem not raised by Niebuhr within his Euramerican framework, but it cannot be avoided in the study of cultural relations in the Third World. Is there yet another type to add to Niebuhr's five, that of Christ-oppressing-culture? It would probably be more accurate to raise the problem of Christian cultural oppression in relation to all five of Niebuhr's types.

It is difficult to talk about Christ transforming Asian culture, for example, without falling into Christian centrism. C.S. Song suggests that the mission of the church in Asia is not "the territorial expansion of the institutional church or statistical increase in membership." Rather, he says:

> The mission of the church is the more fundamental task of informing the Asian spirituality, shaped by Asian cultures and religions, with the love and compassion of God in Jesus Christ. In addition, Asian Christians together with people of other faiths and ideologies must seek to transform Asian society on the basis of freedom, justice and equality.[5]

The transforming of culture is a common human task.

The nature of our Euramerican cultural centrism is indicated in our academic biases. We are considered theologically literate when we have studied European languages. Our assumption is that only Euramerican cultures yield theological truth. On the contrary, it could be contended that we are not theologically literate unless we have studied a non-western language and culture. Certainly the Christian community is the poorer for its linguistic narrowness.

Aloysius Pieris, a Sri Lankan Jesuit, suggests that the integrity of
Asian theology, at least, depends on getting away from the constric-
tions of European languages in order to discover an Asian theology
of liberation hidden in the folk cultures as well as in the literary
cultures of the continent. Euramerican, including Latin American,
theology is communicated within the same family of languages. He
goes on:

> It is therefore regrettable that Asians... are not able to
> consult each other's hidden theologies except in a *non-
> Asian idiom*, thus *neutralizing the most promising fea-
> ture in our methodology*. We Asians professionally
> theologise in English, the language in which most of us
> think, read and pray. The theological role of Language
> in a "continent of languages" has been grossly under-
> estimated and our stubborn refusal to consult each
> other's linguistic idioms, or even to be familiar with
> one's own cultural heritage, will remain one major
> obstacle to the discovery of a truly Asian Theology.
> This is not an appeal for chauvinism but a plea for
> authenticity imposed on us by what we have defined as
> the Asian context.[6]

If Asian theologians want to do theology in Asian languages and
contexts, it may be asked, why then is it cultural centrism for western
theologians to do theology in European languages? If we recognize
the Euramerican context as one relative cultural situation in which
to do theology, and not claim that it is the centre of authentic
theology, then we are already moving beyond cultural centrism and
its ancillary distortions.

Christ and the Centrism of Class, Gender and Race

Christian cultural forms have their oppressive side, then; this is
not taken into account in Niebuhr's typology. Take his fifth type,
Christ-transforming-culture. He described it as a median type which
affirms both Christ and culture but keeps them separate. We could
ask, however, whether a Christ-against-culture starting point is not
necessary before transformation can take place. Every radical position of cultural rejection needs to be analyzed to ask whether "culture" as such is being opposed, or a particular oppressive form of
that culture. For example, the Pentecostal movement displays
clearly the traits of a Christ-against-culture type. However, in the
early 1970s, the Pentecostal churches in Chile, which were made up
almost entirely of the very poor within the society, came out in
support of Allende's socialist movement. The Pentecostals were
"against culture" in one sense, but they supported social and cultu-

ral transformation when the opportunity presented itself. The culture they were against was the culture which oppressed them.

Is the accommodation of Christ and culture (Niebuhr's Christ-of-culture type) a neutral theological position or an attempt to use Christian justification for preserving an unjust class structure? Is the Christ-above-culture type an ideological justification of ecclesiastical power? Does holding Christ and culture in paradox simply allow for making a deal with state power when it is convenient while holding it in judgment at other times?

At the outset of his study, Niebuhr describes our experience of Christ in terms of love, hope, obedience and faith. Any notion that people may experience Christ as oppressor is far from his consciousness. Today, though, we are very much aware that this distorted use of Christ is not uncommon.

To counteract just such a distortion Tom Driver insists that our teaching about Christ begin with ethics. "The church should teach nothing about God or Jesus which does not make a positive contribution to social justice."[7] The difficulty is that this misuse of Christ is deeply rooted in our cultural thought patterns and not just in our teachings.

How Christ can be an oppressor is illustrated in an illuminating "theological" discussion between two uneducated black women, Celie and Shug, in Alice Walker's novel *The Color Purple*:

> Then she say: Tell me what your God look like, Celie.
>
> Ah naw, I say. I'm too shame. Nobody ever ast me this before, so I'm sort of took by surprise. Besides, when I think about it, it don't seem quite right. But it all I got. I decide to stick up for him, just to see what Shug say.
>
> Okay, I say. He big and old and tall and graybearded and white. He wear white robes and go barefooted.
>
> Blue eyes? she ast.
>
> Sort of bluish-gray. Cool. Big though. White lashes, I say.
>
> She laugh.
>
> Why you laugh, I ast. I don't think it so funny.
>
> . . .
>
> ... Then she tell me this old white man is the same God she used to see when she prayed...
>
> . . .
>
> Ain't no way to read the bible and not think God white, she say. Then she sigh. When I found out I thought God was white, and a man, I lost interest.[8]

Who told Shug and Celie that God was white and male? The whole culture did. Who can blame Shug for losing interest?

Christocentrism and Cultural Centrism: Future Agendas

What does it mean to make Christ the centre of our lives? Does our Christocentric approach inevitably fall into Christian centrism, with all its androcentric, ethnocentric, bourgeois and Euramerican characteristics? Tom Driver has argued against Christocentrism, noting that to make Christ the centre is to oppress.[9] This is a difficult point to deal with since our teaching and our liturgical practice have concentrated on making Christ the centre of our lives.

The prophet Amos warned the people of Israel about cultural centrism:

> "Are you not like the Ethopians to me,
>   O people of Israel?" says the Lord.
> "Did I not bring up Israel from the land of Egypt,
>   and the Philistines from Caphtor
> and the Syrians from Kir?" (Amos 9:7 RSV)

The people of Israel thought that they were the only ones for whom God cared. Our Euramerican, white, male, bourgeois cultural centrism has been subtly shrouded in the theological language of Christocentrism.

Where do we go from here on the Christ-and-culture question? It may be understandable that defensiveness or discouragement is the response of many in the dominant structures. This is unfortunate. The possibility of dealing creatively with the issue in the western context is greater today than ever before. The courageous stands of blacks, women, native peoples, ethnic minorities, Third World peoples, Jews, and many others who have taken the risk of naming cultural imperialism and the oppressive use of Christ in the world have made this opportunity possible. As we should know, however, when a great deal is at stake the battles are not won easily, nor perhaps ever.

Elisabeth Schüssler Fiorenza has made liberation a starting point for the interpretation of history and scripture. Any doctrine or principle which is oppressive is opposed to Christ and the gospel. Doing theology is precisely the process of struggling against any use of Christ to oppress or exploit. She writes:

> The basic insight of all liberation theologies, including feminist theology, is the recognition that all theology, willingly or not, is by definition always engaged for or against the oppressed. Intellectual neutrality is not possible in a world of exploitation and oppression.[10]

In grappling with issues of Christ and culture particularly, we cannot escape into intellectual neutrality. Once this insight is grasped, the issues of cultural centrism and Christocentrism are put into a different framework. Whenever we use Christ to support male, white, Euramerican, bourgeois thought forms, we are involved in oppression and are unfaithful to Christ's spirit.

The cultural agenda of the western churches is immense. We have barely begun to reformulate the structures, liturgies, programs, theologies, ethics, and projects of our churches in the light of the new understandings that have emerged in the past thirty years. We have not dealt with the way the Christian ethos has contributed to racist, sexist, elitist and imperialist attitudes within the culture as a whole. We have to be clear that answers and solutions are not going to come from the old citadels of church and academia in the West. Perhaps the most difficult agenda for the white, male, western church leaders to take up will be that of listening to the once silent voices which are now speaking of liberation. These voices will be teaching us new truths if we can hear. They are not only Christian voices.

Where is Christ in the liberation of culture? Christians have tried to keep Christ in a kingly role, to be above culture or opposed to culture or transforming culture. In the process we have distorted the meaning of Christ, using reference to Christ to support cultural imperialism. We need to empty ourselves of Christian cultural centrism and the desire to dominate.

> Have this mind among yourselves, which you have in
> Christ Jesus, who, though he was in the form of God,
> did not count equality with God a thing to be grasped,
> but emptied himself, taking the form of a servant...
> And being found in human form he humbled himself
> and became obedient unto death, even death on a
> cross. (Philippians 2:5-8. RSV)

These words of the Apostle Paul should remind us that Christ's way is not one of domination. When we understand this we may be able to discern that power, which Christians call the Christ, active in the world beyond any of the structures and any of the oppressive thought forms which we have created. To be true to the spirit of Christ is to relinquish oppressive power, to listen to the powerless ones and join their side, and to celebrate every instance of liberating struggle.

NOTES

1 H. Richard Niebuhr, *Christ and Culture* (New York: Harper, 1951).
2 Elisabeth Schüssler Fiorenza, *In Memory of Her* (New York: Crossroad, 1983), p. 29. My taking this clue from Schüssler Fiorenza does not mean that she would necessarily agree with the analysis which follows.
3 T.K. Thomas, "Bad Language" in *One World*, no. 40 (October 1978), p. 11; quoted in C.S. Song, *The Compassionate God* (Maryknoll, N.Y.:

Orbis Books, 1982), pp. 63-64.

4   Song, *The Compassionate God*, p. 64.

5   C.S. Song, *Third Eye Theology* (Maryknoll, N.Y.: Orbis Books, 1979), p. 119.

6   Aloysius Pieris, S.J., "Towards an Asian Theology of Liberation," in *The Month* (May 1979), p. 149.

7   Tom Driver, *Christ in a Changing World: Toward an Ethical Christology* (New York: Crossroad, 1981), p. 22.

8   Alice Walker, *The Color Purple* (New York: Washington Square Press, 1982), pp. 176-77.

9   Driver, chapter 3.

10 Schüssler Fiorenza, p. 6.

Communication Across Class Barriers

John Rowe

It is becoming acceptable in the Church of England and is considered by many even desirable that men (women are still not eligible for the priesthood here) should be ordained to the ministry while remaining in their normal employment in the world. Everyone knows this has something to do with lack of money for the stipends of full-time clergy. The parochial system is helped to keep going by an injection of voluntary labour. But already some of these people before ordination, and more of them after it, are aware of dimensions in ministry which are invisible in the conventional setting. If only through a sense of being unfairly used by the institutional church, there is a development of thinking among "auxiliary pastoral ministers." More than that, it is inevitable that people trained in theology and exposed to broader theological perspectives by their preparation for ordination will, from the standpoint of secular employment, begin to see their priesthood in a fresh light. They will write and they will meet and they will think about the church and the world and they will create a mode of communication across the boundary between the two which must provide a mass of new material for thinking and research, whatever it may or may not achieve for the Kingdom of God.[1]

For one who has been a "priest in secular employment" for a good many years there is an element of irony in the newfound popularity of the "non-stipendiary ministry."[2] For one finds that what seemed the crucial issue to some of us all those years ago — the alienation of the church from the poor — simply does not figure in this modern movement.[3] What is being bridged is not a *class* barrier but only that which divides an institution from its own characteristic hinterland. And as the institution is predominantly a middle-class one it follows that its non-stipendiary ministers, seeing no reason to forsake the avocations which are normal to them, are for the most part teachers, civil servants, social workers, technocrats — anything other (in the great majority) than manual workers.

It is as if, when a conversation begins to approach the heart of the matter in question, by some unconscious sense of danger or embarrassment, or by the sheer weight of the trivia which people love, it veers away again to find its centre elsewhere, leaving perhaps in one or two a vague feeling of frustration.

If our problem is about "the sacred and the secular," "the church and the world," there is so much to talk about, and so many interesting facets of the subject to explore that everyone can join in confidently and have something to say. People can even be hurt and so there is room for self-discipline, mutual consideration and the civilized virtues. Nobody needs to get off his or her chair and walk out in exasperation and anger. But, if the issue is what can possibly be "good news to the poor" and from what stance can it realistically be announced, there comes a whiff of sourness in the air, perhaps even of fear. Not that "class" cannot be discussed in a civilized way. It is the suggestion that this issue might cut right across every possible consideration of church polity, doctrine, liturgics, vocation and finance which raises the hackles. "After all, the church has got to deal with the world the way it is, not with some ideal world." Quite so, let's get back to the church and the world. Let's talk about "communication across class barriers," in particular communication between the church and working-class people.

Nobody should imagine there isn't a great deal of communication or that it was ever lacking. Great Britain is divided into Anglican parishes, each of which has a parish church of some sort. These are a visible witness. In addition, people are seen going in and out of these buildings. The clergy associated with them are not invisible either but are more or less involved in their communities. Then there is the recurring appearance of religious and clerical matters in the media, services broadcast on radio and TV, episcopal pronouncements on public affairs and so on. It is impossible for ordinary people who do not go to church not to have images of the church in their minds. Communication from church to common people certainly takes place. Some people like to think that what is conveyed is not a true picture and this consideration could cause a person like myself to spend many years of frustration trying to correct false impressions. But I have come to think that on the whole the projection of the church's image and of its message toward working-class people is correct. What is seen is bodies of people principally devoted to services of worship but also to a certain amount of social service and personal help to the sick and suffering. Their leadership mostly moves within socially superior, educated circles and speaks in an idiom appropriate to them. They promote an ancient mythology which most ordinary people can hardly take seriously but they also seem to bring to the church an uncompromising commitment which makes a certain kind of sense, even if you reject it for yourself.

However, it seems that church people are just as confused as everybody else about how an absolute commitment is to be lived or practised. If occasionally it is suggested that Christ meant things to be different, intended the exalting of the humble and meek and the sending of the rich empty away, this is not backed up by any kind of political will. This would, in any case, contradict the inevitably non-political character of religion. Thus, a strong impression of humbug and ineffectuality is often conveyed, with notable exceptions from time to time. There may be "something in" religion but it hardly seems necessary as a source of inspiration for unselfish service to your neighbour. The latter can occur without it. Most people feel they can manage very well without religion. Even if ultimate questions niggle at one from time to time, why get involved with something so problematic?

This, roughly speaking, is the way churches figure in the minds of the people who surround me here in the east end of London. What of communication the other way? I think I would distinguish between the perceptions in the minds of the church-people in working-class areas like this and those evoked in more suburban, rural and prosperous localities. Here, where congregations are small and made up of folk who live nearby and where the clergy are in constant contact with local life, the image of "working people" (by which shorthand expression I mean those whose incomes come from manual or lower-level clerical jobs, for the most part) is not wildly inaccurate. It is a picture first of people mainly engaged in getting and spending. The range of income is considerable. Two or three wage-earners in a family can allow a mobility and a style of life not normally associated with poverty. On the other hand, low wages and unemployment limit the lives of very large numbers and their effects are obvious. The overall impression is therefore probably not an unsympathetic one. People here are seen to contend not only with the pressure of "materialistic" values exerted constantly through the media but also with a depressing physical environment, poor educational traditions and a long history of deprivations which have left lasting marks on bodies and minds. Present economic conditions and governmental policies depress people disproportionately in areas like this. Yet, although recreational and artistic facilities are poor, for whatever reasons, people can be surprisingly buoyant. This comes out in the pub culture, at weddings and parties, in the markets and in the characteristic cockney humour which takes some of the hurt out of the underlying feeling of being victimized.

It has to be said, though, that since the dominant preoccupations of the clergy (and indeed of the whole church tradition) are what they are, the population of an area like this is perceived primarily as it were from outside, from "above." The church is not and never has been indigenous in the sense in which, for example, the Labour Party has been. Local leadership is nearly always subordinate to imported leadership which in any case rarely stays for a lifetime. All this reflects a continuing failure of imagination as to the potentiality of working people and as to what sort of church might be truly theirs. It also illustrates that although its congregations consist of local people, it is in essence a bourgeois institution. I would like to say that my knowledge of the local clergy and the local church gives rise more to sorrow than to anger considering the obstacles which would stand in the way of transforming such an institution into a genuinely working-class one. In fact, though the clergy here are a mixed bag, as anywhere I suppose, and no doubt this and that could be "done better," there is no reason to suppose that any other group of clergy, no matter how enlightened, could change the situation significantly.

There is of course another image of the working people in the mind of the church at large, a picture of crowds of men led by the nose by irresponsible trade union leaders and trouble-making and politically motivated shop stewards. Although it is plainly a more prejudiced and crasser view than that common in localities like my own where working-class people predominate, it arises from the same root cause as the other: namely, that the church exists, politically speaking, to reflect and bless things as they are. The division of society between poor and rich, between dominators and dominated, is not to be considered an offense in the eyes of God. It is more or less as it should be, or at least must be, human nature being what it is. No doubt there are responsibilities to be exercised toward the underdogs and these are variously interpreted at different times. The church may be listened to when it asks for alms (nowadays called programs) of one sort or another for the poor, but not if it really countenances the underdog acting as if he wants to upset the whole applecart.

Communication between church and common people then exists, but perhaps there is not enough of the right sort? Perhaps something is needed which goes deeper, which reveals to the workers the "true" objectives of the church and to the church the true character and situation of the working people? Such, I suppose, might sympathetic observers consider the aims of the worker priest. How well does he fulfill them?

Nobody would expect a person in my position to be self-satisfied on this score, but perhaps he should at least be able to say where he might have succeeded if he'd been a better man or an abler one. Certainly one might have put oneself forward more, become a sort of authority on the church/common people divide. Seminars could have been arranged between trade unionists and church people, lecture tours and sermon series undertaken. But if this sort of thing was too ambitious, and a little out of character, there was surely the daily exchange which must take place in ordinary life. You go to work every day and find yourself among people. You perform as best you can according to your faith. Inevitably there is conversation, opportunity to serve; there are even from time to time close relationships. People know you are a priest. Surely truth is exchanged? Surely a few people at least gain a truer understanding of what Christianity is about and are challenged by it? Seeing the devotion of the priest among them, must they not turn more hopefully toward the church which sent him? And, on the other side of the exchange, the church must surely benefit as the worker-priest moves in its circles correcting its stereotypes, undermining its prejudices? Maybe. But if the answer to these questions is yes, there is precious little evidence to prove it, and, in any case, none of these hopeful conclusions reckons with the changes which can take place in the priest himself. As he lives at this interface between the institution and the people, he may begin to have thoughts which are as awkward for himself as for any one on either side of the divide. Here he is, an agent of the Gospel, taking it for granted that the historical dissociation of the church from the poor is a Bad Thing and needs to be reversed. Of course the institution needs to be revolutionized in order to accommodate the poor, but the church is still the church and he is still its representative. After all, though, *can* the church be revolutionized, and in what sense can it properly be said to be the Body of Christ if it *needs* to be revolutionized?

No doubt other contributors to this volume will draw attention to the part played by the Society of the Catholic Commonwealth in the lives of Cyril and Marjorie Powles. I am among those who shared with them the high inspiration of that fellowship. One of the ideas we learned from F.H. Smyth, the founder of the SCC, and which gave us hope despite our sense of the betrayal of the Gospel by the churches, was that somehow the church might be "re-founded" in cells of people living in a revolutionary way while both associating with and criticizing contemporary revolutionary movements. Believing that the church's true nature was being denied by its compromises with capitalist society, we insisted that the basis of such a refounding must be orthodoxy in doctrine, in ministry, and in sacramental practice. It is a testimony to the power of the assumptions behind this idea, assumptions which have been mine since earliest childhood, that only now, long after the demise of the SCC, am I able to question it seriously. Perhaps after all the church's separation from the poor is as much a judgment of God as a betrayal in itself, and who should try to reverse God's judgments? Perhaps the Gospel of Christ has nothing to do with the Christian church any more and is up for grabs by another "nation" (Matt 21:43)? Certainly, whenever I approach what I understand to be the meaning of the Gospel in conversation with my mates at work, whether it has to do with repentance and personal transformation, or justice and a new society, or indeed any of the crucial teachings of Christ, we seem as far as possible from the church and its concerns. And by the same token, when the worker-priest vests himself as it were to fulfill his functions among the faithful, he finds himself somehow divested of the Gospel. It is just as well, for it would only offend the institution as it did in Christ's day.

At this interface the problem of identity is very great. What can it mean to be a priest who cannot either in fact or in conscience lead the people around him toward the worshipping community? And what can it mean to be a workman who turns away from the locus of the Gospel — the common herd and its struggles — to join with a specialist society in saying its prayers? The priest may not cut himself off from the Body which commissioned him. The man may not abandon the place where the action is. But these are not simply two sides of his life — they are two polarities. Could it be a fair item on the "agenda for the church" to authorize and encourage more men and women to be worker-priests when this is to be their experience? It appears to me now after all these years that it may be too much to ask. Of course, some would find the internal conflict easier if they kept the two sides of the life apart and did not look too hard for the Gospel, or worked out their commitment to it entirely in terms of service to others, or felt they had, as it were, a contemplative vocation to pursue. But if the Gospel is to be sought as something which might enliven the downtrodden, set them free within themselves in order that they might free this wretched society from its chains, indeed, from its shroud, how can a priest be fairly asked to be its minister? In all honesty the church's valediction to the neophyte worker-priest could not be "Godspeed!" but rather: "For God's sake hang on to us, but not too tight! Let go, but not entirely! Keep the secret of our compromise with the world and we'll pretend you're our man among the people."

NOTES

1   There is now a "Newsletter among Ministers-at-Work" with a subscription list of about 250, edited by Michael Ranken, 9 Alexandra Road, Epsom, Surrey KT17 4BH.
2   See Mark Hodge, "Non-Stipendiary Ministry in the Church of England," a report prepared for the General Synod of the Church of England (London: CIO Publishers, 1983). This estimates the number of NSMs as 773.
3   Since 1957 the Worker Church Group, now the Shop Floor Association, has united men and women, priests and laity, in the commitment to serve the Gospel from within the status of wage workers.

II

The Experience of the
Japanese Church

Christianity and the People in Japan

John Takeda

In this paper I shall point out problems of Christianity in its encounter with "people" of Japan and with their traditional life and customs. The "people" (*minshū*) of Japan, though the word is expressed in the same Chinese characters as its counterpart in Korea (*minjung*), hardly appear to have the same features today as previously. We may even say that the Japanese Minshū and the Korean Minjung (with Asian people in general) stand in contrast. The majority of those notorious tour groups from Asian countries are actually Japanese Minshū. Those hectic Japanese businessmen in Third World countries are from the Minshū. Those common soldiers who, during the war, outraged innocent people in many places such as Manila and Nanking were Minshū. Today the Minshū are the ruling rather than the ruled, the haves rather than the have-nots. Before the beginning of the modernization of Japan, the Minshū as such did have the characteristics that are associated with the Korean Minjung. In the process of modernization, however, the Japanese Minshū lost the characteristics of the oppressed and exploited people.

The individual Minshū never present themselves as typical self-reliant modern human beings. Rather, they have little self-confidence and tend to depend on the powerful and conform to the majority. Neither do they seem to be secularized. The survey of the religious consciousness of the Minshū by the Asahi Press in 1981 provides some statistics: 62 percent put no trust in the established religions, but 60 percent believe in the immortality of the soul, and 54 percent have a sensitivity for the supernatural; more than 80 percent have household altars in their homes with Shinto or Buddhist practices; 72 percent believe they will be punished for evil acts; 58 percent feel peace of mind when staying with their family at home; 55 percent carry some kind of amulet.

One of the most popular services in the Japanese church is the memorial service for the dead. In an ordinary parish church in both rural and urban areas, it is almost routine practice that the priest read the names of the dead members and commemorate them in the main Sunday Eucharist. Many families ask the priest for a memorial service for their dead members at their home or beside the grave. This demand originates in their fear of the spirits of the dead, a fear that lingers even after they have become Christian. It is believed that the spirit of the dead wanders around for some time after death and that it must be commemorated faithfully by the living so that it may rest in peace.

From early times the spirits have been particularly associated with the mountains. When the army of the fifth-century Yamato clan invaded the local communities, most of the villagers surrendered and eventually intermingled with the invaders, but some of the respected men such as the village elders and others of integrity who were ashamed to surrender, instead of attempting a hopeless resistance, withdrew into the mountains. Separated from the everyday life of the village community, they started a hermit-like mountain life. The people's feeling toward the "mountain men" (*sanjin*) was ambiguous: they had a guilty conscience and a sense of fear toward them, but they also felt love and a sense of dependence. They would be able to find their own identity only when they had a sense of being with the Sanjin. Gradually there came to be many local legends about the Sanjin, in which the amalgamation of the Sanjin with *onryō* (the avenging spirits of the deceased) was made.

Mountains became the locale of Buddhist ascetic practice in the second main phase of Buddhism, the ninth-century Heian period (compare the scholastic Buddhism of the nobility in the cities in the sixth- and seventh-century Nara period). This second phase was esoteric and mystical. Its spiritual exercise put great emphasis on physical exercise, sometimes such strenuous exercise that the person could slip into a trance and see a vision. The *gyōsha* (spiritual exerciser), after spending a certain period of time in the mountains, would return to "this world." On his return, the people would treat him as a respectable man with charismatic gifts such as healing, telepathy, soothing the avenging onryō, and the like. He became a sort of mediator between the people in the village (this world) and the gods in the mountain (the other world). He would play the role of spiritual leader and adviser for the people.

The gyōsha usually came from among the common people, but after becoming a gyōsha, though working for the people's welfare, he would not settle down in any village community as a member. He would separate himself from his community and home. He would become a wandering traveler, visiting people in any village to help them. The gyōsha sometimes became leaders of village insurrections when taxes or labour duties became unbearable. When the rulers put these insurrections down, the gyōsha was arrested as the instigator, tortured and put to death; then he would be remembered by the people. There was also a strange custom among some of these gyōsha from around the tenth century, especially at times of turmoil. This custom was called *dōchū nyujō*, voluntary burial alive. The gyōsha actually became a scapegoat for the people. All in all, the spiritual activity of the gyōsha was not for his own spiritual growth but for the salvation of the people.

Although the people admit that the Ultimate Being (Tathata in Buddhism, the Great Ancestor Goddess Amaterasu-o-mikami in Shinto) deserves their respect, they are not quite attracted by these supreme deities. Rather, they put their trust in subordinate deities who are in the world striving for truth and suffering with the people. The Bodhisattva (Jizō Bosatsu), the avenging spirits (*onryō*), the "mountain men" (*sanjin*), and the mountain ascetic (*gyōsha*) have common features, the gyōsha being an expression in human form of compassionate suffering. The traditional spirituality of the people of Japan seems to underlie them all.

It would be good to take up any cases of Christian gyōsha that may have existed. But instead of that, I am compelled to deal here with the question of why it is *not* easy to find such Christian ministry among the people of Japan.

It has often been pointed out that the Japanese generally have no sense of suffering but have an emotional feeling of transitoriness and self-pity in the face of supernatural powers. That may be correct as far as Japanese poetry and literature are concerned, for example, in works such as the eleventh-century *Tale of Genji*. But these works, though written movingly and with highly refined literary skill, were complacent in their self-pity. They do not express the reality of the people's suffering for they were written by authors who did not understand this reality.

When Protestant Christianity was introduced into Japan in the latter half of the nineteenth century, the initial Christian converts were not from the Minshū. Those who became interested in this new religious teaching were primarily intellectuals from the ruling class of Meiji society. Although they belonged to the group of the samurai which was excluded from the current ruling party, they were nevertheless men and women of great self-respect, well-educated and well-to-do. They were trying to rebuild Japan with new knowledge and ideology from the western world. Christianity was one facet of this new wisdom, so they were attracted to it as well. As they held Confucianism as the basis of samurai moral principles, they were already rationalistic in their training. As Christians, they did have a concern for the common people, but their approach was paternalistic and philanthropic. They treated the Minshū as ignorant people and their religious beliefs and customs as primitive, superstitious, pagan, and syncretistic.

Kanzō Uchimura (1861-1930) is an example of a samurai Christian. He was the founder of the Mu-Kyōkai (the Non-Church Movement), and was a much-respected Christian leader in Japan. Uchimura was one of the samurai intellectuals seeking new western knowledge from the missionaries, but still with the self-consciousness of the old ruling warrior class, and in the spirit of Zen Buddhism and Confucian ethics. Uchimura belonged to the official academic circle which had been founded by the new government for training the leaders of the new modern nation. He was a teacher of the First High School, a kind of preparatory school for the Imperial University. He once explained the relationship between Jesus and the disciples using the analogy of the samurai society, i.e., the feudal lord and his retainers. This analogy could hardly be understood by the common people in Japan. His attitude toward the people seemed to be as an enlightened teacher who looked down upon the people as ignorant and pagan.

In contrast to the philanthropic type of Christian is another type of Japanese Christian. Tōson Shimazaki (1872-1943), a famous poet who was baptized when he was a student at Meiji Gakuin (a Reformed school in Tokyo), was a romantic, individualistic intellectual, interested in Christianity's ideal of love. However, he used this idea of love as a basis for seeking a self-indulgent freedom rather than the responsible freedom given by the grace of God. His type of Christian was indifferent to anything happening in the outside world, and was rather complacent.

Uchimura and Shimazaki represent the two characteristic types of Japanese Christians in the initial period. Eventually Christianity spread to the Minshū as they began to have middle-class traits, due to their transformation. However, the features represented by these two types of Christian have been maintained in Japanese Christianity as a whole. Today the church in Japan consists mainly of middle-class people in urban areas who are seeking a stable family life in the city, who are well-educated, and who are white-collar workers. The schools founded by the missionaries have thus had the remarkable role in modern Japan of training the Minshū, promoting them to a higher middle-class, bourgeois, status and giving them the hope of identifying with the values of the traditional upper class.

In a typical parish church, the majority of the members are college graduates. They enjoy a solemn atmosphere at Sunday Eucharist. There is some kind of "intellectual" Bible study and members with their own family problems may come to the priest to ask for spiritual advice. For philanthropic purposes, fund-raising charity bazaars are held, but the "social fellowship program" sponsored for church members is enjoyed much more. Although the members are seeking a higher social status, they expect their church to be their "spiritual asylum" and to have the function that the traditional household religion had for previous generations of the Minshū. So the church as a whole tends to conform with the current political power and is somewhat reluctant to stand against it. Also, the church is not positively concerned with the reality of the lower class of the Minshū and the marginalized minority people. The church's sense of mission is lacking.

What should be the role of Christian spirituality in this kind of situation? I understand Christian spirituality as letting the Holy Spirit work more effectively in us, in the church, and in the world. My agenda, then, consists of three reflections on the work of the Holy Spirit.

First: Let the Holy Spirit, the Strengthener, work in the church and in individual Christians in order that they may stand more firmly as a self-reliant church and as self-reliant individual Christians before God and proclaim more courageously the Lordship of the One Transcendent God to the Minshū and to the ruling powers. When in 1709 Giovanni B. Sidotti (1668-1715), an Italian missionary priest from Manila, called on Hakuseki Arai (1657-1725), a high official in the Shōgun government, to ask him why the Japanese government had made Christianity an illegal religion, Arai answered, "Because Christians worship Absolute God. Only the Emperor has the right to worship Absolute God and if the common people begin to worship Absolute God, we would not be able to govern the people." Arai really had a good insight about Christianity: he knew that it was the religion which could turn the world upside down!

Until the establishment of State Shinto in 1870, there had been frequent local insurrections of the Minshū against the oppression of landowners and the local magistrates. These insurrections were often stimulated by the Minshū's private religious beliefs and mobilized by the itinerant gyōsha. They were suppressed after the Restoration of Imperial Rule and the establishment of State Shinto. Perhaps Christian spirituality could more effectively stimulate the Minshū's latent strength than their old religious beliefs did, and enable them to struggle in commitment against the injustice of the political and economic powers.

Second: The encounter of Christian spirituality with popular Shintoism must begin, from the perspective of Japanese Christianity, with the recognition that the Holy Spirit has been working in the Minshū's religious beliefs. The prerequisite for this kind of discernment is to reflect on and to reappraise the role which Christianity has played in the history of the modernization of Japan. In some aspects Christianity must be given credit for its role in modernization, but so far as the attitude towards popular Shintoism is concerned, Christians have regarded it as a mere primitive, animistic religion of the superstitious Minshū, and accordingly despised it. Further, the church requires catechumens to denounce it. On the other hand, we must notice that until the disestablishment of State Shinto in 1945, Christianity, except for a small number of individuals and groups, had tried to avoid conflict with the imperialistic and militaristic policy of the government based on State Shinto ideology. We must also notice today's phenomenon of many Christians desiring to have a closer contact with highly developed Buddhist teachings and practices such as Zen or Shinran's Pure Land teaching. But so far as popular Shintoism is concerned, almost no attention has been given it by Japanese Christians. Even in Japan's academic circles, although the studies of "formal traditional religions," i.e., Buddhism and establishment Shinto, have been highly advanced, popular Shintoism as the "private" religious tradition of the Minshū has not been given much attention. In short, both Christianity and academic religious studies are concerned only with the religions of the establishment. But if it is the mission of the church in Japan to meet and be responsible for the spiritual needs of the Minshū, then it should discern the works of the Holy Spirit in popular Shintoism, and reassess the spiritual values of Shintoism that remain in the Minshū to this day. Special attention should be given to the religious beliefs, customs and piety of the Minshū, such as the *matsuri* (local festivals), spiritual exercises, popular devotion to the Bosatsu, respect for spirits, belief in nature, and so on.

Third: Let the Holy Spirit, the Guide to all truth, lead the Minshū Christians to realize who they essentially are. It will be necessary for the Minshū today, who have now taken the form and consciousness of the bourgeoisie, to encounter the real oppressed Minshū in Japan who have features in common with the Minjung and other peoples of Asia, so that they may understand who they really are: the Minshū — the people. They have to meet those whom they have been exploiting and discriminating against: Korean residents in Japan, the Ainu, the Buraku (unclean) people, people in Okinawa and those who have been victimized by economic development and pollution. Perhaps the Holy Spirit is speaking to the Minshū Christians today as he spoke to St. Peter when Cornelius sent to him his three servants (the Gentiles whom St. Peter was avoiding encountering because his people discriminated against them): "Behold, three men are looking for you. Rise and go down, and accompany them without hesitation; for I have sent them" (Acts 10:20). It is only by the work of the Holy Spirit that the Japanese Minshū Christians shall be able to be open to and accompany those marginalized people without hesitation and be made the people of God together with them. Although this has not been the pattern of Japanese Christianity, today there are some signs of the Holy Spirit working toward this goal. Gradually the realization is growing of what it means to be a Christian today in Japan. There are increasing numbers of honest attempts to create solidarity with the minority peoples and to speak up and take action for them. At the same time, the problem of the Imperial ruling structure and ideology (*tennō-sei*) as the essential cause of suppression of the rights of the Minshū is being taken up in many quarters of the church.

Some Reflections on the Missionaries' Right to Preach the Gospel: With Special Reference to Uchimura Kanzō (1861-1930)

Yuzo Ota

The religion which can unite people in the same faith can also be an important dividing factor for humanity by contributing to what Konrad Lorenz calls "Scheinartenbildung" (pseudo-species-formation)[1] which induces members of one group to regard those outside it as outside the pale of humanity itself and might lead them to show no sensitivity to what they hold sacred. It is regrettable that we must affirm, with Lorenz, that a religious war is not yet a thing of the past for us living in the twentieth century.[2] The shadow of a religious war in one form or another will continue to haunt us if religions encourage fanatical belief which denies to other people any legitimate deviation from one's own values and ideas.

The question of tolerance seems to be particularly important for people brought up in the western Christian tradition. After all, Christianity has remained a missionary religion in the sense that Shintoism or Confucianism is not. Even today there are as many as 2,000 Christian missionaries in Japan, virtually all of them from North America and Europe.[3] In what spirit and with what aims are these missionaries working in Japan and elsewhere? Are they still aiming primarily to convert natives to Christianity? What kind of expectations do the Christians at home have of them? Are the majority of western Christians intellectually and spiritually open to non-Christian and non-western traditions as was, for example, Pierre Teilhard de Chardin, who thought that, in order to come of age, the earth required contributions from all its people?[4] Are they ready to learn, instead of just trying to teach? These are some of the questions which occur to me, who, as a non-Christian born and brought up in Japan, would like to see Christians and non-

Christians related in a natural way based on mutual tolerance and respect both at home and abroad.

In this context I had an interesting experience during the academic year 1982-83, when I included in the list of required reading for one of my courses at McGill University biographical and autobiographical works on two of the most well-known Christians of modern Japan, namely, Niijima Jō (Joseph Hardy Neesima) (1843-1890) and Uchimura Kanzō (1861-1930).[5] What surprised me was that for the majority of my students who had come to know them through these works, Uchimura was felt to be a much more sympathetic figure than Niijima, despite the fact that he was much more critical towards the west than Niijima. In this I believed I saw a reflection of the increased complexity of the world view of North American people, and consequently a greater openness on their part to other world views, in comparison with the time when Niijima and Uchimura studied in the United States, between 1865 and 1874 and between 1884 and 1888, respectively. In this essay I would like to expound the thoughts stimulated by this "discovery" with the hope that they may in turn stimulate readers' thinking about the way Christians (especially those in the west) and non-Christians (especially, those outside the west) should be related to each other.

Niijima, the first Japanese graduate of an American college and the first Japanese to be ordained a Christian minister, is remembered today as the founder of the Doshisha, an important educational institution in Kyoto. He entertained, in my opinion, a very simplistic picture of the world after having first-hand experience of the United States. To him his country Japan was "the benighted Japan"[6] and, so to speak, a realm of darkness. He believed the native tradition should be rejected more or less in toto as "heathenish customs."[7] The United States, the country of his benefactor who enabled him to receive a good education and to prepare himself for his future activities in Japan, was a wonderful country and a realm of light. Niijima's mission then was to make Japan like the United States. How should he do this? What was the secret of the excellence of the western civilization in general and that of the United States in particular? Niijima's answer was again simple — it was Protestant Christianity which was "the true secret of the progress of civilization,"[8] and, thus, what he should do was to propagate Christianity to his fellow Japanese.

Many Americans at that time held a similar view. S. Wells Williams, who accompanied the Perry Expedition to Japan in 1853 and 1854 as the first interpreter, saw "the real source of our superiority in the momentous truths of the Bible."[9] After he had had some chance to observe the behaviour of Japanese people, he wrote, "the unblushing effrontery of these fishermen, as indeed of most whom we have seen, shows how much Japan needs the gospel of purity and love."[10] Williams was probably quite typical of Americans of that time for his matter-of-course assumption of the superiority of his country over "heathen" Japan.

Though early converted to Christianity, Uchimura was a much more disturbing and irritating figure to contemporary Americans than Niijima. When Uchimura actually came to the United States in 1884, the idealized picture of the United States which he had formed at home was shattered by the discovery that "Christian" America, with its frequent robbery, money worship, racial discrimination, and so on, was not better than "heathen" Japan as far as manifestations of various social vices were concerned. "Is this the civilization we were taught by missionaries to accept as an evidence of the superiority of Christian Religion over other religions? With what shamefacedness did they declare unto us that the religion which made Europe and America must surely be the religion from on high? If it was Christianity that made the so-called Christendom of today, let Heaven's eternal curse rest upon it!" (p. 91) So wrote Uchimura with his characteristic vehemence and rhetorical exaggeration.

It is relatively easy to affirm the superiority of one country over another in tangible matters such as the amount of automobile production, but to judge if the ethical or spiritual level of the United States of, say, 1880 was higher than Japan's is not easy. Despite Niijima's conviction that Japan needed a moral regeneration through Christianity more than anything else before she could become a rich and prosperous country, it is not easy to prove that the Japanese of the Meiji period were ethically at a lower level than the Americans of the same period. "A foreigner, after remaining a few months in Japan, slowly begins to realize that, whereas he thought he could teach the Japanese everything, he finds to his amazement and chagrin, that those virtues or attributes which, under the name of humanity are the burden of moral teaching at home, the Japanese seem to be born with," observed Edward S. Morse, an American scientist who came to Japan in 1877.[11] To many Christian missionaries, as well as to native converts of the early Meiji period, native religions were idol-worship which could only lead to complete moral depravity. Morse, however, after living in Japan for some time, had the following words to say about "paganism." "Now this is paganism — to be kind and obliging, courteous and hospitable, generous with their food and their time, sharing their last bowl of rice with you; and whatever you may be doing, — collecting, pulling up a boat, or anything else, — jinrikisha men, or fishermen, always ready to lend, or rather to give in abundance, a helping hand."[12]

William Smith Clark, who came to Japan in 1876 to be the president of the newly established Sapporo Agricultural College had a somewhat similar experience to Morse's. "Speaking of his absence in a foreign land [Japan], he [Clark] said he had had a good deal of conceit taken out of him since he went away. He had found as good men in heathendom as there were in Amherst," reads a report of his talk after his return to the United States.[13]

It is not wise to construct a picture of nineteenth-century "heathen" Japan solely on the favourable testimonies given by people such as Morse and Clark. The testimonies given by Christian missionaries are, as one might expect, generally more gloomy. "In morals, they [the Japanese] are like all pagan peoples, untruthful, licentious and unreliable," was the judgment of James C. Hepburn, one of the first Protestant missionaries who arrived in Japan in 1859.[14]

If people such as Morse and Clark were unduly favourable towards Japan and the Japanese, the missionaries were very likely equally prejudiced in the opposite direction. It was Uchimura's experience in the United States that, if in a speech at a mission convention he referred to admirable Japanese customs and traits or to great people Japan had produced, the audience would react unfavourably and manifest great dissatisfaction.[15] This was very likely because the western Christians, who wanted to justify religion (Christianity) in terms of culture (the western civilization) before the "heathens," saw in the low moral standard of the "heathens" one of the most eloquent justifications for missionary activities. However, if the claim of the ethical superiority of the Christian nations over heathen nations were not factually tenable, what kinds of justification, if any, were left for sending Christian missionaries to non-western countries or for native converts to preach Christianity to their own people?

This question occupied Uchimura deeply. Unlike the Christian missionaries who normally talked only about blessings of accepting the Christian faith, Uchimura was deeply aware of the various troubles and difficulties which a conversion to Christianity could entail. "It is a veritable misfortune to have embraced Christianity in this country [Japan]. It causes very serious difficulties for you in your life,"[16] said Uchimura in 1897.

As Uchimura's words indicate, when the Christian gospel was preached by a western missionary to individuals who belonged to different cultural and religious traditions, all sorts of problems could arise for them. An introduction of an alien religion could occasion considerable social disruption as can be seen in many anti-Christian riots in China in the nineteenth century. An alien religion could denationalize and make *déracinés* of converts — a danger the nationalistic Uchimura was particularly aware of.[17] An alien religion could also cause a violent internal tumult in the soul of a new convert by destroying his inner peace. Uchimura himself was in fact a good illustration of difficulties which a conversion to an alien religion could entail. He lost his job at the Number One Higher Middle

School in 1891 for his hesitation to bow deeply in a manner somewhat reminiscent of religious obeisance before the imperial signature
attached to a copy of the Imperial Rescript on Education, due to his
Christian scruples.[18] As for the internal tumult in the soul of a new
convert, Uchimura was no stranger to it: "I was to see New England
by all means, for my Christianity came originally from New England
and she was responsible for all the internal struggles caused thereby"
(p. 112), wrote Uchimura.

It was in the last chapter of *How I Became a Christian*, "The Net
Impression of Christendom — Return Home," that Uchimura
addresses himself in detail to the question of the justification of
preaching Christianity to "heathen" people. "Is Christendom after
all better than Heathendom? Is Christianity worth introducing to
my country; or is there *raison d'être* of Christian mission?" (p. 148),
he asks himself.

His answer to the former question is neither a simple affirmation
nor a negation. Uchimura maintains that in Christendom both
goodness and badness are more extreme than in Heathendom.
According to him, "One characteristic of Truth is that it makes the
bad worse and the good better" (p. 154). So, Christianity as Truth
"develops badness as well as goodness" (p. 154). The worst kinds of
evil to be found in Christendom are then no longer signs of the
failure of Christianity but rather evidence of the intensity of the light
shed by Christianity, Uchimura seems to be arguing; for, as he
metaphorically expresses it, "The same sun that melts wax hardens
clay" (p. 154).

Uchimura's interpretation may represent a more honest attempt
to tackle the question of vices in Christendom than just overlooking
their existence or committing the inconsistency, as pointed out by
Simone Weil, of taking heathen religions to task for various vices in
heathen societies but maintaining that vices in Christendom exist in
spite of the perfection of Christianity.[19] Nevertheless, his interpretation seems to be of dubious merit. Uchimura's assertion that Truth
[Christianity] "makes the bad worse [instead of good] and the good
better" is not only a very arbitrary statement (Uchimura writes, "It is
useless to ask why this is so." [p. 154]), it seems to have serious
deterministic implications.

In the last analysis, the position taken by Uchimura is rather
conservative. He reaffirms the conventional exclusive claim of Christianity: "Christianity is more and higher than Heathenism *in that it
makes us keep the law*. It is Heathenism *plus* Life. By it alone the
law-keeping becomes a possibility" (p. 152). Uchimura also reaffirms the *raison d'être* of Christian mission by such statements as:
"You cannot make yourself perfect without making others perfect.
An idea of perfect Christendom in midst of encircling heathenism is

impossible. In Christianizing other peoples, you Christianize yourself" (p. 162).

I shall not dwell upon what to me seems an obvious contradiction between his claim that Christianity alone "makes us keep the law" and his admission that vices in Christendom are often worse than in Heathendom. There are too many seemingly contradictory statements to comment on at this time. As we have seen, Uchimura admits that both on individual and social levels Christianity is not necessarily an unmixed blessing. What makes him prefer Christianity to "heathenism," all the same, seems to be something akin to the Romantic love of drama and power. "Heathenism I always consider as a *tepid* state of human existence; — it is neither *very* warm nor *very* cold. A lethargic life is a weak life. It feels pains less; hence rejoices less. *De profundis* is not of heathenism. We need Christianity to intensify us" (pp. 166-67), he says. However, many people will feel that when Uchimura implies that a butterfly and pink rose should be changed to an eagle and an oak (see p. 167), he is simply forcing his taste on others.

Uchimura in *How I Became a Christian* does not provide a real basis for genuine dialogue among believers of different religions. He tries to be fair to heathenism up to a point. He says, "We will meet our enemy in his best and strongest" (p. 151). It was also one of his great "discoveries" during his stay in the United States that the Christian God had been guiding even "heathen" Japan:

> "I recounted to myself all the great men of my own heathen land and weighed their words and conducts [sic]; and I came to the conclusion that the same God that spoke to Jeremiah did also speak to some of my own countrymen, though not so audibly as to him; that He did not leave us entirely without His light and guidance, but loved us and watched over us these long centuries as He did the most Christian of nations. The thought was inspiring beyond my power of expression. Patriotism that was quenched somewhat by accepting a faith that was exotic in origin, now returned to me with hundredfold more vigor and impression" (p. 110).

However, I suspect that Uchimura never really tried to understand "heathen" traditions from within. He had imbibed the dominant nationalistic spirit of Meiji Japan from his childhood and he, as a representative of Christians with a heathen background, tried to wage a battle against patronizing and self-righteous Christians of Christendom; but towards real "heathens" in heathendom, he was, in the last analysis, virtually just as patronizing and self-righteous. Who among the real "heathens" would not feel the arbitrariness of his claim, "Indeed, I can say with all truthfulness that I saw *good men* only in Christendom" (p. 157)?

Simone Weil compares the change of religion for an individual to the change of language for a writer.[20] The implication is that, although there are exceptions, both normally lead to poor results. Probably she is right. Her reminder that one can hope to understand other religions only with a kind of empathy seems to be important for those who are genuinely interested in interreligious and inter-cultural communications.[21] Moved by nationalistic desire for self-assertion and self-justification, Uchimura studied the Japanese "heathen" tradition somewhat, but he does not seem to have accorded them full attention as something valuable in themselves. He seems to have studied only to gain weapons for self-defense against western Christians whose unconscious arrogance had hurt his nationalistic sensitivity. I believe that those Christians of the present day who want to live peacefully with people who do not share their faith should approach non-Christian traditions with a greater amount of humility than did Uchimura.

NOTES

1 Konrad Lorenz, *Das sogenannte Böse: Zur Naturgeschichte der Aggression* (1961; München: Deutscher Taschenbuch Verlag, 1974), p. 86.

2 Ibid., p. 87

3 *Kirisutokyō nenkan: 1983* (Tokyo: Kirisuto Shinbusha, 1983), pp. 739-60.

4 Pierre Teilhard de Chardin, *Lettres de voyage 1923-1955* (1956; Paris: François Maspero, 1982), p. 104.

5 They are: Arthur Sherburne Hardy, *Life and Letters of Joseph Hardy Neesima* (Boston and New York: Houghton, Mifflin and Company, 1892) and Uchimura Kanzō, *How I Became a Christian*, *Uchimura Kanzō zenshū*, XV (Tokyo, Iwanami Shoten, 1933), pp. 1-169. *How I Became a Christian* was originally published in a book form in 1895 and it is written in English. Subsequent quotations from Uchimura's writings in this essay, unless otherwise stated, are all taken from *How I Became a Christian* and they will be indicated in the text itself by the page numbers of *Uchimura Kanzō zenshū*, Vol. XV.

6 Hardy, p. 65.

7 Ibid., p. 86.

8 Ibid., p. 103.

9 S. Wells Williams, *A Journal of the Perry Expedition to Japan* (1910; rpt. Wilmington, Delaware: Scholarly Resources, Inc., 1973), p. 148.

10 Ibid., p. 164.

11 Edward S. Morse, *Japan Day by Day* (1917; rpt. Tokyo: Kobunsha Publishing Company, 1936), I, p. 44.

12 Ibid., I, p. 246.

13 *The Amherst Record*, 1 Aug. 1877, p. 4, col. 3.

14 William Elliot Griffis, *Hepburn of Japan* (Philadelphia: Westminster Press, 1913), p. 97.
15 "Ani hitori Tamura-shi nomi naranya," *Uchimura Kanzō zenshū*, II (Tokyo: Iwanami Shoten, 1933), pp. 199-200.
16 "Konnichi no konnan," *Uchimura Kanzō zenshū*, II (Tokyo: Iwanami Shoten, 1933), p. 776.
17 See also *How I Became a Christian*, pp. 163-64.
18 Ozawa Saburō, *Uchimura Kanzō fukei jiken* (Tokyo: Shinkyo Shuppansha, 1961), pp. 9, 66-67, and 78.
19 Simone Weil, *La Pesanteur et la Grâce* (1948; rpt. Paris, Union Générale D'Édition, 1979), p. 138.
20 Simone Weil, *Attente de Dieu* (Paris: Éditions Fayard, 1966), p. 177.
21 Ibid., pp. 177-78.

Sowing and Reaping:
A Christian Leader in
Post-Hiroshima Japan

John F. Howes

The New Testament contains many metaphors of growth which compare the spread of the faith to the sowing of seed. Generations of missionaries have started their professions with a sense of pioneering adventure. They have felt within themselves the potential of a new seed just planted. While these missionaries have continued to work, reports home have educated their fellows in the development of new churches. When the missionaries return home for the last time, communication often stops. Those at home who have devoted money and prayer to nurture new congregations lose contact with what they have helped start.

Actually, in many parts of the world the new churches surpass their parent organizations in dedication and vigor. Less known than many other young communities is that of Japan. It has not grown as fast as many, but it deserves close attention. Secular conditions in Japan increasingly resemble those of the nations which sent it missionaries. In these circumstances, Japanese Christianity has produced a significant core of leaders rich in dedication, personality and accomplishment.

One of these is Fukatsu Fumio. His life in many ways reflects the changes which have come about in Japanese Christianity since 1945. Rev. Fukatsu was born in 1909. He grew up in Manchuria, the vast northeastern section of China whose fertile plains attracted so many Japanese. In 1933, when a Tokyo theological seminary graduated him, Fukatsu dedicated himself to an enthusiastic and active ministry. He was the pastor of a church in Tokyo when the bomb at Hiroshima ended World War II in 1945.

A recalling of the last few months of the war introduces an autobiography which covers the twenty postwar years of Fukatsu's life.* The autobiography chronicles the growth of Fukatsu's personality and thought as he gradually became aware of the problems faced by ex-prostitutes and as he developed a special settlement for them. The following analysis is based on these recollections.

The description of events which begins the book demonstrates how one night of firebombing near the end of the war clearly separated what happened later in Fukatsu's life from what had gone before. He had retired after meeting with a number of friends to read Genesis in Hebrew. When the bombs dropped and fires sprang up, he started to spray water on nearby buildings. To get sufficient pressure, two other people had to operate a pump while he controlled the stream of water. They fled, and all he could do was remove some of the books from the doomed buildings. By the next morning, half of Tokyo had burned. Fukatsu had lost the church, a student dormitory and his home. He and his wife cleaned up and moved into the kindergarten. A few months later Fukatsu, like most Japanese, heard the recorded voice of the Emperor announce the end of the war. "While listening to his voice, tears welled up in my eyes, but somewhere within the depths of my being I thought, 'Good, good'" (p. 40).

As the shock of defeat passed, Fukatsu realized that he alone remained alive from a group of three students who had pledged to work together after seminary. This circumstance seemed to devolve a particular responsibility onto him. His book covers three major stages in his activity as he responded to this inner need. For ten years he continued at the church. When he resigned, he went on to found an order of Protestant women dedicated to service. Out of this came the movement to start a "colony" for ex-prostitutes. Through his description of this career development one discovers in Fukatsu a man who views his life as a series of encounters with history. He gradually changes his own view of his calling as a Christian, finally, to accomplish his aim, finding himself enmeshed in the practical ways of the world, far from the life for which he trained.

Fukatsu remembers that he began to recover from the shock of the fire after two days. Sleeping on kindergarten tables pushed together, he could "look out at the night sky and the crescent moon hanging in it. This was enough to entice quiet thoughts from within me" (p. 31). Working with this resilience, Fukatsu found himself over the next few years audaciously attempting to remake the United Church of Japan, breaking with the missionaries who had helped support his church, and founding an order of lay people.

The reform started with a suggestion by Russell Durgin, a missionary friend from Fukatsu's school days. Durgin had returned to

**Ito chiisaku mazushiki mono ni* 'Unto the least and the meanest of these' (Tokyo: Nihon kirisutokyo shuppan kyoku, 1969).

Japan as an advisor to the Occupation forces. At that time, a high priority of the Occupation was to bring those responsible for the war to justice. Political and military leaders were being tried in highly publicized proceedings. The leaders of the United Church had cooperated with these government officials during the war and some of their critics felt that they also should be tried. Durgin told Fukatsu that his policy instead was to encourage reform from within. He challenged Fukatsu to act as a spokesman for change.

After quick consultation with like-minded friends, Fukatsu led a few of them up the rickety steps to the dingy office which served as the headquarters for the United Church. These young turks called for a General Assembly of all the pastors to discuss the problem of war guilt. "Do you know how much it would cost to bring them all together? Can you raise that kind of money?" asked the General Secretary.

"The General Secretary says that he lacks the money to convene a General Assembly, but if the General Secretary of an organization cannot for years on end convene a General Assembly required by the regulations, is that not in itself a sufficient reason for him to resign?" responded Fukatsu.

The embattled official responded with a reddened face and the curt comment that Fukatsu was a "Communist" (p. 56).

In the pinched days immediately after the end of the fighting, everyone lacked money. Contributions to the church fell drastically, as the General Secretary knew. But to Fukatsu, enthused with reforming zeal, this official attitude could be summarized as the "ethics of a corpse" (p. 49). Fukatsu's restless enthusiasm led him a short time later to confront another man that circumstances forced him to cooperate with — the German missionary whose superiors controlled the property on which Fukatsu's church stood.

The church was part of a large "compound," to employ the word that was often used in those days. The Germans had bought it more than half a century earlier and erected on the spacious premises a number of homes in addition to the buildings mentioned earlier. Intended for missionaries, they were rented out when there were no missionaries to fill them. However, with both Germany and Japan devastated by war, this property became an increasingly valuable resource and the possibility of other uses occurred to Japanese in the neighborhood as new buildings replaced those that had been burned out.

The land problem which resulted caused Fukatsu's separation from mission work. The record shows that the property must have bothered former missionaries as much as it did him. In 1943, the missionary then in charge had rented out two-thirds of the sanctuary to a German business. Though enough space remained for the regular congregation, this action made Fukatsu wonder what the missionary had considered his main aim. The Germans ceased to be allies of Japan after Germany surrendered in the spring of 1945. The missionary and his family were interned. After Japan surrendered, another missionary with his family of six moved into the same house as the Fukatsus. During this time one large room and kitchen on the ground floor plus a church sanctuary served as cooking, eating and relaxing space for two families. When that family returned to Germany, another missionary moved into the house; this time Fukatsu found another home nearby.

In 1952 the next missionary came with his wife. Fukatsu tells us that he and his flock awaited the arrival with great anticipation, but that their hopes were dashed, for the man seemed at once contentious, shallow and pretentious. Now, seven years after the end of the war, the area around the compound had been built up. The mission property, still largely open, seemed particularly attractive. Fukatsu, as a father of children in the school next door, realized the justice of its claim for part of the space as a playground. Yet, both repair of existing buildings and new uses for the other space had to await the decision of the missionary, for he alone had the legal right to deal with the problem. However, the missionary seemed incapable of decision and Fukatsu found himself in frequent conflict with the man. In one of his greatest moments of self-doubt, Fukatsu asked, "Why was it that I, who listened calmly to whatever sort of complaints from a Japanese, couldn't take similar talk from a foreigner?" (p. 119) Fukatsu's Japanese neighbors blamed him for the delay. Under pressure, he dreamed that someone had stabbed him, but that no one among his neighbors standing nearby would help.

The answer to his dilemma appeared shortly thereafter. He would resign and move from the neighborhood. The missionary could handle the property as he saw fit and the new pastor of the Japanese church could hardly do worse than Fukatsu. He might even do considerably better. In retrospect, Fukatsu realized that his resignation had been for the best. In this move he declared independence from the control of property which so bedevils the relations between missionaries and young churches. Fukatsu would continue for the rest of his career to work closely with Christians from abroad, but they would not control the material resources with which he worked.

Fukatsu then decided to continue with a project which had interested him for some time. This was to found an order of celibate women dedicated to Christian service. The deaconess movement had started in Germany and two of its young members had come from the German mission. Their every act reflected to Fukatsu piety, purity of purpose and adaptability to Japanese living conditions. This last characteristic was, particularly for Japanese, a "source of great joy" (p. 155). Within a short time, a number of young Japanese enrolled. Fukatsu devised several additions to the system as it had

developed in Germany. Most significant of them was the requirement that each candidate secure ten sponsors who together would
support her with funds and prayers. In addition to this spiritual and
material support for the candidate, the groups of ten increased
public awareness of the program. A small monthly journal which
Fukatsu edited linked them all together.

In all three of these developments — his defiance in the face of the
church hierarchy, his separation from the missionaries and his
founding of the deaconess movement — Fukatsu had demonstrated
courage and innovation. In the bleak years immediately after the
war, he had managed to keep his family fed and discover in the
disorder of society a matrix for innovation.

His theological position shifted as he worked through the results
of his decisions. He gradually changed from a pastor concerned with
the spiritual health of his flock into a reformer dedicated to imple-
menting Christian imperatives throughout society. He ended with a
special concern for one group whose lives had been changed for the
worse by Christian-inspired reform.

In 1945 Fukatsu was leading a small congregation whose main
body consisted of no more than twenty individuals and families. Yet
these few viewed their belief and its role in their lives as more
important than anything else. Fukatsu, convinced that the church
would have to start with the young if it was to grow, had started his
career with a kindergarten complex on the outskirts of Tokyo. With
the passage of time this effort had produced a small church. Fukatsu
also led it while he worked with his main parish in the city.

Fukatsu tried to learn as much as he could from the great leaders
of Christendom who came into the newly receptive atmosphere
provided by the Occupation. They included Paul Vieth, professor of
religious education at Yale, James Muilenburg, professor of Old
Testament at Union Theological Seminary in New York, and Emil
Brunner, the Swiss theologian. In both this pastorate and this search
for personal inspiration, Fukatsu resembled many other pastors.

He differed from them in what he did with his new knowledge.
Brunner assured Fukatsu that the bureaucratic cavil he had encountered in the church hierarchy resulted from the nature of the church
itself. He added that circumstances often required bold action outside the church. Muilenburg gave Fukatsu confidence that the Old
Testament studies his little group had started could produce valid
results. And Vieth taught him the importance of actions as opposed
to inactive faith. At first Vieth's concern with audio-visual equipment made Fukatsu wonder that a person could get an advanced
degree based on such gimmickry. But slowly Vieth's enthusiasm
caught hold. The Christian's every action is in itself instruction in the
Christian life, Fukatsu learned. Thus Christian education continues
throughout one's lifetime; it is not limited to childhood.

Fukatsu first turned to making the Gospel more broadly relevant. He wrote a text on the Old Testament for Sunday school teachers, but objections to his liberal views by an outspoken literalist layman persuaded the timid church leaders to cancel publication. They returned the manuscript they had requested without the fee they had promised. Brunner consoled Fukatsu that this was the way of the church.

Then someone asked Fukatsu to do a short stint of religious broadcasting. He discovered that others were reading university-style lectures and appeared to give little or no thought to their audience. Fukatsu realized that many listeners had little academic training and no time to concentrate on the profuse details that gushed out of their receivers. Aiming at everyday concerns and skillfully employing his rich baritone voice, Fukatsu soon became the best-known individual in Japanese religious broadcasting. He designed his own program for Sunday mornings. It used new long-playing records from Europe and North America to present a Bach cantata each Sunday. His commentary linked the words and music to the church year and to the Christian faith in general, thus bringing effective witness to a nation longing for western music and spiritual direction. Fukatsu became a renowned lecturer and writer.

Encouraged by Vieth, Brunner and his own experience, Fukatsu began to seek ways to use the graduates of his deaconess-training program. Under his direction they started a home for delinquent girls. So confident was he in the power of the deaconess' Christian dedication that he told the authorities, "Send us those no one else will take" (p. 217). They did. Most of the girls flourished in the new surroundings. Volunteer students in work camps built facilities. The complex came to number seven buildings, including sheds for raising hogs and chickens, a laundry and a bakery. Fukatsu dreamed of what he called a "colony," a larger version of the same facility. This would provide a haven for prostitutes forced out of their homes by Japan's new national anti-prostitution law.

Those Christians concerned with social reform had long tried to abolish Japan's legalized brothels. During the 1950s they succeeded. This success meant that the women who had lived in the brothels were cast out on the street. Fukatsu's work with delinquents had taught him that most of the prostitutes had very low intelligence. Outside of business hours, the brothels had provided them with a home and companionship. The reforming zeal of the Christians had cost them this sense of family which alone had mitigated the harsh conditions of their life. By themselves, they lacked the ability to do anything except return to their old profession, but now without the security of a home and the protection of the law.

By this time Fukatsu had come far from his original calling of parish pastor, and he had become a social reformer. The warning

from the leader of the German deaconess movement that one should
not waste time trying to reform prostitutes only encouraged Fukatsu
and his colleagues. For nine years they persevered in attempts to get
government sponsorship for a colony. This involved Fukatsu in
detailed negotiations with the bureaucracy. Interested members
within it urged him to set his sights high, to think big. However, once
funds became available, construction delays meant buildings could
not go up within the legal time limits. The same officials then helped
Fukatsu with the quasi-fictitious reports to the government that the
occasion demanded. He became the indispensable symbol his vision
required. As his wife drove him in their battered Volkswagen mini-
bus to one of many formal appearances, he told her, "If I die, don't
have a funeral . . . Just say, 'He is sick. [I have come] in his place . . .' "
(p. 330).

Finally the work ended. Fukatsu saw the new colony for six
hundred girls take shape on a slope which looked out across the
Pacific. A parade of government and church dignitaries came to
participate in the opening. Fukatsu rejoiced with them but recognized in a short poem the true state of affairs:

At last the colony has been built,
But the colony has not been built.
Everything
Begins now (p. 357).

For the succeeding eighteen years Fukatsu has continued at the
site in charge of his creation. His work seems to have endowed the
word "colony" with a special meaning. As in other parts of the
world, Japanese social workers have come to think that to separate a
particular group of unfortunates into a mini-society, however well-
intentioned and endowed, may not work in their best interests. As a
result, they have gone beyond the idea of a colony. But Fukatsu's
success remains as a tribute to his prescience and devotion.

Several aspects of Fukatsu's story represent characteristics common to other Japanese Christians. Perhaps foremost among them
are the vexed relations with the representatives of the nations who
sent the faith in the first place. Japanese Christians from the first
tried to gain and maintain their independence from foreign control.
Fukatsu served under missionaries who retained legal title to property longer than most. Yet, having freed himself from their control,
he immediately started up the deaconess movement as an offshoot of
the German original. And he continued to find inspiration in the
ideas and personalities of western Christian thinkers. Independence
from mission control did not mean rejection of sympathetic foreigners and attractive foreign ideas.

The fruits which Fukatsu harvested from the seeds sowed by
missionaries may not appeal to some members of the churches in
North America or Europe. One would hardly expect that they would

satisfy everyone. What Fukatsu's experience does demonstrate is that the spirit of Christ and his teaching has taken vigorous roots in Japan. The shoots have spread so that the growth must be taken seriously by those who plan national policies.

Learning from these new Christian communities constitutes an important agenda item for the contemporary western church. It is quite distinct from what seemed so important a century ago. At that time, the great need was to evangelize the whole world in our generation, as the enthusiastic founders of the Student Volunteer Movement phrased it. They succeeded, not as well as they hoped, but very well indeed. Christianity exists, even thrives, in the countries to which those inspired by the Student Volunteer Movement went. That these churches are now contributing to the international community of believers is clear from meetings such as those held recently by the World Council of Churches in Vancouver.

The voice of the church in Japan did not ring out in Vancouver. Representation, based on membership, allowed the Japanese to send very few individuals. Hampered in part by problems of language, these few said practically nothing. Over 650 representatives of the world media covered every aspect of the meetings. About twenty percent of them came from the United States. At most international meetings Japanese reporters appear as numerous as those from the United States, but it seems that in this case the Japanese were simply not interested. Even their own Christian press did not make it to Vancouver.

One could conclude that Christianity has little to say in Japan. One would be wrong. Fukatsu's story helps us understand two important aspects about the faith as it lives there.

The first is the relation between giving and receiving. The motives behind nineteenth-century Christian outreach were varied. Certainly one was the desire to share the bounty occasioned by new technology and the fruits of a newly cultivated land. Western Christians believed that giving was more blessed than receiving. Freely giving of themselves and their resources, the missionaries felt no desire for gifts in return. Yet they often seemed not to give what a true gift requires — the trust that it will be properly used.

In Japan the leaders of the new church came from the samurai elite. They were the custodians of their nation's spiritual heritage. One of its main imperatives was that no gift can be simply received. Every gift requires repayment. Where there is no obvious form of repayment, the recipient finds himself perplexed at how to expunge the burden caused by the need to repay. He expects the missionary to want something in return. Frequently the missionary's hope that the convert would join his denomination instead of another seemed to be the price. The Japanese in general have felt little sympathy for the sectarian divisions which have seemed to warp the Christian message to fit various historical developments in the west. To them the selection of one denomination from among many seemed a high price to pay for the missionary's gifts.

Fukatsu had grown through these concerns. He does not tell us if he came of samurai stock and, of course, a century after the abolition of the samurai class it makes little difference whether or not he did. But his bearing and attitude represent the conscious self-control the samurai admired. From this background Fukatsu shows us that he can receive, as from the scholars Vieth, Brunner and Muilenburg. He expects to give and receive in partnership with the German missionary whose tradition he admires. He cannot realize that the property his neighbors covet is one of the few remaining assets of the mission board which has sent the missionary. Fukatsu only knows that he must get out when it appears that the missionary can do nothing to accede to the desires of his Japanese neighbors. And Fukatsu realizes that other people may work out solutions where he has failed.

What we learn here from Fukatsu is the difficulty of cooperaton across great cultural barriers. True cooperation requires trust, and the missionary did not seem to trust Fukatsu. His story shows us the strains that receiving, in this case, placed on the recipient. And as we in the western church turn to receive, we will increasingly feel the need to learn how to accept with grace.

Fukatsu's story tells us about another element of his nation's encounter with Christianity, namely, Christianity's influence. To learn that only about three-quarters of one percent of the Japanese can be counted as Christian might make one conclude that Christianity is a puny force. This conclusion does not seem to square with Fukatsu's belief that Christians were responsible for the passage of the anti-prostitution law. Yet both facts are true. The numbers of those who commit themselves to the body of convinced believers is very small, but they and others who share their concern for social justice, in large part based on Christian ethics, have accomplished a great deal in modern Japan. In no field has this been greater than in women's rights.

Fukatsu recognized that in their great victory over the social ills of licensed prostitution, the Christians and their well-wishers seemed about to inflict another social injustice upon those most hurt by prostitution. In his appreciation of the forces that had led to the ban, he showed his understanding of Japanese history. In his correct perception of the new injustice, he recognized the perplexities of any attempt at ethical perfection. Rather than bask in self-congratulation over the original success, he allowed himself to become the symbol of the need for further effort. Thus, in a society just accustoming itself to the concept of personal rights, he fought through to an acceptance of the rights of those who must sell their bodies to live, and he found that even here moral ambiguities abound.

We notice also how in his advocacy of the rights of ex-prostitutes, Fukatsu thought less and less about the church. Though a convinced believer, he found that in order to accomplish a clearly Christian objective, he had to distance himself from the body which in the west is usually seen to represent Christianity. Christian influence in Japan rests upon an admiration for Christianity's ethical achievements and the Christian Bible. In comparison with these two elements, the church seems less important. The fact cannot be denied. The Japanese press showed no interest in the World Council of Churches' meetings, because, at least in part, the Japanese do not equate the church or churches with Christianity. Fukatsu's experience, and that of many Japanese, seems to ask whether or not the church is necessary to achieve Christian social justice.

III
Foundations for Mission

Experiential Theology:
Fad or Foundation?

Don Thompson

Schools of theology and training centres for ministry have experienced a bewildering number of challenges throughout this twentieth century. Many factors have changed the "horizon" of human living — from world wars, post-colonial imperialism, racial genocide and the threat of nuclear warfare to uncontrollable inflation, economic depression, and global food shortages. Yet these devastating events of our century are set within what can also be described as an exciting post-industrial and technologically progressive era. Hence our century is experienced as one of great contradictions and contrasts, and one that has not lent itself to simple understandings and solutions (although individuals and politicians still market "simple" truths). Rather, we see such complexity and interrelatedness in so many of our actions, programs, and discoveries that never before has an understanding of the world and its ways been so crucial to living the Christian life of faith.

These characteristics of twentieth-century living have gradually forced (and are still forcing!) a new "agenda" upon our schools of theology and ministry. Centres of learning were generally unprepared for many of the issues that this century would present. Further, seminaries and divinity faculties had emerged historically along the same line as university faculties. There was the assumption of a body of knowledge to be "learned" (i.e., the content of the theological disciplines of the "Christian faith"). This coincided with the societal assumptions as to *how* it was to be learned (i.e., as a "Christian gentleman"), with the classroom, library, chapel and common room providing the chief contexts for learning. The role of minister as graduate followed suit: the minister was "learned gentleman" within cities, neighbourhoods, communities, etc. But twentieth-century issues soon challenged that. As urban poverty began to

be recognized as an "open wound" in society, evangelical and
Catholic alike ventured out to explore what "Word" or "Sacra-
ment" would mean in such a setting. Then the devastating experience of war brought the discovery of "God in the trenches" — a
"newly discovered" place where *everyone* was supposedly transformed from sceptic to believer! New organizations such as the
Student Christian Movement in the universities began both to bring
the plights of industrial work and poverty within the horizons of the
ivy-covered walls and to encourage students and graduates to experience life "overseas" or in the "colonies," at least to round out one's
education. But the crucial questions emerging from these experiences — such as the graduate suddenly facing the realities of unemployment, abuse, or death within a parish — had *not* been dealt with in
classes on systematic theology, or even in the classes of the kind-
hearted (but ineffective) priest teaching "pastoralia." Yet these
unprepared graduates increasingly became our clergy, and only later
did their questions become focused back on the schools of theology
and ministry. Those schools and faculties were pressured to make
response.

There were, in fact, many responses that appeared after the Second World War. The issues of National Socialism in Germany had
touched all the theological "greats" from Barth and Brunner to
Tillich — as well as creating a twentieth-century theologian-martyr
in the person of Dietrich Bonhoeffer. His protests of the church's
"cheap grace," its need to hear the *real* "cost of discipleship," and its
need to explore a new "religionless Christianity" perhaps most
clearly signaled the era of a new agenda for schools of theology and
ministry. Theology *did* respond to that task at hand by taking more
and more seriously a new philosophy of the twentieth century:
existentialism. As these philosophers rejected the abstract intellectu-
alism and "objectivity" of a once classical and coherent world view,
so theologians followed suit — and found in figures like Jaspers,
Kierkegaard, and Sartre a welcome return to the *actual* existence of
human beings in all of their concrete living, acting, and doing. What
this meant was that there was a new reference point for theology: not
an abstract metaphysics, but rather the human subject itself. Yet,
who *was* this actual human subject who had become a re-discovered
reference point for theology? What were his or her thoughts, needs,
hopes, fears, etc.? Where and what was theology in his or her world?

In North America in the mid-sixties, a study undertaken by the
Association of Theological Schools by Charles R. Feilding of Trinity
College, Toronto, provided a turning point in training for ministry
— and thereby influenced the focus of theology for ministry. Feilding identified the "person in crisis" as the representative human
subject, one that could be found in almost any nearby healthcare
facility. Through appropriate programs, students of theology and

ministry could meet these "persons in crisis." Their experiences and concerns could be brought back to the theological schools as those of the exemplary "human subject" whose needs and issues should be attended to in the "doing" of theology. Over the next decade, these Clinical Pastoral Education programs became not only the focus of a student's field education, but also for much of the theology taught in the seminary itself. "Persons in crisis," as an almost cross-cultural human experience, had begun to shape not only the whole pastoral dimension of ministry, but theology itself.

But not all schools had focused on Clinical Pastoral Education. Field education programs which included a range of pastorates, social service agencies, jails, and inner city centres had also proved to be valuable contexts for revealing the human "subjects" whose issues-in-existence were also the focus for theology and ministry. Yet the variety of their contexts revealed substantial differences in the horizons of their experiences: issues of life, health, and death there continued to be — but there also appeared *another* set of issues, such as (un)employment, power(lessness), and social roles. Here the human subject was more typically experienced as *structured* (i.e., controlled) by his or her society. Sin became more clearly identifiable as *social* rather than individual; healing was the result of transformative and just responses *in society*, rather than only the physical or spiritual healing of an individual. Programs such as the Canadian Urban Training Program developed in many cities as resources for schools of theology — providing another reference point for theology of "societies in crisis." While rather more suspect than its C.P.E. counterpart, urban training did provide another "subject horizon" for theology and ministry, and in particular a substantially different social and collective view of who might be "persons in crisis." It also raised a new question for theology: if human experience is a reference point in theology, *whose* experience is to be used?

Also, by the mid-sixties to seventies, schools of theology (and social service professions in general) had been experimenting with still a further reference point. In vogue were human relations training, "T" Groups, sensitivity and interpersonal relations groups, and the whole new "science" of group dynamics. Such group techniques and processes enabled students (and faculty) of theology and ministry to become aware of *their own* subjectivity as a reference point for theology. With the horizon of subjective experience so readily at hand, these human relations groups, not surprisingly, assumed considerable prominence as a framework for theology and ministry. They projected issues of human growth such as personal authority, integrated personhood, and maturity as central to theology. Yet these issues were gradually recognized as those of the late adolescent seminary constituent about to embark upon a professional career! Again was revealed the critical question: *Whose* experience is to be used? While it came to be seen that a *seminarian's* experience was too limited a reference point, the residual effect of the "growth" movement on theology and ministry was that *education* for ministry must itself be "experiential," meaning that any basic theological insight must be capable of originating in, or at least paralleling, one's own *experience*.

A major challenge to these rather limited expressions of human experience emerged by the seventies, in what came to be referred to as "liberation theologies." The tide that had for so long brought "educated thought" to the "underdeveloped world" suddenly reversed. Third World thinkers, and specifically theologians, were suddenly heard. Probably raised up through the platform of Vatican II and World Council of Churches Assemblies, the horizon of *their* experience was now viewed through eyes that *did* see, as never before. Persons in crisis and societies in crisis now became *nations and cultures in crisis*. Terms like exploitation, violation, and injustice were added to the other descriptive terms of human experience (psychological and sociological) that had become the reference points for theology and ministry. More than any other movement in twentieth-century thought, "liberation theology" forced First World theology to recognize the degree to which it very uncritically assumes its culture's prevailing *ideology* — a discovery that becomes very apparent when Christians of one culture dialogue with those of another. But it also raised once again that very disturbing question: *Whose* experience is the reference point?

Finally, one of the most recent challenges to the prevailing descriptions of experience has come from the feminist movement. Through a combination of ears that finally could hear and mouths that dared to proclaim, the still not-so-obvious was publicly declared and affirmed: That a man's experience and a woman's experience are *not* the same thing! Re-appropriating and uplifting the experience of women in narrative, symbol, and language, this movement has most thoroughly shaken the assumptions of theology and ministry in this century by being an incarnate issue of liberation in the very midst of the First World. Not an issue of cultures with an unequal voices here, but rather an issue of the unequal voice of a whole gender of persons *within* a society itself. Little wonder that the insights of this movement are still far from being incorporated into North American theology and ministry; the oversight is almost too much for some to admit, and the re-definition of what human experience is — for *women* as well as for men — strikes at the very heart of our theological heritage and practice of ministry. And it raises still again the question: *Whose* experience is the reference point?

There are two ways the foregoing history could be read. One would be to conclude that human experience should *not* be a reference point in theology; it is obviously fraught with difficulties and might be interpreted as very misleading in this century. Another conclusion would be that we have been merely discovering some of the *implications* of referencing theology to human experience; it remains the task of this generation to find a sufficient method of doing theology such that the pluralism and complexity of human experience can be adequately dealt with, rather than denied. This latter, as will be evident, would be my choice. For if we go back to a theology referenced only to the religions and revelatory experience of the early Christian centuries, we go back to a theology *implicitly* dealing with the issues of a community either living in what it thought to be the last days, or surviving in times of persecution, or trying to resolve the religious and racial tensions between Jew and Gentile, etc. Critical history makes us aware that the history of Christian origins is still full of implicit personal, social, and cultural assumptions which *were* the experiential issues of those times. Ought they to become absolutized for all of Christian time? Or do we rather deal with the issues of our own century and decades — *explicitly* — such that we are both faithful to the human experience of *our times* and faithful to the apostolic tradition which has grounded our community of faith? Obviously, my choice would be the latter.

A sufficient method for doing theology amidst the pluralism and complexity of twentieth-century global human experience would first of all have to be capable of dealing with *complexity itself.* We inherit eighteenth- and nineteenth-century notions of a simple life, typically rurally based; these understandings of a far more simple lifestyle have to be *unlearned.* In their place has to be a procedure by which we automatically seek to explore *other* people's experience, as well as our own — and we must by no means assume we will find but a mirror of our own experience! For we should variously look to our personal experience, then to the experience of the group or community to which we belong or in which we live, then to the experience of others in different cultures or societies likely related to such an experience, and last, but not least, to those historically who seem to have been dealing with a similar experience.

Of course, we will come up with a diversity of experience, and some analogy may be needed to help us cope with that. One such analogy would be "perspectivism," in which we all understand ourselves to be looking towards the same mountain (the issue shaping our experience), but from radically different perspectives. Only dialogue among the perspectives will reveal the mountain as it actually is — sheer cliff on one side, gradual incline on another, a second smaller peak on the third, etc. Another analogy might be a notion borrowed from mathematics — probability theory. As we look to multiple experience, we find that we can see trends or generalities within certain understandings and experiences. How "probable" or "less than probable" has been *our* version of the experience? Does such probability direct us here or elsewhere for a sufficient understanding?

Whatever the analogy, we have to get used to understanding or responding to something when we are *not* presented with a sharp and clear picture of it, but rather one which we will have to "descramble" (to use a communications term) and reconstruct in order to get it sufficiently balanced and comprehensive. Above all, it will be an understanding that is built upon *differences* rather than similarities in experience; its test will be how many differences it can faithfully hold.

The second key component for doing theology in this century has to do with the recovery of a different theological language — and with it, another set of understandings about God. Our liturgies, prayers, and hymns of the last four hundred to one thousand years were oriented to the individual living largely in a world over which he or she had no control. The social and political conditions of human living were tenuous at best, and all one could hope for was some semblance of order, fair economic exchange, and some protection from wanton theft and killing. Far more important would be fair weather, good crops and flocks, and the relative absence of disease or other afflications. But since death did come at any time, one had at least to be prepared to "meet one's Maker," having regularly confessed one's sins and continually reaffirmed one's intention to live the "new life," following the commandments of God, etc.

In our day, we do have much more control over all our environment — and it is the abuse or "sinfulness" of this control we exercise over each other that is now the focus of our theological concern. Luckily, the early Christian centuries were times of civil, economic, and cultural oppression — so our New Testament narratives already contain some theological *language* referring to victim, oppression, abuse, liberation, healing and transformation. We must recover the sharp, prophetic edge of this language, being able to see that God *is* concerned and involved in our plight, stands in judgment upon the various oppressors, and declares liberation for those that our societies and nations have bound. It is in this oppression, part of the *experience* of twentieth-century living, that God stands as a Liberator, Healer and Creator — and our theological language has to reflect that understanding.

In all of this, then, in our experience and that of others, is laid the foundation for what we should attend to in theology and ministry. To look at what we are experiencing in our times, is not merely a "fad," it is a search for God's activity and truth in those transitory experiences of living — there is no "other" place where life takes place! And what we will see will have that stunning quality of revelation itself ... that the "good news" is for the captive Third World, that "release" is for the women in our midst, that there must be "recovery" for those who have been dispossessed of their work and living, that political prisoners and opponents must be "set at liberty," and that faithful people all over the world must strive to make *this* year "an acceptable year of the Lord." This is theology at its foundation: the activity of God in originating human experience.

Theological Education and the Mission of the Church

Virginia A. Peacock

Not so very long ago, it seemed clear what was meant by "theological education." Theological education involved acquiring a knowledge of (1) dogmatics or systematic theology; (2) the scriptures, including the biblical languages; and (3) the history of the Church and of Christian thought. Dogmatics or systematic theology, especially, served to provide an organizing world view incorporating an interpretation of human life. Dogmatics or systematic theology reigned supreme as the necessary operative understanding for the application of a theological education, which was almost always realized in ordained parish ministry. The trouble with this approach to educating theologically was that a knack for the actual practice of ordained ministry in the parish scene, involving certain pastoral skills, had to be assumed. More often than not, this approach encouraged a highly individualized style of pastoral care which, in turn, encouraged a very privatized style of the practice of religion among the faithful.

More recently, a concern for the practice of ministry within the church has led to the development of a second approach to theological education. This approach can be thought of as specifically goal-oriented or dictated, because it is designed with the intention of producing good practitioners in ministry. The approach is indebted to a shift in a kind of "cultural wisdom" whereby a knowledge or understanding of our humanness (what it is to be human and to live a human life) is deemed, either implicitly or explicitly, a more central knowledge, a more important knowledge, than is a knowledge of subjects.[1] In this view, a knowledge of subjects is regarded as secondary to a knowledge probably most accurately identified as self-knowledge, whether that term is meant to designate individual self-knowledge, or socio-cultural self-knowledge, or both. This prevailing "cultural wisdom," dominant at the present time, whether or not it is recognized and articulated, gained ascendency following the rise of the social sciences, particularly psychology, and the approach to theological education indebted to it has been and continues to be most influenced by psychology. An evidence of this is the requirement of many theological schools and ordaining authorities of some form of "pastoral education" which is geared to increase the self-insight of the student or candidate.

A problem resulting from the second approach to theological education, not obvious initially but increasingly manifest, is that many of its products and adherents tend to operate out of various "theologies" at various times and under various circumstances. The core of the problem appears to be the failure of graduates to develop a centering, integrating theology out of which to function. When the one who ministers has failed to develop a grounding theology out of which to minister, there is a danger that differing particular circumstances, with differing predominant pastoral needs, may provoke the application of somewhat narrowly focused and even conflicting "theologies" at different times. Thus, one "theology" might be relied upon in a pastoral situation in which the problem addressed is the breakdown of a marriage, another "theology" serving when the pastoral need is the support of grieving parents, and so on. While the importance of appropriate supportive pastoral care cannot be denied, the lack of an overall, integrative interpretive theology which encompasses a view of the world and of life is nevertheless unacceptable if Christian theology and Christian thought today is to bear any resemblance to the inherited tradition with which it has always been identified. Theology has an ongoing character. Perhaps the essential task of theology is to communicate a *tradition* — a task which requires continuity. Christian theology cannot really remain truly Christian theology without continuity with its own past.

While the "second approach" to theological education has not totally replaced the first, and the two, in reality, exist side by side in most theological schools today, this very fact exacerbates rather than modifies the problems of the situation. Recognizing the loss of an integrating "system" of theology where emphasis has followed the second approach, many are calling today for a "back to basics" in theological education — meaning back to the predominance of "content" in the form of dogmatics. Yet, we cannot really go backward to a situation as it was before the awareness of the role of self-understanding in all human knowledge. To do so would be to attempt to separate theology from the context of culture, whereas the ongoing character of the task of theology requires stating the "good news" of the Gospel and the Reign of God in different and changing cultural settings. For theology to renege on the task of speaking within the context of culture would be as sure a path to the

failure of theology truly to be theology as the path of discontinuity
with theological tradition. But the task of speaking adequately
within modern culture involves reworking the manner in which
theology states the tradition which it is obligated to communicate.
We now recognize — on sound theoretical basis and not just on the
basis of reigning "cultural wisdom" — that the building of a complete, fully integrated intellectual system of interpretation, such as
was intended through classical dogmatics or systematic theology, is
impossible.[2] Concept as reality, however helpful conceptual thought
continues to be as a tool, is no longer a possible option for theology.
A complete and all-embracing systematic theology is and will
remain an illusion.

An objection to the "resulting product" of either a classical style
theological education or the more current approach emphasizing
ministry is that both approaches encourage a privatized understanding and practice of Christian faith. This has been a result in spite of a
realization — shared by both approaches and supported by the
governing interpretations behind the approaches — that, accurately
understood, the practice of Christian faith demands a sense of
corporateness and an acknowledgement of the fundamental nature
of relation and of the importance of relatedness.

Although there is more that could be said about the failings of
either approach to theological education — the one which aims for a
grounding in the "content" of "the faith" or the other which aims to
turn out good practitioners of ministry — the real point and purpose
of this paper is not so much to critique what is or has been as it is to
offer a suggestion for a possible alternative foundation for the
organization and design of theological education. Carrying it one
step further, I would suggest that we have come to a point — made
evident, perhaps, by the obvious uncertainty today concerning what
theological education is or ought to be — at which the very presuppositions assumed by theology for the theological task are in need of
careful and serious critical analysis and evaluation.

Let me begin at the beginning and, at the same time, return to a
point already suggested. Theology, at its origins, historically, did
what it did within a cultural context which assumed philosophy.
That is, classical philosophy *defined* the world view or way of seeing
things in the Greco-Roman world in which theology first spoke.
Theology, at its origins, assumed not only a philosophical way of
thinking but also a philosophical way of seeing and being in the
world. (Philosophy, here, means metaphysics, whereas philosophy
today almost always means epistemology. In a world view which
assumes metaphysics, there is a "reality behind" what is or can be
observed. In a world view in which metaphysics has been abandoned, the relevant questions shift from the observed to the
observer, from what is known or can be known to the knower, what

the knower is able to know and the nature of knowledge. Philosophy as epistemology introduces questions about the limitations of knowledge and postulates a gap or discontinuity between knower and known whereas metaphysics assumes continuity between knower and known.) In a world in which philosophy (metaphysics) is not assumed as foundational, such as our own today, concept as truth can never have quite the same weight or authority or ultimacy as in a world in which philosophy (metaphysics) is supreme. But the biblical world and the world in which Jesus lived and ministered — the worlds in which Christianity had its true origin and out of which it directly grew — were worlds which did *not* assume philosophy (metaphysics or epistemology). Thus, there is good reason for thinking we can find a legitimate basis today for theology — and for theological education — which does not assume philosophy as the necessary foundation of its language.[3]

In the biblical way of thinking, what is *is*, and it is not necessary or appropriate to assume a "reality behind" what is. Moreover, what is, is as act. Is is not as "being" or "essense"; is is as actor and action. Hence, God is deliverer or redeemer — one who delivers, one who redeems. God is known through the act of deliverance, through the act of redemption. The delivered, the redeemed, who know the experience of deliverance, the experience of redemption, know God — who God is. Who God is is known through the experience of what God does.

Jesus gave instructions for his followers. He said they would be known as his followers through their following a commandment. The commandment was to love one another. They were to be defined as his followers by an action toward one another. Loving one another was to follow the example Jesus himself gave. "Love one another," he said, "as I have loved you." Then Jesus took the course of action which led to a cross. Jesus gave himself for his others. He said that was how his followers were to love one another. To give one's life away for the other is to love the other. Jesus said he came not to be served but to serve. Jesus demonstrated what he meant by serving by washing the feet of others — and by a whole ministry of service toward others by whom he was moved to compassion. Jesus said that he himself was served by those who would serve him when they served the least among them. Jesus sent his followers out to a whole world. They were to preach about the Reign of God, about the Good News of the Gospel of Christ and the redemption through his action out of love for the world, and they were to take his place, so to speak, to be Christ in the world, to be as a servant — like him — in the world, if they would be his followers. They would be known as his followers by their actions — as he was known to be who he was through what he did.

Jesus' followers were commissioned. They were sent on a mission.[4] The mission was defined on the basis of what they were to *do*. Mission was to be defined in terms of *action*, in terms of *doing*. What they were to do was to be determined by the need they found — just as it was for Jesus himself. Jesus' own action was in response to human need. What the mission of Jesus' followers ought to "look like" is to be determined by the need in the world found by the would-be follower.

Now, what does all this mean for the task of theology? First, theology retains the task of having to say what it has to say in different cultural settings, in various places and times. It will continue to have to articulate who God is and who Jesus is by being able to say what they do and how that action is to be seen and even how that action is to be "understood" as delivering, redeeming, serving. But, before we jump to the conclusion that things don't seem so different after all if we base our theological understanding upon descriptions and interpretations of actions rather than of essences, it had better be pointed out that a description of who Jesus is and how he is to be understood in terms of actions done is quite far removed from a description of who Jesus is in traditional dogmatic theological terms of "sonship" and of his "divinity," etc. (Yet, such a statement should not be taken as a denial either of Jesus' sonship or divinity. It is, really, a rejection of a way of talking because it is considered inadequate precisely as a way of talking.)

Second, theology has gained a new task of fundamental importance, subordinate only to the first, which remains talk about God and about Christ. That new task involves defining the need of the world in which the action of discipleship — the act of the church as church — is to take place. A new emphasis for theology upon the world in which mission takes place, or the world in which the church ministers comes to the fore here.[5] Understanding the world in which the church ministers and its need, which the church as church is obligated to view with compassion and toward which it is to be drawn into serving action — even healing action, because reconciliation is, after all, healing — becomes, in this view of theology, a major task of theology.

Such a task for theology was always a derivative one — theoretically, anyway. In classical systematic theology or dogmatics, such a task never formed an essential part of "the system" such that the system couldn't "hold together" or be complete without it. And, such a task for theology was never primary, even in a view of theological education which took the stance that the foremost goal of theological education was to produce good practitioners of ministry, because this approach saw pastoral needs in a very narrowly defined and limited way.

Now, let me return to what began as my major focus of concern: theological education. How can what I have said about theology and the theological task be taken as significant for organizing and structuring the process of theological education and for setting its aims and goals? As a beginning, theological education needs to be governed by a requirement to educate for mission in a world defined as a world in need. Understanding the action of God and of Jesus Christ as modeling mission in the world would be a theological foundation for such theological education. Insight into self — individual and cultural-societal — would continue to be seen as necessary for understanding both world-in-need and the genuine act of mission and, thus, as necessary to the process of theological education and as a desirable goal of theological education. If anything, self-understanding, seen as serving the purpose envisioned here, would have to emphasize the cultural-societal dimension more fully than has been the case.

Seeing the goal of theological education as preparing for mission in and to a world in need of being served, both by ordained and lay members of the *laos* (people of God), might serve to help integrate all the pieces which contribute to theological education in a way in which they have not been integrated before. Finally, ethics, through this approach which envisions a foundational emphasis upon *action*, might achieve the prominence which, in my view, the Gospel intends — both in what we may want to continue to call theological understanding or interpretation and in the defining purpose of theological education.

The purpose of this article and of this volume is better served if what is said here remains suggestive rather than prescriptive regarding the spelling out of a curriculum for theological education. One point, however, is obvious enough to deserve expression. That is, an adequate analysis and understanding of the world in which the church ministers require at least some awareness, on the part of those who minister, of the analyses of the social sciences — beyond psychology — i.e., the analyses of sociology, economics, and anthropology, including minority, feminist, and Third World critiques. Thus, concern for ways toward such awareness becomes a concern of curriculum design.

NOTES

1   "Subject," here, is used in the sense of organized knowledge about something, as in "academic subject." Such knowledge is characterized by its content.

2   The work of mathematician Kurt Gödel has pointed to a general principle of the non-self-sufficiency of any system as a system. Consistency and completeness are not possible to maintain together. As a system approaches completeness, consistency drops out and inconsistency creeps in. I first became aware of the implications of Gödel's

work in a course called "Science and Biblical Theism" taught by Charles K. Robinson in The Divinity School of Duke University (1971). Awareness of thinking and ways of thinking within twentieth-century science, especially physics, is important for thinking theologically today, I believe.

3 I am rejecting philosophy as both metaphysics and epistemology here. Epistemology is rejected as well as metaphysics because it introduces the notion of a gap or discontinuity between knower and known which is as foreign to the biblical way of thinking as are the assumptions of metaphysics.

4 I am using "commissioned" here in the sense of "charged" and "given authority." I am using "mission" in the sense of "task."

5 The phrase "the world in which the church ministers" has often been used by Marjorie Powles.

Social Action and Mission in the Eighties

Roger Hutchinson

In the 1960s the social passion which has characterized recurrent periods of social gospel activity within the churches was rekindled.[1] This social justice awakening revitalized the churches' efforts to attack problems such as poverty, racial discrimination and war. To increase their effectiveness, and to sharpen their focus on particular issues, Protestant and Roman Catholic churches jointly sponsored a number of social action coalitions. Interchurch initiatives such as the GATT-Fly Project (dealing with Canada's aid, trade and economic policies), the Inter-Church Committee on World Development Education (Ten Days for World Development), the Taskforce on the Churches and Corporate Responsibility, the Inter-Church Committee on Population, Project North and the Inter-Church Committee on Human Rights in Latin America are examples of the groups created and the issues and concerns addressed by the churches with renewed zeal.[2]

During an optimistic, expansive period such as the sixties, new initiatives could be added to existing programs and a pluralistic attitude towards ways of pursuing the churches' mission could be encouraged. Now that the general mood has shifted from expansiveness to restraint, there is growing concern about priorities and about the criteria by which distinctions will be made between what is central to the churches' mission and what is secondary and expendable. In this paper I will attempt to provide both a framework for discussing priorities and a criterion for assessing them.

The first step will involve tracing shifts in attitudes towards social action from a "service *to* the world" orientation to "the development *of* peoples" to "solidarity *with* oppressed groups struggling for liberation." Next, I will suggest that a "mutuality between partners" model represents not simply a fourth stage or a movement beyond the other three orientations but it also serves as a criterion for assessing particular approaches to service, development and liberation. I will conclude that it is appropriate to combine a pluralistic attitude towards different types of social action (e.g., aid, development, advocacy) and areas of church life (e.g., social action and evangelism) with a non-negotiable commitment to mutuality and to empowering rather than enfeebling relationships.

As a criterion for assessing priorities a "mutuality between partners" model must be applied concretely in particular contexts. Thus, it is part of the framework for discussing priorities and for developing skills in practical moral reasoning.[3] I am assuming that a commitment to mutuality is not in itself contentious. In my experience, most disagreements about policies and priorities centre on differing understandings of what is going on and conflicting assessments of the extent to which a particular program or policy will enhance or undermine this shared goal.

Since I will be focusing on differences and defending a pluralistic outlook, I should make it clear at the outset that I am not simply relativizing all positions. My conviction that mission in the eighties should be characterized by a non-negotiable central affirmation can be illustrated with an anecdote. At a meeting between church leaders and businessmen during the Mackenzie Valley pipeline debate, one of the businessmen rather angrily suggested that the churches should stick to their main task of filling the pews. One of the church leaders replied that filling the pews was not the churches' main job. The central responsibility of the churches was, he said, to witness to the truth.

The commitment to witness to the truth remains constant and non-negotiable. However, views about which beliefs and which ways of acting have primary importance have varied from time to time and place to place. For Paul, the situation in which Titus found himself made it essential to reaffirm the central fact that through Christ "God has justified us ... and made us heirs, in hope, of eternal life." He urged Titus to "speak about these matters with absolute certainty, so that those who have believed in God may concentrate upon a life of goodness." He advised Titus to "steer clear of stupid arguments, geneologies, controversies and quarrels over the Law. They settle nothing and lead nowhere" (Titus 3:7-9). In this attempt to clarify different assumptions about mission, I hope both to avoid stupid arguments and to identify basic truths about which we should speak with absolute certainty.

The findings of a Lutheran-Roman Catholic committee which met during the 1960s provide a good illustration of a "service to the world" orientation.[4] This committee decided that "the best hope of ecumenical progress lies in working together for the world and its needs rather than in tackling directly questions of doctrine and worship."[5] These humanizing tasks were thought to be both important in themselves and instrumental to the more basic task of working with God to convert the human into the divine. Salvation as wholeness served as a criterion both for including social action as an integral part of the churches' mission and for insisting that it was necessary to go beyond meeting human needs for food, shelter and justice. The churches' total mission, according to Frederick Crowe, one of the members of the committee,

> necessarily involves the word of God or the Gospel, with its power of transforming the meaning of life. It necessarily involves a reference to the death and resurrection of Christ, and therefore a reference to the sacrament by which we are baptized into his death (Rom. 6:3) and to the Eucharist in which we show forth the death of the Lord until he returns (1 Cor. 11:26).[6]

A recent history of the ecumenical movement provides a second example of the view that social action involves service to the needy neighbour and that it is instrumental to more basic aspects of the churches' mission:

> One rejoices that otherwise divided Christians sometimes cooperate in political and social action intended as loving service to the neighbor in need. Indeed, liturgical, doctrinal, and constitutional unity would be a sham without an ethical counterpart. Yet the primary purpose of harmony among Christians remains doxology.[7]

There is general agreement among Christians that doxology, "liturgical formula of praise to God" (Oxford Dictionary), is important. There is less agreement, however, about its relationship to other aims. For some Christians the primary purpose of harmony among Christians is to witness to the unity and interdependence, not simply of the various Christian traditions, but of the whole human family. This can be detected in the shift in emphasis from service to the world as a means towards Christian unity to the development *of* peoples as an end in itself.

In his 1967 encyclical "On the Development of Peoples," Pope Paul VI struck a resonant chord in many churchpeople with his claim that:

> The development of peoples has the Churches' close attention, particularly the development of those peoples who are striving to escape from hunger, misery, endemic disease and ignorance; of those who are looking for a wider share in the benefits of civilization and a

more active improvement of their human qualities; of
those who are aiming purposefully at their complete
fulfillment.[8]

This emphasis on the development of peoples has been assessed in
different ways. In his book *The World Council of Churches and the
Demise of Evangelism*, Harvey Hoekstra complained that:

A definition of mission has emerged that many feel is
too horizontal — and too closely associated with other
ideologies. Those who subscribe to this wider definition seem primarily concerned to work for a better
society; they place their emphasis on human dignity
and human rights. Such participation in the social
struggle is a worthy objective as long as it does not lead
to the eclipse or neglect of the churches' responsibility
to win others to faith in Christ. But this has often been
the result. Rather than giving member churches "support ... in their worldwide missionary and evangelistic
task," WCC programs have too often tended to divert
those churches from that task.[9]

Similar concerns were expressed within Canadian denominations,
even though there was general support for social justice and development programs. For example, some Mennonites complained that
the work of the Mennonite Central Committee (Canada) focused on
Jesus as Lord but neglected Jesus as Saviour. Of particular concern
was the work with native peoples. A commission set up by the Board
of Spiritual and Social Concerns of the Canadian Conference
"acknowledged the validity of the justice issues related to Native
peoples." It asked, however:

Are Native peoples not, like the rest of us, fallen and
outside of Christ until they come to personal faith? In
reading some of the documents one almost gets the
impression that if only the land question could be
settled, if industrial development virtually stopped, if
hunting rights could be restored, then the Indians
could live happily. But surely, in the light of the gospel,
their biggest need would still be unmet.[10]

The mainline liberal response to these evangelical complaints has
been to reaffirm a both-and stance regarding evangelism and social
service. A division of labour is taken for granted between departments of evangelism and social service and between development
agencies and mission boards. Occasionally different emphases are
related to factors such as generational differences. For example, the
report to the 1972 meeting of the Inter-Church Consultative Committee on Development and Relief (ICCCDR) from the Development Education Committee prompted the secretary to record in the
minutes:

It would appear that the discussion is still going on in terms of the relationship between "mission" and "development," and that those of the younger generation respond more readily to projects of development while the older generation still responds to and thinks in terms of mission.[11]

At its 1979 meeting, ICCCDR was warned against widening "the scope of this Committee to include other things, like mission. Development has enough issues." In this context, mission appears to be equated with evangelism and church growth. The implicit assumption is that these activities are related more obviously than social justice activities to the inner spiritual lives of individuals and to the mandate to extend Christianity to all corners of the world. In relation to this both-and stance regarding development and mission, the radical wing of the social gospel of the 1930s, and the liberation theologies emerging in the 1960s in Asia, Africa and Latin America, and among blacks, indigenous peoples and women, are both more radical and more obviously religious. Radical social gospellers and liberation theologians not only provide an analysis of structures of domination, they articulate a social justice spirituality for individuals who experience the presence of God in the struggle against oppression. From this standpoint, the relationship between social action and other aspects of mission has been reversed. Action on behalf of justice is not only a constitutive dimension of the preaching of the Gospel, as the Roman Catholic bishops said in their 1971 synod report, it is the primary expression of the mission of the people of God. From this point of view, social justice activities would receive top priority in a period of restraint.

The evolutionary picture I have thus far presented gives the impression that shifts in emphasis from service to development to liberation, and from the primacy of evangelism to the primacy of social action, are in themselves relevant for assessing priorities. In fact, the situation is more complicated than that. A more precise criterion, and a more contextual approach are required. As I mentioned above, I believe that the current emphasis on "mutuality between partners" provides a useful norm in relation to which programs and priorities can be assessed.[12] It provides a basis for speaking with absolute certainty about the centrality of human dignity as the goal of our striving and as the essential meaning of the gift of God's kingdom. It provides a basis for insisting that all people ought to be treated as active subjects of their own histories rather than as objects of our charity, development projects, political advocacy or evangelization efforts.[13]

The image of mutuality between partners directs our attention two ways. On the one hand, it stands in contrast to hierarchical and individualistic understandings of human life and it affirms a vision

of persons-in-community in which self-determination and interdependence are held together in dialectical tension.[14] On the other
hand, it asks about the categories of people excluded from community and denied the status of equal partners even when mutuality
between partners has been affirmed as the goal and criterion. An
emphasis on assumptions about the boundaries of the community
was a central feature of the writings of Gregory Vlastos, a leading
spokesperson for the Canadian social gospel in the 1930s. In
response to Reinhold Niebuhr's tendency to treat love as an impossible ideal and justice as a pragmatic balancing of interests, Vlastos
pointed out that love and justice were both grounded in the fact of
community. Thus, it was crucial to notice how and by whom community was defined:

> Love is the recognition of community. Justice is the protec-
> tion of individual rights in that community. If the community
> recognized is an exclusive, arbitrary one, the rights to be
> protected will be likewise exclusive and arbitrary. When the
> community is broken up into castes or classes, (races or
> sexes), the prevalent sense of justice will enforce these
> divisions.[15]

The mutuality between partners model draws attention to important developments within aid and relief organizations regarding the
relationship between rich and poor, donors and recipients. For
example, the World Council of Churches' Commission on Inter-
Church Aid, Relief and World Service stresses the importance of
mutual respect and sharing even in cases where the flow of material
aid is in one direction. Leon Howell points out that in spite of
built-in difficulties, CICARWS programs in the drought-stricken
Sahel region of Africa support "the participation of people at village
level in the decision-making process that determines what is to be
done to make their community more sustainable." He suggests that
the work of CICARWS is "intended to exemplify a process of
mutual aid ... not a one-sided action where the rich or strong partner
helps the poor and weak." It is "a process of sharing."[16]

Advocates of development and liberation have, or course, placed
a great deal of emphasis on listening to the victims of oppression and
on being in solidarity with those whose material conditions place
them on the side of liberation struggles.[17] However, mutuality
between partners remains a relevant norm or ideal even for advocates of liberation for at least two reasons. Actual efforts on the part
of highly motivated, well-trained church activists to treat poor people and marginalized racial minorities as partners will always leave
room for improvement. It is also possible that other categories of
people will not be treated as partners. Ordinary lay people and
members of local congregations occasionally complain that they are
treated like passive clients to be educated, animated and conscienti-

cized. When there are grounds for feeling this way the mutuality between partners criterion is being violated.

An examination of documents written in the 1960s and 1970s advocating a mutuality model which would include the poor as partners reveals a further way in which the boundaries of the community were arbitrarily drawn. For example, in his otherwise progressive message to the Secretary General of the U.N. on the occasion of the launching of the second development decade, Cardinal Roy expressed the hope that:

> economic man is beginning to give way a little to the full vision of man as a responsible moral agent, creative in his action, free in his ultimate decisions, united to his fellows in social bonds of respect and friendship and co-partner in the work of building a just and peaceful world.[18]

Mission in the eighties will be characterized by a much higher level of awareness than was the case in the sixties and seventies when such exclusive language symbolized and perpetuated the exclusion of women from full membership as partners in the community. The fact that God could not have intended this fate for half of the human family is a matter that is being spoken of with absolute certainty. As Paul advised Titus regarding similar non-negotiable matters, those who remain argumentative after two warnings should be ignored! There will continue to be debates about what counts as a case of unacceptable sexism, and there will need to be strategic discussions about what to do about it. Such discussions will take place, however, within the context of a non-negotiable commitment to the struggle against sexism, racism and classism, that is, against "the global 'web of oppression' with its particularly enfeebling effects on the poorest of the poor."[19]

Promoting empowering relationships and avoiding enfeebling effects ought, in my view, to be a central feature of mission in the eighties. The question remains, however, how this non-negotiable commitment to empowering relationships and to a mutuality between partners model relates to evangelism, and in particular to the traditional concern about missions to non-Christians.

This issue was debated by the Roman Catholic bishops at their 1974 synod which was called "Evangelization of the Modern World." In their report to the Pope, the bishops wished "to confirm anew that the mandate to evangelise all men constitutes the essential mission of the church." For most of the bishops this meant that the emphasis should be on "the necessity to proclaim the Gospel to all nations and to every individual man." According to Tom Harpur, who covered the event for the *Toronto Star*, some participants whose voices were heard at the synod had a different view. They

> believe that Christ is decisive for them without insist-

ing that He must be decisive for all men. They believe
that God has spoken in and through other religions
and that His light is not absent from anyone. They
want to share their vision of Christ as liberator with all
men without asking for conversion in return.[20]

This attitude towards Christian missions to non-Christians, which
I share, does not necessarily entail a rejection of evangelism — i.e.,
sharing the good news. It does, however involve assumptions about
how that task should be carried out and what its aim should be. It
counsels humility regarding dogmatic claims about the state of
anyone else's relationship to God and about the relationship
between one's own verbal protestations and actual fidelity to God's
will. From the standpoint of a mutuality between partners model,
approaches to evangelism deserving support will be based on respect
for all persons. This will include teaching respect for non-Christians
as Hindus, Jews, Muslims, etc., and no longer reducing them to
objects of Christian missions.[21]

I pointed out above that the shift in emphasis regarding social
action from "service" to "development" to "liberation" does not in
itself constitute a criterion for assessing priorities. I must now counteract the opposite impression. I have implied that different types of
social action have equal claim to scarce resources, and that evangelism and social action are equally deserving of support in a period of
restraint. My main point, however, is that priorities should be
assessed concretely and contextually rather than in relation to
abstract categories such as the ones used to distinguish types of
social action and areas of church life.

It is also important to notice that I have been wearing two hats. As
a detached, academic observer, I have been attempting to clarify
different assumptions about mission. As an engaged participant, I
have been advocating a particular agenda for mission in the eighties.
The different emphases I have identified should be useful as a
discussion framework for persons who do not share all of my
assumptions about the churches' priorities. The purpose of any
attempt to clarify differences is to facilitate discussion among persons who do not already agree about everything.

In my proposal of a criterion for assessing priorities, I have
assumed that mutuality between partners is a widely shared general
goal. It is an ambiguous criterion, however, for two reasons. First, it
embodies a permanent tension between the legitimate demand for
the self-definition and self-determination of individuals or groups on
the one hand, and the equally central commitment to relationships
and interdependence on the other. In some cases, the situation will
demand a divisive emphasis on self-determination. In other cases, it
will be appropriate to stress cooperation, reconciliation and the
well-being of the whole community. A second source of ambiguity is

the constant need to interpret what is going on in particular situations. That is why it is so important that priorities be discussed concretely and contextually by the people responsible for and affected by particular policies and activities. Only in the context of particular debates will it become clear what it means to advocate a pluralistic attitude towards types of social action and areas of church life and a non-negotiable commitment to mutuality and empowering relationships.

NOTES

1 Richard Allen, *The Social Passion: Religion and Social Reform in Canada, 1914-1928* (Toronto: University of Toronto Press, 1971).

2 See my "Ecumenical Witness in Canada: Social Action Coalitions," *International Review of Mission*, LXXI, 283 (July 1982), pp. 344-352.

3 For a good discussion of what I am assuming about practical reason, see John Howard Yoder, "The Hermeneutics of Peoplehood: A Protestant Perspective on Practical Moral Reasoning," *Journal of Religious Ethics*, X, 1 (Spring 1982), pp. 40-67.

4 Frederick Crowe, S.J., "Salvation as Wholeness: Theological Background for an Ecumenical Programme," *Canadian Journal of Theology*, XIV, 4 (October 1968), pp. 228-237.

5 Crowe, p.228.

6 Crowe, p.236.

7 Geoffrey Wainwright, *The Ecumenical Movement: Crisis and Opportunity for the Church* (Grand Rapids: Eerdmans, 1983), p.2.

8 "Populorum Progressio: On the Development of Peoples" (March 26, 1967), in *The Gospel of Peace and Justice: Catholic Social Teaching Since Pope John*, presented by Joseph Gremillion (Maryknoll, New York: Orbis Books, 1976), p.387.

9 (Wheaton: Tyndale House, 1979), p.10.

10 "Speak more of Jesus as Saviour, says commission," *Mennonite Brethren Herald* (October 24 1980), p.25.

11 Minutes of the Inter-Church Consultative Committee on Development and Relief, April 19 & 20, 1972. Anglican Church of Canada, General Synod Archives.

12 Christians have always talked about mutual respect and love, but it is interesting to notice how during the 1960s mutuality, interdependence and partnership regained potency as symbols in which the essential meaning of human life and the central core of the Gospel were fused. See, for example, Robert W. Sopford (Bishop of London), *None of Us Liveth To Himself* (London: Geoffrey Bles, 1964). Reporting on the Anglican Congress held in Toronto in 1963, he said: "Most of all there came to us the vision of our Anglican Communion reformed to a new mutual acceptance of responsibility and a new interdependence" (p.10). "The Church's mission to the world ... is not what we do for somebody else; it is what we do in the proper stewardship of all that God has given us. It involves sharing and receiving as well as giving. It

makes irrelevant and obsolete the old description of some churches as 'older' and others as 'younger' — or some as 'sending' churches and others as 'receiving'. It is a mutual, united obedience to God, who calls us all to be His fellow-workers in His mission." For Western Anglicans to discover Asian and African Anglicans as partners in mission was an important first step towards a more inclusive mutuality between partners' understanding of mission.

13 For excellent treatments of this theme in the Asian context, see Kim Yong Bok, ed., *Minjung Theology: People as the Subject of History* (Singapore: The Commission on Theological Concerns of the Christian Conference of Asia, 1981).

14 See Gregory Vlastos, "What is Love?" *Christendom*, 1, 1 (1935), pp. 117-131 and R.B.Y. Scott, "The Biblical Basis," in R.B.Y. Scott and Gregory Vlastos, eds., *Towards the Christian Revolution* (Chicago: Willett, Clark & Company, 1936), pp.75-97.

15 Gregory Vlastos, "Love and Justice," *The Canadian Student*, 50, 2 (1936), p. 6. Vlastos was an active member of the Fellowship for a Christian Social Order, a Canadian Christian socialist movement which existed between 1934 and 1945. For an analysis of his debate with Niebuhr, see my "Love, Justice and the Class Struggle," *Studies in Religion*, 10, 1 (Fall 1981), pp. 473-479.

16 Leon Howell, *Acting in Faith: The World Council of Churches since 1975* (Geneva: World Council of Churches, 1982), p.45.

17 GATT-Fly, *AH-HAH! A New Approach to Popular Education.* (Toronto: Between the Lines, 1983).

18 Gremillion, p.482.

19 Constance F. Parvey, ed., *The Community of Men and Women in the Church: The Sheffield Report* (Geneva: World Council of Churches, 1983), p.9.

20 "Christianity in Crisis: Church urged to liberate men as well as save their souls," *Toronto Star* (Nov. 2, 1974).

21 Gordon Turner, *Being the Christian Story: A Not-So-New Approach to a Christian Style of Living.* (Toronto: United Church of Canada, 1982).

Dialogue with Evangelicals

Gregory Baum

In this article I wish to show that the church's justice mission demands dialogue with evangelical Christians. First I shall examine the difficulties of finding an appropriate vocabulary in this area. Then I shall point to a recent development: the emergence of evangelical Christians for whom faith implies a commitment to social justice. Finally I shall suggest that with the emergence of the faith-and-justice perspective the older categories of "conservative" and "liberal" are no longer useful for describing the significant conflicts in the Christian church. I shall conclude that the church's mission in society includes the effort to create solidarity and widen the common ground among all Christians dedicated to serving God's coming reign.

I

It has become customary to distinguish between "ecumenical" and "evangelical" Christians. The opposition to the World Council of Churches (WCC) on the part of conservative Christian churches that call themselves evangelical is well known. Yet this terminology is not wholly adequate. In the first place, all Christians want to be evangelical in the sense of walking the way of the gospel. Conversely, evangelical Christians are faithful to the ecumenical councils of antiquity that produced the Christian creeds and hence have every right to be recognized as ecumenical. A second difficulty emerges in Canada where the ecclesiastical situation differs significantly from that of the United States. In Canada Christians are less polarized. Christians who call themselves evangelical exist in the Anglican Church, the United Church, the Presbyterian Church and the Lutheran Church. Canadian Baptists, moreover, who define themselves as evangelical, participate in various ways in ecumenical projects, either through the Canadian Council of Churches or through other

inter-church connections. In Canada it cannot be said that evangelicals stand apart from the ecumenical movement. Large sectors of
Canadian evangelicals support the ecumenical endeavours of their
churches.

Do we have a better vocabulary? In Canadian churches tensions
exist between "liberal" and "evangelical" Christians. What is meant
by liberal in this context? Liberal Christians, I propose, feel free to
reinterpret Christian doctrine in the light of new experiences and do
not mind if they come to deviate from the great tradition; they feel at
ease with the application of the historical-critical method to the
interpretation of scripture; they are in dialogue with the world and
tend to understand the church's mission as a service rendered to
society. If this description is correct, then it is impossible to equate
"liberal" with "ecumenical," for there are many ecumenical Christians, including especially Roman Catholics, who are doctrinally
conservative, have reservations about a purely scientific application
of the historical-critical method, and regard the church in dialogue
with the world as the mediator of supernatural life.[1]

There is no perfectly adequate vocabulary to designate the gap
between the churches associated directly or indirectly with the WCC
and the conservative evangelical churches that oppose the WCC,
have little ecumenical sympathy for Roman Catholicism, and put
singular emphasis on the mission to convert the world. Still, despite
this shortcoming, I wish to use the distinction between "ecumenical"
and "evangelical" Christians, in the hope that the reader will keep in
mind that some Christians insist that both designations apply to
them.

In recent years we have witnessed the return of the social gospel in
the Christian world. In the major Christian churches, including the
Roman Catholic Church, we find Christians whose faith includes
commitment to justice in an unjust world and for whom discipleship
means solidarity with the poor and oppressed. All Christians stand
for justice and love in a general way. All Christians wish to embrace
the human family. For the faith-and-justice Christians of whom I
speak this general orientation has become more specific: their solidarity is first of all with the lower sector of society, with the poor, the
marginalized, the oppressed. The Latin American Bishops' Conference (Roman Catholic) held at Puebla in 1979 defined "the preferential option for the poor"[2] as a spiritual conversion constituted by two
dimensions: 1) the willingness to look at society from the viewpoint
of the people at the bottom, and 2) the readiness to express this
solidarity in public witness and social action. In a society that is
gravely divided by structures of injustice, it is impossible to embrace
all members with the same act of solidarity: here solidarity must first
be partial, preferential, reach out to the oppressed, and aim at the

reconstruction of society in greater justice so that solidarity may then become truly universal.

Faith-and-justice Christians exist in the Canadian churches. In many instances, Canadian church leaders have endorsed the preferential option for the poor in public declarations. When the Roman Catholic bishops published their "Ethical Reflections on the Economic Crisis" (January 1983), based on the preferential option for the poor, they were supported by the leaders of the other Christian churches, including the Anglican Primate of Canada, Ted Scott, the United Church Moderator, Clark MacDonald, and the Presbyterian Moderator, Wayne Smith.[3] In the 1976 Labour Day Statement, the Roman Catholic bishops admitted that the members of their own church who followed this way of the gospel were "a minority," albeit "a significant minority,"[4] significant because they summon the entire church to greater fidelity. For the faith-and-justice Christians in all the churches, the preferential option for the poor is the contemporary form of discipleship.

II

The gap between ecumenical and evangelical Christians is cause for sadness. For faith-and-justice Christians it is particularly sad: they realize that in most countries, especially in the United States, evangelical Christians tend to belong to the lower sector of society. Evangelicals tend to represent "the hinterland" of society, either the hinterland of underdeveloped regions or the hinterland of neglected groups in large cities. The distinguished Canadian sociologist S.D. Clark has shown that in Canadian history the tension between the wealthy "metropolis" and the poor and underdeveloped "hinterland" has expressed itself in religious terms, in the protest of "the sects" against "the churches."[5] Christian congregations defined by gospel preaching and religious experience expressed their distance from the metropolitan churches of the successful, which were better educated, more liberal, more integrated into society, and more compromising with respect to the dominant culture.

Even today evangelical churches flourish most in hinterland situations. There, people are exposed to the ever-growing cultural influence of the industrial and commercial centre, the metropolis, which threatens to rob them of even their social identity. Even at this distance from the centre, people are persuaded to eat the same food, dress in the same way, listen to the same music, enjoy the same pleasures, and share in the same consumer values. The evangelical movement embodies the protest against the power of the successful, well-educated, sophisticated metropolis. This protest includes a certain hostility to the liberal churches that are comfortable in the metropolis, assimilate the cultural ideals of the upper crust, and

express the Christian message in terms that make sense to people
with a college education.

There are several historical signs that prompt faith-and-justice
Christians to long for serious dialogue with sectors of the evangelical
churches. *First*, there is the remarkable movement of radical evangelicals in the USA, accompanied by similar currents in Canada. Best
known here is the Sojourners Community in Washington, D.C.,
founded by Jim Wallis. It promotes its understanding of the Christian message in a journal called *Sojourners*.[6] Jim Wallis' *Call to
Conversion* lays the theological foundation for this shift in the self-
understanding of evangelical Christians.[7] Small groups of radical
evangelicals exist in towns and cities all over the USA and Canada.
In Toronto, doctrinally conservative Reformed Christians, who
have no objection to being called evangelical, have formed the social
movement Citizens for Public Justice which publishes *Catalyst*.[8] In
Winnipeg, radical evangelicals publish a paper called *Seeds*.[9]

In what sense are these evangelicals faith-and-justice Christians?
For them the Word of God includes a judgment on present society.
They offer a critique of society based not simply on the neglect of
private virtue (as many evangelicals do) but more especially on the
existence of unjust structures, structures that inflict economic exploitation, racial discrimination, and violations of human rights. This
radical judgment on society implies, moreover, that the traditional
Christian concern with almsgiving, with helping the poor at home
and overseas, however praiseworthy, is no longer enough. What is
required is a new critical approach to society as a whole. For the
radical evangelicals, Christian faith calls for commitment to peace
and justice.

A *second sign* is the emergence of faith-and-justice Christians
among Hispanic evangelicals in the Caribbean, Central America
and South America. The best known author is here Orlando Costas,
a Baptist theologican from Puerto Rico. His book, *The Church and
Its Mission: A Shattering Critique from the Third World* (1974),[10] the
first book he wrote in English, became a signal for the new movement. Since then, both the movement and its theological literature
have grown.[11]

In a study titled *God So Loved the Third World*,[12] Thomas Hanks,
an American Baptist preacher and missionary, tells the story of his
conversion to this new orientation. Seeing the great masses of impov-
erished people in Central America, he became moved by compassion and yearned for the arrival of biblical justice. He felt that under
these conditions he could no longer preach the Christian message as
if its meaning were restricted to personal salvation and personal
holiness. He first turned to Latin American liberation theology,
elaborated largely, though not exclusively, by Roman Catholics.
While he approved of their conclusions, he was unable to follow

their argument. Catholic liberation theology tried to clarify the meaning of the Christian message in Latin America with the help of insights drawn from the social sciences. As an evangelical, Thomas Hanks could not do this. For him the Bible was the unique source of Christian wisdom. From the Bible his preaching derived all its authority. He therefore turned again to the Bible to find its teaching in regard to poverty and destitution. What amazed him at that time was that the standard works on the scriptures, including biblical encyclopedias, were not very helpful on this topic. The tenured professors who had produced them had not been preoccupied with this issue. Hanks decided to re-read the Bible himself, underline every reference to poverty and misery, and work out for himself what scripture in its various parts teaches about the dispossessed. The conclusion he came to was startling: the Bible taught that the cause of poverty was oppression. Poverty was no accident: it was produced by people and resulted from the conditions of oppression. Hanks did not need the social sciences. The Bible was sufficient. And since the God of the scriptures was intolerant of oppression, Hanks realized in what direction his evangelical mission had to go.

The *third sign* is the emphasis on social justice found in the leadership and among the intellectuals of the evangelical movement. The leaders of the movement have found the need to organize Christian outreach on a world-wide basis to give witness to the universality of the Christian message. Several such international assemblies have been held.

In 1974, at Lausanne, Switzerland, an evangelical covenant was formulated which included this declaration: "We affirm that God is both the creator and the judge of all men. We therefore should share his concern for justice and reconciliation throughout human society and for the liberation of men from every kind of oppression."[13]

Support for these new directives, strengthened by subsequent international assemblies, is found especially among the intellectuals of the evangelical movement, in particular the professors of scripture and theology teaching at evangelical seminaries.[14] Since these seminaries have become interested in academic accreditation, they have acquired faculties whose members have studied and received their academic degrees at accredited universities and theological faculties. These well-trained evangelical theologians are eager for dialogue. Many among them are deeply touched by the threat of nuclear war and the ravages produced by economic exploitation. They have become convinced that obedience to Jesus Christ includes concern for justice and peace.

In this context I wish to mention the remarkable theological study, *The Growth of the True Church*,[15] produced by Charles Van Engen, an evangelical scholar. This work brings out the fruitfulness of serious dialogue between ecumenical and evangelical Christians.

Van Engen belongs to the Church Growth Movement in the United States. When he found that this movement was criticized for lacking a sound ecclesiology, he went to the Free University of Amsterdam to study theology in dialogue with the Protestant and Catholic traditions. He produced a study of substantive value which offers an original analysis of the ecclesiological debate in the entire Christian church. Since the conclusions of his book are important, I wish to summarize them briefly.

Van Engen elaborates a theological concept of what used to be called the *notae ecclesiae*, the marks of the Church. After showing how this concept was used and misused in the history of theology, he retrieves a contemporary understanding of these *notae* that would be acceptable to Catholics and Protestants alike. The marks, in particular, unity, catholicity, apostolicity and holiness are 1) gifts of God revealing the divine plan of salvation in the Church, 2) tasks given to the Church and hence tests by which the Church examines its own life, 3) dimensions of the community's self-understanding and as such belong to the order of religious experience, and 4) signs visible to the world, proclaiming the Good News.[16]

As Van Engen examines contemporary theology and, in particular, the documents of church councils and the Second Vatican Council, he finds that the new concern for the world, shared by many modern Christians, emerges in this literature as a mark of the Church.[17] The Church's relation to the world is seen as part of the Church's substantive definition. The new relationship to the world is described differently as "Church as mission," or "the Church for others," or "Church as servant of the world," or "the Church in solidarity with the poor and the oppressed." What is important is that in all these texts this shift of pastoral policy appears not as a tactical modification of ministry but as visible manifestation of the Church's essential character: as *nota*, as gift of God revealing God's redemptive economy, as test by which the Church examines its own life, as dimension of the Church's self-understanding nourished by religious experience, and as witness to the world proclaiming the gospel. This emerging unanimity on the meaning of the Christian message, Van Engen argues, must be taken seriously by the evangelical communities and be a starting point for dialogue.

Conversely, Van Engen examines the evangelical literature on the Church's mission. Here he finds dedication to the conversion of the world. For evangelicals, Jesus Christ is the powerful reality that affects every aspect of human life and relativizes all secular values so that no Christian activity deserves the name of mission unless it tries to communicate to others the great saving reality of Jesus Christ. Some evangelical Christians, especially in the Church Growth Movement, have made the Church's outreach and its numerical growth a criterion for evaluating the Church's fidelity to the Lord.

Van Engen deals with this literature critically. What he retrieves from this literature, what remains valid after a biblical testing, is an element often forgotten and repressed by the major Christian churches, namely the "yearning for the ingathering of God's dispersed people."[18] After reading Van Engen's theological treatment, theologians of the mainstream must ask themselves whether they have not too readily reduced Jesus Christ to a symbol of God's universal offer of humanization and hence neglected the concrete, present, transcendent reality of Jesus, as the Way and the Life, as the One Mediator Between God and humanity. Dialogue with evangelical Christians must examine what precisely this yearning for the ingathering of God's dispersed people means when Jesus Christ is seen as messiah, as God's eschatological messenger, as saviour-and-liberator of the human race.

There are three signs, then, that urge ecumenical Christians to seek communication and solidarity with evangelicals committed to social justice.

III

It is becoming increasingly clear that it is quite misleading to divide Christians into "liberals" and "conservatives." Where would one locate the faith-and-justice Christians among the evangelicals? Is the Sojourners Community liberal or conservative? The question does not make sense. In their pastoral letter "The Challenge of Peace" (May 1983), the American Roman Catholic bishops asked their people to dedicate themselves to peace: they are to promote a spirit of national repentance in their land, they are to intensify their prayer and express the longing for collective metanoia by observing the Friday fast and abstinence. Was this return to an abandoned custom conservative or liberal? The question is meaningless. With the emergence of a radical faith-and-justice perspective, the old debates have been partially transcended and the significant conflicts in the Christian church are defined by new criteria. What counts here is whether or not the formulation of the Christian message recalls the world's poor, the history of human suffering, and the power of the Spirit to transform the face of the earth. What counts here is whether or not faith in the good news implies a socio-political thrust, an option in favour of society's victims, and a public gesture of solidarity with them. Who is this Jesus? Can we define him without reference to the world's poor? Can he be proclaimed without promising the newness of life?

It seems to me that faith-and-justice Christians, especially in countries where they struggle against repression, are spiritually closer to evangelicals than to liberal Christians. For radical Christians life is deadly serious: life is an urgent wrestling with demonic powers. God is an exciting, massive presence in their lives that

demands fidelity every minute of the day. For them, as for evangelicals, the encounter with the world is full of temptations. Betrayal
lurks around every street corner. Daily life demands ever new acts of
fidelity to Jesus Christ. Their public behaviour symbolizes their
distance from the mainstream. They are strangers in the world,
longing for God's redemption.

Liberal theology creates a more moderate climate. God's grace
and God's call are here perceived as inclining people more gradually
toward personal growth and the reform of society. Christian faith
tends here to be seen as the right perspective on the world and the
trusting engagement in doing the right thing in it. Liberals do not
share the sense of urgency that is important for radicals. Neither do
they share their sense of alienation. Liberals do not know what to do
with the apocalyptical passages of the New Testament. They are
puzzled by evangelicals who feel like strangers in this world. They
are equally amazed by radical Christians who yearn so passionately
for a society more conformed to the biblical promises that they find
it existentially impossible to be reconciled to a society characterized
by structural injustice.

Evangelicals and many radical Christians are doctrinally conservative. While liberals try to weaken aspects of Christian doctrine
that go against modern, enlightened sensibilities, radicals in the
church try to unfold the revolutionary content of Christian dogma.[19]
Take, for example, the biblical promises of eternal life. Evangelicals
readily speak of death and eternal salvation, while liberals tend to be
shy on this issue. Liberal theologians are concerned with promoting
more human forms of dying, yet they often wonder how important it
is to believe in life after death. For the radical Christians of Latin
America the New Testament message on death and resurrection is
central. But it is not their own personal death that stands at the
centre of attention, but the death of "the other," the death of the
innocent, the death of the oppressed, the death of Jesus Christ
crucified. For them the resurrection of Jesus proclaims the vindica-
tion of all the victims in history. What about the poor who are killed
in the struggle for justice? If there is no life beyond death for them,
they remain in death what they have always been, the cheated, the
invisible, the forgotten. Then there is no gospel for them. When
Archbishop Romero of El Salvador was warned that his life was in
danger, he said that he was not afraid: for if he were assassinated, he
believed, he would be a better pastor to his people in the Risen
Christ. The military that killed him, and the governments that
supported them, thought that they could get rid of the Archbishop
by putting a bullet in his heart, for they did not believe in resurrection. They did not realize that he would remain alive in the resistance
of his people and in their demand for justice.

I wish to conclude that the time has come for ecumenical Christians to engage in dialogue with evangelicals. This dialogue will deal with the meaning of discipleship in the age of Auschwitz, Hiroshima and the nuclear arms race. This dialogue will examine the nature of the Christian life in a world marked by an unjust distribution of food, power and honour so wicked that it cries to high heaven. The church's mission is here to expand solidarity in a sinful society and gather all Christian believers into a community of resistance and hope.

NOTES

1   See G. Baum, "Liberation Theology and 'the Supernatural'" *Ecumenist*, XIX (Sept.-Oct., 1981), pp. 81-87.
2   Final Document, n. 1134. See J. Eagleson and P. Scharper, eds., *Puebla and Beyond* (Maryknoll, N.Y.: Orbis Books, 1979), p. 264.
3   See G. Baum and D. Cameron, *Ethics and Economics* (Toronto: Lorimer, 1984), p. 61.
4   "From Words to Action," Labour Day Message, 1976, n. 7. See also Appendix 2 of G. Baum and D. Cameron, *Ethics and Economics*, p. 165.
5   S.D. Clark, *Church and Sect in Canada* (Toronto: University of Toronto Press, 1948).
6   *Sojourners*, 1312 Otis Street N.E., Washington, D.C. 20017.
7   Jim Wallis, *Call to Conversion* (San Francisco: Harper and Row, 1981).
8   *Catalyst*, Citizens for Public Justice, 229 College Street, Toronto, Ont. M5T 1R4.
9   *Seeds*, 155 Canora Street, Winnipeg, Man. R3G 1T1.
10 O.E. Costas, *The Church and Its Mission* (Wheaton: Tyndale, 1974).
11 See O.E. Costas, *Christ Outside the Gate* (Maryknoll, N.Y.: Orbis Books, 1982), "Prologue: A Personal Word," pp. xii-xvi.
12 T.D. Hanks, *God So Loved the Third World* (Maryknoll, N.Y.: Orbis Books, 1983).
13 J.D. Douglas, ed. *Let the Earth Hear His Voice* (Minneapolis: World Wide Publications, 1975), p. 4.
14 See also Douglas D. Webster, "Evangelicals: Growing Social Consciousness," *Ecumenist*, XVI (March-April, 1978), pp. 33-37.
15 Charles Van Engen, *The Growth of the True Church* (Amsterdam: Rodopc, 1981), distributed in the U.S. by Humanities Press, Atlantic Highlands, N.J. 07716.
16 Ibid., pp. 84-85.
17 Ibid., pp. 95-112.
18 Ibid., pp. 442-453.
19 J.B. Metz, *Faith in History and Society* (New York: Crossroad Books, 1980), pp. 200-204.

IV
Women and the Church

Beyond Father and Son

Mary Rose D'Angelo

In 1982, a group of women from Wycliffe College at the Toronto School of Theology asked me to set their concern for the use of less exclusively male language for God into the context of the Bible and tradition. Part of their purpose was to defend a letter to the Doctrine and Worship Committee of the Anglican Church of Canada. Signed by women and men from Trinity and Wycliffe Colleges, the letter urged that revisions include options for more inclusive language, requesting, among other things, that one of the five Eucharistic prayers replace the titles "Father" and pronouns for God with language that is not specifically masculine. Thus, they especially desired me to show that the use of exclusively male language for the Trinity belongs to and evokes a theological context that has been abusive of women, to answer the question whether the Bible and tradition permit us to rethink and reword our understanding of the Trinity, and to suggest ways in which the Bible provides female language and imagery about God. This essay is a revision of my response to them, and proposes their (and my) agenda for the church.[1]

A few words about my presuppositions are in order. First, the essay is written from a feminist perspective. I begin from the assumption that language that prescribes, assumes or reinforces the subordination of women cannot be adequate as language about God. Second, this essay is directed toward the issue of revising liturgical use in the churches with a strong concern for the tradition, and, therefore, focused on the sources of liturgy and theology in the first six centuries of the Christian era. Third, I assume that theology and all human language about God are radically anthropomorphic and metaphorical (not merely, but powerfully, metaphorical), and are faithful only insofar as they are constantly qualified and rethought.

First, then, I wish to concur with my friends from Wycliffe that the exclusive use of masculine language about God arose in and evokes a context that is abusive to women. The early Christian theology that settled upon the titles "Father" and "Son" included a schema in which "male" and "female" represented respectively positive and negative qualities, and while that schema alone did not determine the choice of these titles, it infected and continues to infect it to a degree that requires not mental reservations when we use them, but positive antidotes in the use of other kinds of language.

The "male versus female" pattern in theology results from a peculiar marriage of popular misogynism, Platonic theology, and biblical interpretation which emerges first and most fully in the work of Philo, an Alexandrian Jew of the first century, whose life work was philosophical commentary upon the scriptures. The polarity begins from antique views on procreation: "The man sows the seed into a womb as into a field, the woman receives the seed for safe-keeping. . . ."[2] The one is described as activity, the other as passivity: ". . . first, giving birth is wholly peculiar to woman, just as begetting is to man. [Scripture] therefore wishes the soul of the virtuous man to be likened to the male sex rather than the female, considering that activity rather than passivity is congenial to him."[3] "Passivity" and the passions are linked by name and by theory for Philo, and the male/active attracts all good qualities, while the female/passive is credited with everything bad: "The female sex is irrational and akin to bestial passions, fear, sorrow, pleasure and desire, from which ensue incurable weaknesses and indescribable diseases."[4] Thus, femaleness with all its concomitants is distance from God, while maleness with its companion qualities is nearness to God, perceived as Father and maker of the universe: ". . . the male soul assigns itself to God alone as the Father and Maker of the universe and the Cause of all things. The female clings to all that is born and perishes. . ."[5] In this picture, women can have access to the true life of the soul and to God only by "leaving the ways of women," becoming virgin and therefore male.[6]

Although Philo did not influence the New Testament authors, his influence on the great theologians of early Christianity was considerable. But more important even than his influence is the fact that the use of male and female which emerges in his writings is compounded from the same sources and influences as bore upon early Christianity. As a striking case, his work helps alert us to the confluence of biblical and philosophical traditions with conventional wisdom and popular misogyny. Of these the New Testament is not free. The Pastorals share the misogyny of their times (II Tim. 3:6-7), and the generous attention devoted to women in Luke-Acts[7] is made possible by a very conventional view of their role,[8] and perhaps by a strain of asceticism.[9] The letter to the Ephesians makes an explicit association between God as Father and fatherly (patriarchal) authority: "Therefore, I bend my knees to the father (*pater*) from whom every *patria* (fatherhood/fatherland/family) is named..." (2:14-15). It is significant that this same letter speaks of being built up into the "perfect manhood (*anēr*, not humanity), into the maturity of the fullness of Christ,"[10] and enforces the patriarchal family structure as a Christian demand: "Wives be submissive to your husbands... children obey your parents... slaves, obey your masters..." (5:22,33; 6:1,5). While the undisputed letters of Paul never use the schema, it is in the air, in the language: when Paul tells the Corinthians to be courageous he says, "Play the man" (*andrizesthe*; I Cor. 16:13); he has to, as that is the word the Greeks had for it. So also God, when named as author of the universe and of authority, was called "Father"; there was no equally potent word.

The era of the "Church fathers" (second to sixth centuries, an era which also boasted a number of heroines of "manly courage")[11] was the crucible of the doctrine and language of the Trinity. Little attention has been devoted to the connection between the exclusive claim of "Father" and "Son" in naming God and the theological abuse of femaleness and women in this period, but the correspondence among the separation of God from everything female, the abuse of female reality and the demand that Christian[12] and Gnostic women[13] become virgin and/or male has been traced to the theology and the development of ecclesiastical discipline[14] of the period. The occasional assertation of a Gregory of Nazianzus that the title "Father" does not mean that God is male is an important reminder that theology explicitly rejected the identification of God with maleness,[15] but it does not subvert the pattern of separating and alienating the female from God.[16]

Likewise, the damaging aspects of the language cannot be exorcised by continuing to use it with the mental reservation that the titles "Father" and "Son" do not mean to exclude women from imaging God. Too much else in the tradition causes them to do exactly that. The abusive side of patriarchal theology has been described in analyses of theology from the Middle Ages through Barth.[17] And the functioning in western culture of the polarity by which the male signifies transcendence and the female the flesh has been given a psychoanalytic explanation by Dorothy Dinnerstein.[18] While it is possible for one of the Christian communions to deny women ordination on the grounds that their humanity is incapable of imaging Christ's,[19] positive attempts to assert and supply the limits of the language "Father" and "Son" are essential. To my mind, the best avenue is to reduce drastically our use of these terms, especially in the liturgy, and to juxtapose and overwhelm them with a flood of alternative language and imagery.

The recognition of this necessity brings me to the second task the Wycliffe women set, the task of answering the question whether the Bible and tradition permit us to revise the Trinitarian language. Can we express the traditional doctrine (the Niceno-Constantinopolitan settlement) in other language than Father, Son and Spirit, for instance, in the frequently proposed formula: Creator, Redeemer, Sanctifier? I wish to argue not only that we can and, indeed, must do so, but that our understanding of the doctrine would be enhanced by attending to the feminist demand for revisioning the Trinity.

Creator, Redeemer, Sanctifier, like Father, Son and Spirit, is a formula drawn from the Bible that describes the economic Trinity — the Trinity in relation to us. To choose to use the former rather than the latter in communal celebration does not "change" the Trinity, that is, jeopardize our understanding of it. The special claim of "Father, Son and Spirit" is its relation to the technical doctrinal formula which describes the immanent Trinity — the Trinity in relation to itself. The technical terms "ingenerate, generated and proceeding" were developed to give the meaning of the biblical terms "Father, Son, and Spirit" and of the New Testament witness by describing the Trinity as relational, distinguishing the persons while excluding subordination and temporal priority from the distinction. "Ingenerate, generated and proceeding" are rarely used in liturgy and catechesis; their meaning is understood to be carried by the biblical names "Father, Son and Spirit." But "Father" and "Son" have never been fully successful in expressing the doctrine, specifically, in excluding subordination and temporal priority. This defect of the metaphor was recognized as the doctrine was being worked out, and both biblical language and technical terms were supplemented with other analogies. One was the distinction between substance and individuals proposed by Nyssa: as many gold staters [coins] share one goldness, as Peter, James and John share one humanity, so the three divine persons share one Godhood. This analogy required the qualification that unity is of the essence of divinity.[20] A more satisfactory approach was Augustine's use of contemporary psychology to make analogies to the Trinity from "trinities" within the human person: as memory, understanding and will are one, distinct, coinherent and equal, so is God.[21] Augustine's analogies from the human mind have continually played a role in explaining the Trinity in theology, although they have never entered the liturgy and are rare in catechesis.[22]

The radically egalitarian character of feminism and its rejection of titles like king, lord, almighty, as well as Father,[23] can make our demand for rethinking the trinitarian language a benefit to the church's understanding of the traditional doctrine, which has never been able to exclude subordination.[24] To accomplish this we must forego the temptation to substitute a single formula for "Father, Son and Spirit." Instead we must seek a multiplicity of names for God which reflect both the working of God in history — like Creator, Redeemer, Sanctifier, or better, Creator, Liberator, Advocate —

and God's being. For the latter, Augustine's analogies from the human person might provide a model for selecting "new" biblical language to describe the Trinity; I shall make some suggestions below.

Before moving to biblical sources for feminine language about God, I wish to address the objection that "Father" has a unique claim among Christian addresses to God because of its prominence in the New Testament and particularly because it appears to have been used by Jesus. This objection often asserts that the Jesus of history used "Father" in a way that was free of common patriarchal conceptions of the era.[26] There is no disputing the importance of the title "Father" for God in the New Testament, and it is most probable that Jesus used it. It is also true that in the New Testament this address can function not only to support human patriarchy, as it does in Eph. 2:13, but also to defy it: "Call no one your 'father' upon earth, for one is your Father, in heaven" (Matt. 23:9).[27] But arguments that Jesus' use of "Father" was radically different from contemporary Jewish and Greek theology are extremely weak, and frequently tinged with anti-Judaism.[28] Historical and moral responsibility are better served if we assume that this name for God came to Jesus and the church with the heritage of Judaism and spoke profoundly to Jew and Greek alike[29] of God's being as author and sustainer of life and of our being as God's kin. Our obligation to the New Testament witness is not to repeat the title for its sacredness, but to sanctify God's name in words that ever more fully disclose its call upon our being and its challenge to human dominions.

My third task is to offer some options for revisioning God in female terms from the biblical tradition. Here a word of caution is necessary: some feminists are reluctant to use feminine language about God on the grounds that to do so is to return to the anthropomorphic trap.[30] Their fears are given substance by those who insist that "Father" must be retained as the primary title for God, or "Mother" substituted for it, because God must be envisioned as "personal". However clear a philosophical definition can be given to the term "person," feminists like myself suspect that, in practice, the demand for a personal identification for God merges with the expectation that we must envisage God as a "Big Man" or "Big Woman."[31] This suspicion makes us prefer to forego a personal definition for the vision of a "diffused and competent love."[32] While I endorse the attempt to envision God in female as well as male terms, I take this objection very seriously. The basic problem with the Father image and the patriarchal model it evokes is "its expansion, its inclusiveness, its hegemony, its elevation to an idol."[33] Substitution will not do, and "mother" is particularly problematic as a substitute.[34] A multiplicity of language and imagery is required. Sallie McFague's model of friend and Letty Russell's model of partner[35] are important beginnings in restructuring our address to God. In what follows, Augustine's analogies from the human person will have a larger part in guiding my choice of relational terms than the analogy from human generation and familial roles.[36]

Other feminist commentators have already pointed to sources in the Bible and Christian tradition which offer ways of revisioning God in female language and imagery. The best known is the observation that "spirit" is not only not masculine, but in Semitic languages is feminine in gender, and in some portions of early Christianity has a feminine persona. The deaconess can be seen as an image of the Holy Spirit,[37] and some gnostic texts also speak of the spirit as mother.[38] The Gospel to the Hebrews is said to have contained a passage in which Jesus speaks of "my mother, the spirit."[39] The Son/Word is also given the functions and name of mother in gnosticism[40] and in early and medieval Christianity.[41] The title may be a manifestation of the ancient and complex explanation of Christ's relationship to God through the persona of wisdom.[42] Wisdom arose in the Hebrew scriptures and flourished in the Greek Bible as the earliest and most important of a number of female personifications of God's being, especially of God's being — with humanity as creator, sustainer, revealer, providence. Proverbs 8:22-31, Sirach (Ecclesiasticus) 24 and Wisdom 7 were of particular importance in explaining Christ as Word. Sirach 24 is especially striking; in it wisdom describes herself through ancient and powerful female symbols: vegetal imagery of trees, flowering plants and aromatic spices, budding and blossoming vine, abundant fruit (24.12-18); water imagery of river, channel and sea (25-27, 30-32); light joined to water (27, 32). John's call to drink and eat of Jesus seems to have been drawn from this tradition, perhaps even from Sir. 24:18-20: "Come to me, you who desire me; eat of your fill of my fruit," says Wisdom. "The one who eats of me will hunger still; the one who drinks of me will thirst for more." John's Jesus proclaims, "I am the bread of life; the one who comes to me will not hunger, the one who believes in me will never thirst" (6:35). Matthew also identifies Jesus with God's wisdom, causing him to utter her invitation: "Come to me, all you weary . . . learn of me," (Matt. 11:28-30, cf. Sir. 51.23).[43] This identification was important in explaining the second person of the Trinity all through the period of the great councils, and persisted in liturgy and piety as a source not only for understanding Christ,[44] but also the Spirit[45] and the cult of Mary.[46]

Considering the spirit as feminine and wisdom as God's being in Christ is helpful, but if we use feminine language about God only about the second and third persons of the Trinity, we shall reinforce both trinitarian subordinationism and the subordination of women in church and society.[47] It is essential to revision the Father and the relationships in the Trinity. The Hebrew Bible and the work of Jewish feminists[48] are important sources here, and tradition and recent scholarship provide some important clues. One of the best of these is Phyllis Trible's disclosure of the function of the root *rḥm* (womb/mercy/have compassion) as a recurring metaphor in the Hebrew scriptures.[49] This image is vividly female, but not a female surrogate for the "Father". And it belongs to the very center of the scriptures: the covenant and its continual reinterpretation. Another clue of major significance comes from E. Schüssler Fiorenza, who suggests that it is not only the case that the New Testament uses wisdom to explain Jesus' relation to God, but also that like "Father," "Wisdom" was central to Jesus' understanding of God.[50] A favorite biblical image of mine is the image of water source, an image which has ancient female overtones, and which is capable of representing relation in God:

> How precious is thy steadfast love, O God!
>   human kind take refuge under the shadow
>   of thy wings
> they feast on the abundance of thy house
>   and thou givest them to drink from the river
>   of thy delights
> For with thee is the fountain of life
>   in thy light do we see light. (Ps. 36.7-9)

The images of light, water, wisdom, yearning and compassionate mother-love offer us biblical ways of revisioning God as one and relational, in terms of a diffused and competent love. We can revise and revivify our addresses to God by juxtaposing and, for the near future, overwhelming "Father, Son and Spirit" with alternate formulae:

> Creator, Redeemer, Sanctifier
> Creator, Liberator, Advocate
> Wise God, Wisdom of God, Spirit of Wisdom
> God, Source of Being, Christ, Channel of Life, Spirit, Living Water
>   Joy-giving Light, who shone on the world in Christ,
> enlighten us by the fire of your love.
>   Mothering God, make us drink the spirit that flows
> from the breast of Christ.
>   From the womb of your compassion, O God, bring
> forth in us a new order of justice and equality, that the
> spirit may breathe freely in all who share Christ's
> humanity.

And we *must* do so, with inventiveness, vigilance and the continual prayer:

O God, it is only by your gift that we worship you
truly; remove offenses from us, that we may run without stumbling to your promises.[51]

NOTES

1   When I was graciously invited to contribute to this volume, it seemed
    that no offering of mine could be more appropriate than a rethinking
    of my response to the Wycliffe women's request, not only because it is
    so clearly an agenda from and for the church but also because its
    contents are so much a part of my conversations with Marjorie and
    Cyril. Indeed the most powerful justification for the agenda is the one
    with which Cyril explained his decisions to use alternate language in a
    baptism: pastoral necessity. What I have to say cannot replace but can
    only support that justification.
2   *On the Eternity of the World* 69 (Loeb Classical Library 9, 233); cf. *On
    Abraham* 101.
3   *Questions on Genesis* 3.18 (Loeb, Supp. 1, 203); cf. *On Abraham* 102.
4   *Questions on Genesis* 4.15 (Loeb Supp. 1, 203); cf. *Allegorical Interpre-
    tation of the Law* 2.97; *On the Sacrifices of Abel and Cain* 103; *On the
    Cherubim* 8.
5   *On the Special Laws* 3.178 (Loeb 7, 587).
6   *Questions on Genesis* 4.15; cf. *On the Cherubim* 50: "...when God
    begins to consort with the soul, He makes what before was a woman
    into a virgin again, for He takes away the degenerate and emasculate
    passions which unmanned it and plants instead the native growth of
    unpolluted virtues." (Loeb 2,39). Cf. also *That the Worse Attacks the
    Better* 28; *On Drunkenness* 59-63; *On Flight and Finding* 128; *On
    Dreams* 185; *On the Contemplative Life* 68. Many more passages could
    be adduced to illustrate each of the points made above. For a fuller
    description and documentation of this pattern, see R.A. Baer, *Philo's
    Use of the Categories Male and Female* (Leiden: E.J. Brill, 1970). On
    Christian versions of the pattern, see notes 11-13 below.
7   Described by C.H. Parvey, "Women in the New Testament," in *Reli-
    gion and Sexism*, ed. R. Ruether (New York: Scribner, 1974) pp.
    138-146. She suggests that this attention to women is due to the needs
    of evangelization and catechesis.
8   Mark describes women as disciples and ministers (15.41); Luke also
    mentions women who minister, but seems to limit their ministry to
    financial support of Jesus and the disciples (Luke 8.3). See also E.
    Schüssler Fiorenza, "Word, Spirit and Power: Women in Early Chris-
    tian Communities," *Women of Spirit*, ed. R. Ruether and E.C.
    McLaughlin (New York: Simon and Schuster, 1979) p. 52.
9   In the parable of the great supper, Luke includes marriage and a wife
    as excuses for refusing the invitation (14:20) and lists a wife among
    things left for the kingdom (14:26, 18:19). This author omits Mark's
    divorce pericope (Mark 10:1-12), but retains the prohibition of remar-
    riage (16:18), perhaps spiritualizing it. In the later church, celibacy
    permitted women a larger but ambiguous role. See Rosemary Ruether,

"Misogynism and Virginal Feminism in the Fathers of the Church," *Religion and Sexism*, pp. 150-183.

10 Parenthesis mine. The Greek word *anēr* usually refers to the male; the alternative is *anthropos*, usually used to mean human being. It can be argued that the passage has in view full adult humanity. But in a society in which women are released from tutelage of a guardian by the bearing of three children if freeborn and four if freed (Gaius, *Institutes* 1.145, 194), full adult humanity belongs only to men.

11 4 Macc. 15.30 eulogizes the mother of the seven martyrs in this fashion; the description might have been applied by their contemporaries to women like Paula and Eustochium, Melania, Macrina, Eudokia, Pulcheria and the pagan philosopher Hypatia. The point is that the era permitted women more autonomy than formerly at the same time that it abused their female persons. See Ruether, "Misogynism," and "Mother of the Church: Ascetic Women in the Late Patristic Age," *Women of Spirit*, pp. 75-98.

12 Ruether, "Misogynism," and "Mothers of the Church"; see also B.P. Prusak, "Women: Seductive Siren and Source of Sin? Pseudepigraphal Myths and Christian Origins," *Religion and Sexism*.

13 E.H. Pagels asserts (with justice) that Gnosticism, which allowed female deity, also had more room for women ("God the Father/God the Mother," *The Gnostic Gospels* (New York: Doubleday, 1979) pp. 48-69. But see Baer, *Philo's Use*, pp. 69-74.

14 F.J. Cardman, "Women, Ordination and Tradition," *Commonweal* 102:26 (Dec. 17, 1976) pp. 807-810.

15 *Fifth Theological Oration* 7; cf. Arnobius, *The Case Against the Pagans* 3.8. See on this Madeline Boucher, "Authority-in-Community," *MidStream* 21 (1982) pp. 408-411.

16 For a view of the difference between the use óf the analogy by theologians and metaphysicians, and the popular use of the same language, see G.H. Tavard, "Sexist Language in Theology?" *Theological Studies* 4 (1975) pp. 717-718.

17 See the historical studies in *Religion and Sexism* and M. Farley, "Sources of Sexual Inequality in the History of Christian Thought," *Journal of Religion* 56 (1976) pp. 162-176. Sallie McFague summarizes constructive analyses of the patriarchal model of theology in *Metaphorical Theology* (Philadelphia: Fortress, 1982) pp. 147-152. The most thorough-going of these analyses is Mary Daly's *Beyond God the Father* (Boston: Beacon, 1979).

18 *The Mermaid and the Minotaur: Sexual Arrangements and Human Malaise* (New York: Harper and Row, 1977).

19 Sacred Congregation for the Doctrine of the Faith, *Declaration On the Question of the Admission of Women to the Ministerial Priesthood*, pp. 30-31.

20 Gregory of Nyssa, *To Ablabius: On Not Three Gods*, in *Christology of the Later Fathers* ed. E.R. Hardy, (Philadelphia: Westminster, 1954), pp. 265-266. A similar view appears in Christian iconography of the era; the Trinity is depicted on the "Theological Sarcophagus" as three identical human beings, once is represented by three wreaths surmounting an eagle, frequently is figured by the three mysterious vis-

itors to Abraham. See A. Graber, *Christian Iconography: A Study of its Origins* (Princeton: Princeton University Press, 1968) pp. 112-114.

21 Other such trinities were: being, knowing, willing; mind, self-knowledge, self-love. *On the Trinity* 5.12, 15-17; 8.1; 15.5; *Tractates on John*, 99.6.

22 M. Farley, "New Patterns of Relationship: Beginnings of a Moral Revolution," *Theological Studies* 4 (1975) p. 642.

23 See L. Russell, "Changing Language and the Church," *The Liberating Word*, ed. L. Russell (Philadelphia: Westminster, 1976), pp. 92-93. Also McFague, *Metaphorical Theology* 9, pp. 148-149.

24 On the connection between the doctrine of God as relational and the feminist requirement of a change of structure in the church, see Boucher, "Authority-in-Community," pp. 408-413; Farley, "New Patterns," pp. 640-643.

25 This formula was suggested to me by Letty Russell in a conversation with Marjorie and Cyril. See her treatment of it in *The Future of Partnership* (Philadelphia: Westminster, 1979), pp. 33-34.

26 The argument for the non-patriarchal character of Jesus' use of the title is made, for instance, by R. Hamerton-Kelly in *God the Father: Theology and Patriarchy in the Teaching of Jesus* (Philadelphia: Fortress, 1983), pp. 147-151. See McFague's analysis and rejection of such views in *Metaphorical Theology*, pp. 171-172.

27 E. Schüssler Fiorenza, *In Memory of Her* (New York: Crossroad, 1983), pp. 147-151.

28 The argument on which later claimants depend is made by J. Jeremias in "Abba," *The Prayers of Jesus* (London: SCM, 1967), pp. 11-65. Jeremias deduces that "there is no analogy at all in the whole literature of Jewish prayer for God being addressed as Abba"; I suggest that a more sophisticated and sympathetic reading of the same evidence would conclude that Jesus and the New Testament are part of the evidence for first century Jewish use of "Father" in prayer.

29 See George Foote Moore, *Judaism II* (New York: Schocken, 1971), pp. 201-211. Cleanthes, *Hymn to Zeus* (Stobaeus, *Eclogae* 1, 1, 12) points to the contribution to Philo's use of the title.

30 See the cautions expressed by M. Farley, "New Patterns," p. 643. For a defense of the attempt, see Rita M. Gross, "Female God Language in a Jewish Context," *Womanspirit Rising*, ed. C. Christ and J. Plaskow (New York: Harper, 1979), pp. 167-173.

31 See C.P. Gilman's utopian novel *Herland* (New York: Pantheon, 1979), written in 1915:

> "Does God mean a person to you?"
> This she thought over a little. "Why — in trying to get close to it in our minds we personify the idea, naturally; but we certainly do not assume a Big Woman somewhere, who is God. What we call God is a Pervading Power, you know, an Indwelling Spirit, something inside of us that we want more of. Is your God a Big Man?" she asked innocently. (112-113)

32 Ibid.:

> "I see," she said eagerly, after I had explained the

genesis and development of our religious ideals. "They lived in separate groups, with a male head, and he was probably a little — domineering?"

"No doubt of that," I agreed.

"And we live together without any 'head,' in that sense — just our chosen leaders — that *does* make a difference."

"Your difference is deeper than that," I assured her. "It is in your common motherhood. Your children grow up in a world where everybody loves them. They find life made rich and happy for them by the diffused love and wisdom of all mothers. So it is easy for you to think of God in terms of a similar diffused and competent love." (113)

33 McFague, *Metaphorical Theology*, p. 190.

34 Ibid., pp. 183-184.

35 Ibid., pp. 177-192; Russell, *Future of Partnership*, pp. 21-77.

36 See also Farley, p. 642.

37 *Didascalia Apostolorum* 7 (2.25-26); cf. Aphraat, *Homily* 18.10

38 Origen, *Commentary on John*, 2.12.

39 Pagels, *Gnostic Gospels*, pp. 52-53.

40 *Apocryphon of John* 2.9-10; Pagels, *Gnostic Gospels*, pp. 53-58. In calling these representations of deity "second person" I am accommodating the texts for the purpose of comparison with the Christian doctrine.

41 Pagels, *Gnostic Gospels*, pp. 67-68; E.C. McLaughlin, "Christ My Mother: Feminine Naming and Metaphor in Medieval Spirituality," *The St. Luke's Journal of Theology* 18 (1975) pp. 228-248; Carolyn Bynum, *Jesus as Mother* (Berkeley: University of California, 1982); V.R. Mollenkott, *The Divine Feminine* (New York: Crossroad, 1983) pp. 8-14, 15-31, 44-47.

42 G. MacRae, "The Jewish Background of the Gnostic Sophia Myth," *Novum Testamentum* XII (1970) pp. 86-100.

43 M.J. Suggs, *Wisdom, Christology and Law in Matthew's Gospel* (Cambridge: Harvard, 1970).

44 E.g., the hymn *Jesu Dulcis Memoria (Jesus the Very Thought of Thee; Jesus Thou Joy of Loving Hearts).*

45 E.g., the antiphon for the Magnificat at Corpus Christi.

46 E.g., the Mass Propers for Our Lady of Mount Carmel and for the Nativity of Mary.

47 The example from the *Didascalia* above (n. 36) appears to subordinate both the deaconess and the Holy Spirit. See also Farley, "New Patterns," p. 643.

48 E.g., Naomi Janowitz and Maggie Wenig, "Sabbath Prayers for Women," *Womanspirit Rising*, pp. 174-184; "The Shekinah," in Mollenkott, *The Divine Feminine*, pp. 36-43.

49 *God and the Rhetoric of Sexuality* (Philadelphia: Fortress, 1977) pp. 31-71.

50 Schüssler Fiorenza, *Memory*, pp. 130-140.

51 This collect is based on the collect for Proper 26, *Book of Common*

Prayer According to the Use of the Episcopal Church, 1977, and the Latin from which it derives (*Roman Missal* 1962, proper for the Nineteenth Sunday after Pentecost).

Emily's Baptism: A Case Study of Sexism and Authority

Christopher Lind

On May 25, 1981, our first child was born to us — a girl, Emily Ruth Musgrove Lind. Her birth was a wonderful, incredible, ecstatic experience. It was also an intensely religious experience for us and we were moved to celebrate. But the event was also a crisis. In order to celebrate we had to confront our different understandings of what celebration is about. We knew that any struggle to understand religious experience is a struggle to understand yourself, the world and God. With the help of godparents and friends we chose to engage that struggle by writing our own baptismal service. That process turned out to be more prolonged and more revealing than any of us imagined. This is its story.

The decision to write a baptismal service for our own child seemed a natural one. Heather and I are very much children of the age in which we live. In many ways our values are traditional but we have affirmed them only after a thorough-going critique. The decisions to have a wedding and to have it in a church were not automatic decisions for us. They were deliberate and carefully thought out. Having made those decisions we chose to write our own service as a way of struggling with the most profound issues involved. Similarly, church affiliation has not been an automatic affair for us either. As the national statistics on church membership bear witness, most of the people with whom we grew up do not actively participate in church life. During the baptismal service we explained our actions in a talk entitled "For Our Friends Who Ask 'Why Are You Doing This?'"

There were many ideas that we struggled with in the baptismal preparation but four ideas were key. The first was Emily's identification as a child of God. We were clear that, by being baptized, Emily was not paying an admittance fee into God's family. She was created by God and, therefore, was already a member. In this respect the baptism was honouring, marking and celebrating that fact. In more formal terms this refers to our theological understanding of the universal character of creation and the universal fact of salvation. Because this understanding of baptism expresses, like the Eucharist, a fundamental aspect of the Christian faith, we wanted the baptism to take place within the context of a full eucharistic celebration.

A second key idea has to do with salvation. Just as we felt that Emily was not paying an admittance fee, we did not feel that we were purchasing an insurance policy either. As alluded to earlier, salvation is not an expression of God's conditional love but rather an expression of God's unconditional love. Church membership does not guarantee it and it is not, therefore, exclusive to church members. What we were trying to do was to identify the values by which we wanted her to live her life. Through the designation of godparents we were also trying to put into place some structures that would support her moral development.

In the process of trying to separate institutional church membership from guarantees of salvation we were forced to confront a third key issue. What did we understand by the church and why did we want church membership to be part of the package? With the help of our friends and Emily's godparents, it became clear to us that the values with which we wanted Emily to identify were the values of the Bible. While our criticisms of the church as an institution were manifold, our contact with the church was, and continues to be, through a specific congregation and a specific community of people. This is a community which thinks largely, though of course not entirely, as we do. They are the inheritors and interpreters of a tradition and they are the guardians of the record of these same truths and values. Through the actions intended by their faith, like the rest of the Christian church, they enable God's presence in the world. We counted ourselves as one with them and we decided that we wanted Emily to be included, too. For this reason as well, we wanted the baptism to take place in the context of a full Sunday morning worship service.

While there are other issues with which we struggled, it was the fourth key issue which, to our surprise, proved to be the most controversial. One of the deepest foundations of our relationship, of our identity and of our world view is equality. It is central to our theology, central to our politics and central to our life together. Because of this we have been committed to an equal division of labour in the home (keeping in mind that it's easier to say than to do), and we have a clear and shared intention to raise our children in a non-sexist manner (however inadequately we may accomplish it). Our parish has been struggling for a long time with the sexist form of common liturgical language. With this concern in mind we found a lot in the traditional Anglican baptismal service that was less than satisfactory to us and which would be less than satisfactory to the congregation. We wouldn't dream of urging our daughter to go "manfully" into the world and since one of the great problems in the world is its domination by men and by a male culture, it seemed both unfaithful to God and alienating to ourselves to baptize Emily in the name of a God described in exclusively male language.

It is theologically traditional to say that God is neither male nor female, or that both these realities are included in the divine reality. The language of standard ecclesiastical documents, though, is in sharp contrast to this traditional understanding. In our struggle to find new language, we realized that our experience of the triune nature of God was characterized by creation, redemption and sustenance. This is yet another traditional understanding of God and so we felt eminently successful when the celebrant proclaimed,

Emily Ruth Musgrove, I baptize you in the name of God the Creator, God the Redeemer and God the Sustainer. May your life be long and joyful.

After that, the house fell in.

We heard rumours that the priest in charge of the parish, who had not celebrated at the service, was unhappy with the service we had used. In order to avoid a more serious problem and to make sure we weren't making decisions and forming opinions on the basis of rumours, I called the priest and asked if I could sit down with him and also with the priest who did celebrate and discuss the matter. He refused. I was informed that he had been ordered by the bishop *not* to discuss it and that the bishop was going to deal with it from now on. I never heard from the bishop. The celebrating priest, Cyril Powles, did. He was summoned to appear before the College of Bishops (there are now six bishops who share responsibility for the Diocese of Toronto).

At that meeting he was told that the baptismal formula compromised with unitarianism — that is, it didn't adequately express God's trinitarian nature. A paper had been prepared reviewing the history of the use of the baptismal formula. In spite of acknowledged evidence that the formula had changed over time to meet different needs (Peter urged people to be baptized "in the name of Jesus Christ" Acts 2:38), it was asserted that "throughout the centuries all branches of the church have sought to emphasize the Holy Trinity by use of a clear and unambiguous formula, reflecting Matthew 28:19" ("Go therefore and make disciples of all nations, baptizing them in the name of the Father and of the Son and of the Holy Spirit").

One bishop repeatedly wondered whether he could say that the child had actually been baptized. It was finally agreed that they would accept the baptism as having been done but only on the basis that there was clearly an intention that the child be baptized. When asked if they understood why the baptismal formula had been changed, they replied that they did not. When told that it was changed in order to remove its masculine bias and make it inclusive, they were taken by surprise. That thought had never occurred to them. Within two months after the baptism, the bishops of the diocese circulated a letter specifically restricting the number of eucharistic and baptismal liturgies authorized for use.

There seem to be two issues here. One has to do with sexism and the exclusion of women and the other has to do with clericalism and the exclusion of the laity. Both issues point to the question of who has the authority to define reality, and both issues raise the question of whose experience will be used as a basis for our reflections on how we understand our reality. In this case, a group of men, because they had not questioned the restricted nature of their experience as men, were unable to penetrate the motivations for changing the baptismal formula, nor to recognize, without direction, its inclusive character.

Similarly, in their role as clerics, this same group assumed no responsibility for dialogue with the lay people who had drafted the service, nor did they acknowledge any responsibility to these same lay people whose faithfulness they presumed to judge. What they were prepared to assume was complete control over the decision-making process. In their desire to faithfully defend the authentic traditions of the church (which is a responsiblity of their office), they uncritically assumed that their individual experiences were authoritative. As a result, they initiated a process which emphasized their authority over the only people in the chain of events whom they had the institutional power to control. They ordered the parish priest not to discuss it; they summoned the celebrating priest in order that he might defend his actions; and they considered withholding institutional recognition of the baptism. By those acts are the central problems revealed.

In our North American culture, sexism refers to discrimination against women on the basis of their sex. While it is generally used to refer to specific acts of discrimination, as in the unequal allocation of rights and privileges on the basis of sex, it is also used to refer to attitudes which encourage or tolerate discrimination. But the evaluation of acts and attitudes as sexist arises out of women's experience of discrimination. Reflection on that experience produces the evaluation — but it also produces other insights based on this special experience. For this reason, feminism has two foci in its critique of contemporary society. Not only does it criticize specific acts of discrimination and the cultural attitudes which permit them, but it also criticizes the hierarchical way power is ordered throughout society.

Feminists are reflecting on women's experience of being excluded from the positions of power in our society. Some feminists are so convinced of the intrinsic connection between a hierarchical society and a male-dominated one that they characterize such a society as "patriarchy." For myself, I am not convinced of the absoluteness of the connection since it suggests that the participation of women in a hierarchical organization (like the church) will eventually subvert the organization's hierarchical pattern. I do not see any evidence from the experience of any of the churches which now ordain women to the priesthood to support such a claim, nor do I think that is a burden that women alone should have to bear. I am convinced, though, that women's experience of exclusion has provided them with unique insights into the social nature of sin and that these insights are true for us all.

In another article in this volume, Mary Rose D'Angelo has eloquently demonstrated the inadequacies of the traditional baptismal formula. The formula was developed in order to express the triune character of God in the language of the day, without subordinating any one aspect. As D'Angelo points out, on its own terms the formula does so imperfectly.

The concerns of the late twentieth century are different. Today we are less concerned with God's relationship to God than we are with God's relationship to us. When our experience of God is foremost in our concerns, we must pay attention to whose experience is included in official descriptions of reality. In this light, the use of exclusively male pronouns to refer to God is not simply an expression of the inadequacy of language, it is concrete support for an attitude judged as sinful and morally corrupt.

But the concern for inclusive descriptions of reality does not stop with the feminist critique of liturgical language. The second focus of the feminist critique, referred to earlier, raises the question of who has access to the decision-making process and why. The story of the baptism and its aftermath illustrates how a particular group of people who have not plumbed the moral depths of the feminist critique could not understand the motivation which drove the process on which they were sitting in judgment. It also illustrates how the people who were primarily responsible for initiating the controversial event were denied access to the decision-making process. Discrimination against women and discrimination against the laity come together at this point. Indeed, it is a very modern idea to even think of considering the issues separately, since for most of the church's history, discrimination against the laity has been a de facto discrimination against women.

The pattern of relationship between hierarchy and laity in the church was broken at the time of the Reformation. Motivated by the theological proposition that the voice of the poeple was the voice of God ("Vox populi, vox dei"), the Reformed churches adopted new styles of organization which emphasized their accountability to the laity. It is for this reason, I believe, that the Reformed churches have consistently been at the forefront in opening up positions of leadership to women. These new styles of organization did not eliminate the need for a struggle, but they provided the structures for that struggle to take place earlier and in a more coherent manner.

The Anglican Church describes itself as being both Catholic and Reformed. This is manifested by its combination of an episcopal form of church government along with limited lay participation and control. The episcopal structure is maintained because the Anglican Church continues to rely on the doctrine of apostolic succession.

This doctrine has meant many things over time, most importantly, the maintenance of historical continuity with the early Church. But the doctrine has also been associated with the idea that the power of the Holy Spirit is transmitted through the episcopacy by virtue of the unbroken sequence of episcopal consecration. The association of this doctrine with this idea encourages the belief that the church hierarchy receives its power and its authority directly from God. It also encourages the idea that episcopal authority is held individually rather than corporately. Because the feminist critique does not stop at exclusive language but extends to include a critique of exclusive forms of organization, this foundation for church authority is also being called into question. Feminists are relying on their prophetic authority in order to call us to account for our mistaken understandings of episcopal authority.

Feminism is a moral critique of our society. Sexism is a sin and we are all being called to confess and be transformed. But the critique is as much a call for right relationships as it is for a right expression of those relationships. It is a judgment on church structures which do not promote egalitarian relationships as well as on those which do not operate on the basis of egalitarian relationships. The experience of women which issues in this judgment does not simply provide us with insights into female experience, though it does do that. Rather, because of their special experience of exclusion from the structure and the language of the church they are providing all of us with insights into the nature of human life and human experience. Because the feminist critique points to fundamental truths in human life and not just female life, it will not be answered by the ordination of more women into a hierarchical chain of command. The feminist challenge is also a challenge to structure our relationships as people of God in a way which will do justice to our vision of God's justice.

The agenda for the church today is not a new one, yet it must be newly understood. The mission of the church has always been justice. Faithful witness to the truth creates its own disciples. The feminist judgment of liturgical language as sinful in its exclusiveness requires that we adopt a flexible attitude to liturgical experimentation. We are not all being called to write new services to meet our own specialized needs. But the struggle to find a suitable alternative expression in a language with a paucity of inclusive pronouns will be a long one, made even longer by resistance to individual efforts at experimentation.

What is potentially more threatening, though barely acknowledged, is that the questioning of language as an adequate expression of women's experience of God is also a questioning of implicit assumptions about who God is and how we organize our lives in faithful witness to that vision. We are being asked nothing less than to reconsider traditional church structure as well as church language as a question of justice and a question of mission.

Anglican Church Women: In or Out?

Pauline Bradbrook

What is the place and function of women's organizations and "concerns" in the life of the church? This question could not be posed at all if women had always shared equally with men in the government and service of the church. Historically excluded until recent times, women found their own ways to serve the church, in roles usually perceived and described as auxiliary. With newly raised consciousness, many churches have instituted changes aimed at redressing past imbalances and outright injustice. Some of these attempts have had questionable results. It is time for such cases to be documented and critically analyzed. I propose that an integral part of an agenda for church women is the recovery of their history in order to plot their continuing journey.

In 1973, after years of discussion and no little controversy, the Anglican Church of Canada took action which resulted in the "integration" of Anglican Church Women (ACW) "into the mainstream of Church life." This fascinating description, which recurs throughout the archival documentation and which accompanied the dismantling of the national church women's organization, is thought-provoking in itself. I propose that, from the perspective of a decade's experience, one crucial item for the church's agenda is the need for Anglican women to take a keen new look at what actually happened at integration. A number of important questions need attention. What benefits and/or liabilities have accrued from the national decision which was then implemented? Have women been integrated? If not, what must women do to regain lost solidarity and to influence the program and functioning of the church?

I want to begin by discussing the position of church women before integration, briefly reviewing the integration process and pertinent aspects of the surrounding debate, and highlighting one or two indicators of the position of women in the Canadian church today. It is not a complete discussion, but rather a first step. I hope that, reading this essay, women will feel impelled to tell their own stories, adding information where this essay lacks it and correcting it where the picture is incomplete. Essentially, I hope to be sufficiently provocative to engender a new, critical appraisal of the place women occupy in church life.

In the context of social transformation, "integration" is very much a sixties' idea. In North America, the word was particularly associated with the struggle in the United States to overcome racial segregation by the integration of blacks into everyday social, political and commercial life. It is not a word which ever came into vogue in the women's movement, which also sprang into new life in the sixties. In its application to women in the church, however, "integration" had its own peculiar aptness.

Women have always shared with men a common membership in the church. It can be argued that in matters such as attendance at worship, women historically have been more prominent than men. Why then did the idea of "integration into the mainstream of the church" arise? How and why was the ACW outside the mainstream? Were any women in the mainstream? In order to begin to answer these questions, we need to bear in mind the "disabilities" which applied to women in the governing of the church, as well as their "segregation" in women's organizations for the promotion of church life through money-raising efforts for the church at home and abroad.

Up to the time of integration, most Canadian dioceses, by canon or convention, had excluded women from participation in decision-making at all levels from parish wardens and councils to diocesan and general synods. Women became delegates to General Synod in 1946. At the diocesan level, Saskatoon could be considered average, when, at its 1971 spring synod, it deleted "male" from the canon on who could be a delegate, thereby paving the way for parishes to send women as synod delegates. Men inevitably performed the layreading function and, until 1975, women were excluded from the priesthood in Canada. Therefore, up to the decade in which the integration battle was fought, women were absent at the liturgical and governmental level of the church. They had not, however, been inactive.

The ACW had had its beginning in the founding of the Woman's Auxiliary (W.A.) in 1885.[1] With its motto, "The Love of Christ Constraineth Us," the purpose of the W.A. was the promotion of missionary endeavours. From its tiny beginning the W.A. grew into a national organization with an official publication *(The Living Message).* Following the founding of the Missionary Society of the Church in Canada in 1908, the W.A. reorganized itself to conform to the structure of General Synod. Initially, the work of the W.A. included: mission education among girls, with the organization of Junior and Girls' Auxiliaries and Little Helpers' branches; support of women working as missionaries and assistants in Japan, China, and India, as well as on Canadian Indian reserves; community charitable work; and financial support for the education of missionaries' children. In 1910 it established a Pension Fund for women missionaries. In 1912 it assumed responsibility for work with women and children overseas. This included additional budgeted expenditures for evangelism, schools, and hospitals, which by 1919 was extended to encompass the Canadian mission field. In 1931, the W.A. incorporated an expanded social service role by adding a clause to its constitution governing its cooperation with the General Board of Religious Education and the Council for Social Service.[2]

When, by constitutional amendment, the W.A. became the ACW in 1966, it was a substantial and financially healthy organization with a formidable "grassroots" ability at fund-raising. ACW branches at congregational level contributed to parishes and diocesan funds at will, as well as supporting their own ACW activities. The whole organization was run by boards at diocesan and national levels.

By the mid-sixties, at the time the W.A. became ACW, some sort of watershed had been reached in the life of the Anglican Church and its organized women. Many women, and especially the ACW leaders, experienced growing frustration that their work was considered essentially separate and auxiliary to the church and its program, which was quite literally male-run at every level. These women desired that roles in the total life of the church be open to them. At the same time, many ACW groups were experiencing dwindling memberships and poorly attended meetings. Young women did not seem to be attracted. At least one element of the operating psychology of the time was that if the ACW was dismantled as an "exclusive" organization to which one belonged, with its various obligations, then all women would be Anglican Church Women together, sharing equally the responsibilities for parish suppers, fêtes, and so forth. It is not easy to connect the issues of dwindling memberships in ACW and disenchantment with women's essential segregation from church bodies and functions at parochial, diocesan, and national levels, with the perceived remedy of ACW integration at the level at which it occurred.

A pamphlet sent in 1971 by the primate to all archbishops and bishops for dissemination in their areas outlined the history of the integration movement and answered two questions which were being raised across the country: "What is integration?" and "Why has such a goal been set?" Integration was explained as "a national goal jointly agreed upon in 1969 by the National Board of ACW and the General Synod," providing "for the eventual integration of ACW personnel, program and finances into the mainstream of the Church." "It is a way of avoiding duplication of time, energy and expense. It enables women, many of whom formerly worked solely in the ACW, to use their time and talents in the service of the Church as a whole." The integration goal had been set, the pamphlet states, because many church people had come to the realization that it was not "valid to maintain a separate national women's organization to carry out work that is being done by the Church as a whole."[4]

Advocates of integration emphasized that it would take place at the national level first, with dioceses and parishes following in due course if they so decided. The primate's circular, denying the suddenness of the integration agenda, traced its beginning back to 1960 "when W.A. overseas work combined with M.S.C.C." As early as 1966, the year the W.A. became ACW, the National Board of ACW, "stimulated by General Synod, set up a committee to study the integration of ACW and General Synod funds." In 1968 at Banff, the National Board of ACW unanimously accepted its Policy Committee recommendations on integration, and the following year in Hamilton the ACW Annual General Meeting passed the Resolution declaring the goal of integration. Also, in 1969, the General Synod in session at Sudbury passed a resolution of commitment to eventual integration. By 1971 Calgary, Qu'Appelle and Niagara had agreed to be experimental dioceses to see what would happen in dioceses where integration was implemented.[5]

None of these resolutions passed without controversy, confusion, and, finally, a good sales pitch. It is not easy to discern at this point whether the original hope was for the total elimination of ACW at every level, or whether it was rather the aim to consolidate national finances, structure and program. Clearly, if the former had been entertained as a possibility, it must have been recognized quite early that resistance to the complete elimination of ACW would have been impossible to overcome. In any case, beyond the national level, integration was stated to be optional.

At the Annual General Meeting of ACW in 1969, two issues seem to have been especially problematic. ACW leaders emphasized that integration would not mean the end of women's groups. At this stage, it was the national structure that was in question, and women could still return home believing their local groups would be intact (except for those who belonged to the three dioceses which were experimentally undertaking integration). When asked why national integration was necessary, the retiring ACW President, Mrs. John Robertson of Kitchener, was quoted as explaining that "some of the jobs became really too big for us," and cited family life programs as one example.[6]

We may be absolutely sure that wherever integration was discussed, the fear of dissolution of local ACW groups went hand in hand with reservations about loss of decision-making power over money. It is remarkable, therefore, that only two women opposed

the vote for integration at the 1969 Annual General Meeting. The
Hamilton *Spectator* for 13 June 1969 quoted one of those opposed,
Mrs. A.D. McCain of Florenceville, New Brunswick:

> Pointing out that the ACW raised about a half-million
> dollars a year, she said, "I just can't see passing that
> over to the men." She was assured that women would
> have a voice in the allocation of funds after
> integration.[7]

Archival materials contain other examples of this fear which surfaced when diocesan integration was discussed. In a circular letter of
16 March 1973, Bishop D. Hambidge of Caledonia stressed the
avoidance of "hasty" conclusions about finances: "If *diocesan* financial integration takes place, no one will take away ACW Projects
from them, nor overrule in the spending of ACW money."[8] Without
a detailed survey, there is no way to ascertain whether assurances
such as these were influential in swinging votes for integration. One
can only wonder how it was envisaged that ACW would have input
at this level of decision-making if there was no ACW representation
on the bodies which made the financial decisions.

A document on ACW Integration for the Diocese of Rupert's
Land in June 1971 spelled out the meaning of integration. It
affirmed continuation of various parish women's groups where
needed and desired; the involvement of lay men and women in the
whole program of the church on deanery, diocesan, and national
levels; the merger of the ACW organization (as such) at all levels into
the church as a whole, with the discontinuation of the name
"ACW"; and assurance that through the activities of the church as a
whole, "there is no need for women to re-establish a para-church
organization".[9] The document went on to spell out the financial
implications of integration:

> The merging of parish fund-raising programs (for par-
> ish, and extra-parochial purposes) so that parish
> women's groups engaged in such fund-raising are
> doing so for the budget of the parish as a whole,
> including all extra-parochial responsibilities.[10]

Power of decision-making over fund-raising goals could not help but
be lost to ACW by such a merger.

> The merging of programs at various levels will mean
> the increase in budgets (income and expenditures) of
> the various levels of the church organization. There-
> fore, there will be an increase in parish apportionments
> to the national office. Otherwise, church approved
> programs formerly financed from ACW funds will be
> forced to stop as the source of money ceases flowing.[11]

"Integration increase" is the term being explained here. Integration
was going to entail budget increases at all levels — parish, diocesan,

and national. Unless increased direct giving occurred, extra money-raising would inevitably be needed; somehow this was thought likely to occur in the absence of the very group traditionally most responsible for fund-raising. Men and women would now be equally responsible for this activity. To many people, this prospect seemed most unlikely. Brandon's progress report on integration in 1971 noted, "Parishes do not want to lose their ACW groups. Many rural churches would have to close if it were not for the efforts of the women's groups."[12] These sentiments were echoing and re-echoing across the country.

Integration was accomplished on 1 January 1973, when the national ACW budget was transferred to General Synod. The national ACW was replaced by a Women's Unit under the Programme Committee of General Synod, with permanent staff at Church House in Toronto having responsibilities for women's concerns throughout the Anglican Church of Canada. The programs of the ACW were absorbed into the program of the national church. In the whole country, only six dioceses integrated, but even in these, many parishes still had ACW groups. In the integrated dioceses, all the funds raised by the women were remitted either to parish treasurers or to diocesan treasurers towards their respective diocesan apportionments. There was no uniform pattern for unintegrated dioceses. Diocesan ACWs could remit directly to the General Synod Treasurer if they so desired, and these amounts would represent support for the National Program of the Anglican Church of Canada.

We may now fairly ask what integration has meant for the ACW. It still exists at local levels, providing fellowship for its members and a crucial source of support, both physical and financial, for local churches. The 1984 Anglican Year Book lists its membership at 38,920 in 1982.[13] Its Diocesan Presidents meet annually. Yet it exists in a state of limbo — neither in nor out. On the one hand, as an organization, the ACW lacks power to influence decision-making at both diocesan and national levels. On the other hand, women generally are more visible in the church today. We see them functioning as priests, layreaders, church wardens, prolocutors and delegates to synods, and as committee and board members at various levels. The numbers are still out of proportion, however, and the ratio of women to men does not seem to have been on the increase in recent years. Clearly, women's participation in church life has dramatically changed. Unfortunately, it is difficult to attribute this increased participation to integration. Did ACW as a national women's organization have to cease in order to acquire this representation? It is possible to speculate that with the growing awareness from the late sixties onward of the need to include women more fully in community life, the inclusion of women in the roles they now fill would have come inevitably. It is hard to resist the observation that ACW assets were the key motivation for integrating, since the issue of ACW funds is the recurrent theme throughout the archival material. This conclusion, however, must be weighed against several other important factors.

In the same year that Canadian Anglican women were integrated, Elizabeth Howell Verdesi wrote a book of considerable importance for women's history. Her research chronicled the fluctuations in women's power in the United Presbyterian Church in the United States.[14] Twice in this century Presbyterian women had power and lost it through what Verdesi describes as a "process of co-optation." Having defined co-optation as "the process of absorbing new elements into the leadership or policy-determining structure of an organization as a means of averting threats to its stability or existence," Verdesi contends that a process of co-optation operated in the Presbyterian church whenever women gained substantive power.[15] One of her two examples is of particular interest in the context of this paper.

> In the first instance, the power vested in the Women's Board of Home Missions was needed by the larger church structures. Consequently, the women's power base was co-opted through reorganization.[16]

By "formal" co-optation, Verdesi explains,

> an organization publicly acknowledges its need to recognize new elements through appointments to official positions, through inclusion of representatives on policy committees, or through establishing a new organization .... Formal co-optation "does not envision the transfer of actual power." The co-opting group provides participation for the new element but manages to maintain the decision-making power in its own hands.[17]

It is important to note that Verdesi could find no evidence that the loss of power was motivated by any conscious intent on the part of either men or women. Rather, the Presbyterian church women discovered too late that they had had a substantial power-base and had lost it through claims of streamlining and economy.

> Certainly there is nothing to indicate that the *intent* of consolidation of the various boards and agencies was other than to eliminate overlapping programs, to streamline projects, and to manage resources efficiently. These goals the leaders of the Woman's Board understood and supported. Both boards were operating projects in some of the same areas, but there were discrepancies in style and in efficiency of administration ... By becoming the Board of National Missions, the new organization provided "participation" but

managed "to maintain the decision-making power in its own hands." In this way, formal co-optation was used to gain access to the power of the women of the Woman's Board.[18]

Does Verdesi's thesis of co-optation in the experience of Presbyterian women have any relation to ACW integration?

I believe it to be quite unlikely that ACW viewed its organization in terms of a powerhouse. Nor do I think that the women and men who advocated integration were thinking in terms of increased, or decreased, power for women. Increased participation by women was never presented in terms of power for women and not surprisingly so, given the negative connotations associated with "power." The whole concept of the "empowerment" of women is more recent and arises out of the emergence of liberation theology. The declared reason for integration was the awareness that women were called to a wider role in the total life of the church than what was labelled as the separate and auxiliary one provided by ACW. Dwindling ACW memberships in many areas were attributed to this restriction. Second, stress was laid on the wasteful duplication of time, energy, and money associated with the maintenance of programs, personnel, and finance in a structure parallel to and separate from mainstream church life. Though opposition to integration was strong, there is no evidence in the Archives that these reasons were systematically critiqued.

The argument of co-optation raises the central issue of whose idea integration was at the start. The push for integration was perceived to come from the ACW. There is no question that national ACW leaders were firmly committed to this goal. There is some suggestion, however, that the integration idea had been entertained by General Synod at an early stage, since it is reported that the National Board of ACW, "stimulated by General Synod," set up a committee in 1966 "to study the integration of ACW and General Synod funds."[19] Such a study does not suggest women's empowerment as a prime goal. Nevertheless, I could find no evidence that a conscious co-optation was operating.

The true integration of women into the church requires a fervent desire to see that justice is done and the injustices of the past rectified by a real egalitarianism in which power and responsibility for all facets of church life are shared equally. There is no evidence that this could have been accomplished in the integration scheme devised, no matter how sincere the desires of the leaders were that this should be so. Women need to re-examine their roots afresh and decide whether their present position is the best it can be. In order to do this, much greater emphasis must be placed on collecting and publishing churchwomen's history. One recent writer has eloquently referred to our need for maps in plotting the way ahead.

Because our history is destroyed and our present
experience belittled or treated on an individualistic or
ad hoc basis we do not have enough competent maps.
We are cut off from the experiences of each other and
ourselves. We do not know where other women have
been or where they are. We have little idea of even the
outlines of the new world already opened up to us by
the courage of earlier explorers. We do not know how
each little bit of new territory relates to the other little
bits. Not knowing, we blunder into old traps ... Not
knowing, we disturb thoughtlessly the patient work of
other women. Not knowing, we waste time and repeat
errors. Not knowing, our vision is limited to what we
can see for ourselves alone.[20]

This image of cartography is a rich one. The church needs map-
makers. Thankfully, as the essays in this volume demonstrate, pio-
neer "cartographers" continue to inspire women and men to draw
new maps. Maps, however, are essentially tools by and for explorers.
They spring from journeying and exploration, and are helpful only
to the extent that they are used. Women in the Anglican Church
have been exploring new territories for many years. Old maps need
re-assessment and new charts must be drawn before we reach the
"new country."[21]

NOTES

1 Audio-visual material on the early history of the W.A. is available
   from the Women's Concerns desk at Anglican Church House.
2 "Woman's Auxiliary," an anonymous, undated, historical summary.
   Archives, Anglican Church of Canada. GS-76-15.
3 The change from W.A. to ACW was also traumatic, and this story
   needs to be researched and written. It could be that some of the clues to
   the genesis of ACW integration lie in this transition.
4 "ACW Integration." A pamphlet from the Communications Division, Anglican Church of Canada, sent out in December 1971 by the
   primate to all archbishops and bishops. Box 27, Anglican Church
   Archives.
5 Ibid.
6 Hamilton *Spectator*, Tuesday, 10 June 1969. "Go It Alone or Integrate?" by Ann Marie Watkins.
7 Hamilton *Spectator*, 13 June 1969.
8 Circular letter by Bishop D. Hambidge of Caledonia, 16 March 1973.
   Box 27, Anglican Church Archives.
9 Report to the Diocesan Council, "ACW Integration, Diocese of
   Rupert's Land," 22 June 1971.
10 Ibid., p. 2.
11 Ibid.

12 Progress Report on Integration, Brandon Diocese, 1971. Box 27, Anglican Church Archives.

13 *Anglican Year Book*, 1984, p. 11. This, incidentally, lists membership of other women's groups at 20,023 (both figures being considered incomplete).

14 Elizabeth Howell Verdesi, *In But Still Out: Women in the Church* (Philadelphia: The Westminster Press, 1973).

15 Ibid., p. 22.

16 Ibid., p. 24.

17 Ibid., pp. 22-23.

18 Ibid., pp. 77-78.

19 See Footnote 4.

20 Sara Maitland, *A Map of the New Country: Women and Christianity* (London: Routledge and Kegan Paul Ltd., 1983), p. 193.

21 Ibid.

Running Circles Around a Ladder: A Feminine Agenda for the Church

Jeanne Rowles

The agenda for the church in the eighties must be to embrace feminine values, ways of work and styles of organization, and model them in the world. At present neither the agenda of the institutional church nor the way it works are appropriate for the unique ministry of women. It is as though there are two cultures, male and female, with the dominant male culture suppressing the female one which is struggling to gain credibility. At this time, when the competition to possess the earth is bringing about its destruction, the church should be pointing to a different way — a feminine way. The church must get at this agenda at once. For many women and some men it is already too late.

The prevailing male agenda — protecting the faith, defending and perpetuating the institution — is incompatible with the women's agenda to create, nurture, grow and change. Although the current rhetoric and an observation of who is involved in parish life would indicate otherwise, most people know at a feeling level that the church belongs to the men, particularly to the clergy. Men define the faith and dominate the institutions. The struggle to find agreement on interpretations of the faith, and its defense against other belief systems, consume much time and energy. There are traditions to be protected. In addition, the maintenance of institutions requires attention to matters of property, funding and personnel. For most men the defense of the faith and the maintenance of the institutions become the agenda.

Women are not greatly involved in these preoccupations, and their agenda arises from their experience of the family. There the emphasis is on relationships among family members and between the family and the surrounding community. Sensitivity and energy are required to care for those with special needs — the very young and the very old, the victims of accident and injustice. Experiencing within their own bodies the life cycle of birth, nurture, maturity and death, women become attuned to the inevitability of change. Their awareness of the cyclical nature of life brings them closer to the earth and the need to live in harmony with it; women don't speak of conquering or possessing the earth. Women's world view, developed within the context of the human family and community, continues to be contextual; personal actions and public actions are understood as interrelated and inseparable.

The feminine emphasis in the church, then, is on the creation of loving church communities, their nurture, the development of constructive relationships, and the way in which decisions impact upon human beings. The care of "the poor, the broken-hearted, the captives, the blind and the bruised" is important, not only in fostering sensitivity to those needs but in the actual hands-on work of ministry. Women's concern for the overseas mission began early and continues to deepen. The close one-to-one relationships with missionaries have been replaced by one-to-one relationships with Third World women. The majority of those involved in the work of development education have been women. They are concerned for issues of justice at home and in the Third World, and they see personal and corporate, private and public behaviour as requiring the same moral standards. Women place emphasis on the elimination of violence toward human beings and toward the earth. Women, who bear and nurture their children, are both leaders and workers in the peace movement.

When church committees and task forces had one or two women on them, there was little evidence of a different feminine agenda. At the national level of the Anglican Church of Canada, during the inter-synod period 1980-1983, there were a few more women and slight changes began to be noticeable — changes toward a consideration of how ordinary people would be affected by the decisions being made. The church was forced to deal with issues of violence, in particular, woman-battering, of openness to other world views such as in the struggle to understand native spirituality, and of injustice to individuals as experienced by abuses to the conscience clause as applied to women clergy.[1]

With so few women in the decision-making bodies of the church, it is difficult for them to have a significant influence on its agenda, and this is particularly true when the church's way of working is inappropriate for women.

Men have been conditioned to value order and discipline, to be rational, competitive and hierarchical. Women are used to a less ordered working environment, are more passionate in their approach to issues, depend on each other for support to carry out decisions which are often arrived at by consensus. The differences in

the way men and women work are evident early in life. Gloria Durka in
"The Religious Journey of Women," refers to a study of children's games
by Piaget:

> ... boys and girls regard rules in different ways. Piaget
> found that girls, when faced with an argument over the
> rules of a game, tended to end the game and start over
> (or do something else) while boys would legislate their
> way through the issue. This illustrates one aspect of the
> structure with which the girls are operating and which
> the boys' structure lacks: the girls preserve the relation-
> ships of the players of the game, the boys preserve the
> rules.[2]

Masculine and feminine leadership styles or ways of work have
been described as alpha (masculine) and beta (feminine) styles. Betty
Friedan contrasts these two styles. The alpha style, she contends, is
responsible for the scientific method which seeks to discover a single
truth or reality from interactions with the world. The advantages of
alpha (rapid implementation of short-range tasks) are offset in
modern society where interactions with people introduce complex
variables, where there is no perceptible single answer, and where
"fluid shifts of power are needed" for each situation. Unlike alpha's
evolution from confrontation with the physical environment, beta
style is an outcome of resolving day-to-day family crises. It embraces
and integrates "differences and a range of values, goals, perceptions,
hopes and methods." Beta is a long-range rather than a short-range
style. It tolerates ambiguity and resists seeking absolute control in
favour of "a process of incremental adaptation by steps or stages."
Unlike alpha, beta is not orderly.[3]

Friedan's analysis is reinforced by Dawn MacDonald. She points
to studies comparing alpha and beta approaches to management
issues which claim that the beta leadership style will be more appropriate than alpha in future complex problem-solving. MacDonald
describes alpha as "typical of the North American male", i.e., analyt-
ical, rational, measurement-oriented, hierarchical, and avoiding dis-
ruptive change. On the other hand, the North American female and
the Japanese businessman reflect the beta style. Its focus is on
"long-range issues, values and goals, a holistic insight into the
impact of every part of the whole. It has a group rather than an
individual orientation. Relationships that support the tasks and the
people doing them are more important than job descriptions and
defined roles. Time and time again beta beats alpha in creative
problem-solving tests."[4]

In the church, as in other institutions, there are women who have
learned to excel in the male arena, using the alpha style of work.
Women have seen that men's ways win and it is a temptation to try
to get on the winning side. Unfortunately, those women who have

learned this, and do get elected to church committees because of their alpha-type skills, often find themselves without a constituency. They have no point of contact with women, and the men while admiring their skill, won't let them fully into the men's club.

The creativity and strength of church-women is seen in their gatherings, whether in small self-help groups or in larger events. They need each other for support and empowerment, for dreaming up alternatives and for testing their skills (gifts). The very important networking is more easily done when people have met each other face-to-face. Yet, perhaps because of the strength women draw from each other, the church hierarchy has opposed their meeting together without men present. In addition to other arguments marshalled against women's gatherings, strange reactions to what happens at the gatherings are reported. For instance, women were censured recently for dancing Sarah's Circle, although their accusers seemed to have no comprehension of what dancing Sarah's Circle means for women.[5]

The consensus model of decision-making is confusing and messy and very different from the male parliamentary model in which sides are chosen and people speak in support of one or the other side according to a set of rules, deciding by vote which side has won. Women find this intellectual, debating style inhibiting and impractical. They are used to many conflicting demands on their attention, to mess and emotion and no-win situations. They know that if they listen, let all feelings be aired and give time for accommodation, a solution will be found that everyone will be more or less able to support and to help implement.

Women need a flexible form of organization in which leadership is shared. Since women have been expected to respond to emergencies at home, they have never known, when helping to plan an event, whether they would be able to be present at it. They need an organization adaptable enough to accommodate their many different needs and abilities and schedules. They can't make the maintenance of the institution their only priority. In writing about the organization of the future, Toffler has described the alpha and beta organizational styles referred to earlier in this essay as Second Wave or Third Wave. Second Wave principles result in a "classical industrial bureaucracy; a giant, hierarchical, permanent, top-down, mechanistic organization, well designed for making repetitive products or repetitive decisions in a comparatively stable industrial environment".[6] Third Wave principles will lead to new very different organizations. In Third Wave organizations, hierarchies will flatten and be less top-heavy. "They consist of small components linked together in temporary configurations. Each of these components has its own relationships with the outside world, its own foreign policy, so to speak, which it maintains without having to go through the centre."[7]

Unfortunately for churchwomen, they are trapped in a Second Wave institution when they understand and can work with a Third Wave model.

Women have a different agenda, work in different ways, and are developing a different kind of organization. They find that the sacramental life of the church reflects a similar dislocation from their experience. They can find no place for themselves in the liturgy because of a language and symbolism which excludes them. They are not irreligious, but they find that their faith is not being nurtured within the church. Many are asking whether the institutional church is valid for them anymore or whether they will have to move out and form a new church.

Are there two distinct cultures in the church — a dominant male one and a rising female one? Cultural historians have pointed out that cultures decline when they become too rigid in technology, ideas, or social organization to meet the challenge of changing conditions.

> During this process of decline and disintegration, while the cultural mainstream becomes petrified by clinging to fixed ideas and rigid patterns of behavior, creative minorities appear on the scene and transform some of the old elements into new configurations that become part of the new rising culture.[8]

The process of disintegration in European and North American political parties, multinational corporations and many academic institutions is now apparent. According to Capra, the social movements of the sixties and seventies represent the rising culture which, despite the declining culture's inevitable unwillingness to change, will continue to ascend until it assumes a leading role. He argues that patriarchy shows evidence of decline and that the "feminist perspective will be an essential aspect of the new vision of reality."[9] However, patriarchy may not decline before it destroys the earth. Nuclear war is an example of patriarchy gone mad — excessive competition, overemphasis on power and control, an obsession with winning in a situation where there can be no winners.

What would a new, feminine church be like? It would have its share of vision, struggle, success, failure and hope, as has any other Christian endeavour; but it would strive for a way of work and a style of organization which would feature a circle rather than a ladder, sharing rather than competing, and empowering rather than controlling.

The feminine model places the emphasis on the group. Decisions are made by consensus and, if they are to be altered, the group alters the decision by consensus. Individuals are held accountable to the group but there is no super-group or "other" which can impose its will.

Many gatherings or groups are required to develop relationships, provide mutual support and build a kind of rolling consensus.[10] In a country the size of Canada, national gatherings are expensive. A feminine church would have to be prepared to find the necessary funds. The expense of gatherings is reckoned in participants' time also, but ways might be found to minimize that problem. For example, representatives might be chosen from those who have more time to give, such as the unemployed, those who are job sharing, home managers and the retired.

Shared leadership, another feature of a feminine church, would allow its members to pick up and lay down leadership responsibilities as appropriate, depending on a number of factors including the skills needed by the group and the individual's other commitments. No one would need to be oppressed by a leadership role or by a lack of opportunity to use leadership gifts.

Shared leadership would be practised by church members and employed staff working together in the group to reach a decision without the need for either to impose its will on the other or to protect its territory. Trusting relationships would have to be developed before this could happen. There would be less emphasis on staff "experts" and more emphasis on learning from experience together.

For staff members, the feminine style requires the willingness to be more vulnerable, more patient, and to work with less clearly defined guidelines. The urge to push forward must be curbed so that the whole body can progress more or less together. This style allows small groups to work creatively at what they think is important, still within the body but without necessarily being seen to feed into the main thrust. Short-term and ad hoc task groups would add to the fluidity of the organization.

One attempt was recently made in the Anglican Church of Canada to work in a new way. This happened in the Social Action Ministries (SAM) staff cluster when the position of director was about to be created. In the past a cluster director had been appointed by the Executive Director of Program. This time, with the Executive Director's encouragement, the SAM cluster staff elected a person to be called a coordinator and to serve for a two-year term. Staff members also declared their wish to share the work in a less hierarchical style. A further departure from the norm was that the coordinator was a woman. Others in the system were confused and found it almost impossible to take the situation seriously. "If you want to be a director you are called a director and you act like one." It is important to play the game by the rules.

This is an example of long experience in a patriarchal institution negating the attempt to work collegially. Staff members frequently do not expose important decisions to the group process, and those decisions that are made in the group are often changed without group referral. Program is worked out between the staff member and someone "higher up" and the cluster hears by chance, if at all. In this atmosphere it is difficult for the cluster to feel ownership of the work and to get traction to move on it. Cluster members become anxious and uncertain.

A feminine model emphasizes trusting relationships, decisions made by consensus, shared leadership and a fluid organizational style. However unlikely it seems that a feminine model can work in a patriarchal institution, the church must learn a new way. Even though there will be failures during the learning process, the struggle must go on. It is not good enough for the church to speak out against war and for justice and peace; it must model a new way of living itself. It cannot model until it learns an order different from hierarchy, a response different from violence, a power different from oppression. The world still pauses a moment when the church acts. The world wants to be judged to have spiritual and moral values.

It is possible that Christians, held together by their common faith, can struggle out a new way of being that will keep what is valuable from the old and move forward to embrace women's emphasis on life? The attempt to do so must be the agenda for the church in the eighties.

NOTES

1   The "conscience clause," passed at the same time as the ordination of women in the Anglican Church of Canada, sought to ensure that those opposed to the ordination of women would not be forced to act against their consciences or penalized for their views. In practice, the clause has been used to restrict the ministry of ordained women.

2   Gloria Durka, "The Religious Journey of Women: The Educational Task," *Religious Education*, 1982, 77, p.170.

3   Betty Friedan, *The Second Stage* (New York: Summit Books, 1981), p.247.

4   Dawn MacDonald, "The New Public Woman," *Holiday*, 1982, p.3.

5   For a discussion on the meaning of Sarah's Circle see Chapter 2, "Sexuality and Compassion: From Climbing Jacob's Ladder to Dancing Sarah's Circle" in Matthew Fox's book, *A Spirituality Named Compassion and the Healing of the Global Village, Humpty Dumpty and Us* (Minneapolis: Winston Press, 1979).

6   Alvin Toffler, *The Third Wave* (New York: Bantam Books, 1981), p.263.

7   Ibid.

8   Fritjof Capra, "The Turning Point: A New Vision of Reality," *The Futurist*, December, 1982, p.24.

9   Ibid., p.21.

10 Frederick C. Thayer, *An End to Hierarchy! An End to Competition!* (New York: New Viewpoints, 1973), pp. 171-179.

The Ministry of the Laity and the Ordination of Women

Donna Hunter and Elizabeth Wensley

The ordination of women to the priesthood in 1976 was a sign of hope to many Canadian Anglicans. The discussion and action of the 1975 General Synod in Quebec City, followed by a prompt response on the part of both bishops and women candidates for orders in several parts of the country, appeared to signify that the church still possessed the capacity to respond to the Spirit moving in its midst. Many rejoiced that the church had at last transcended its oppressive history with respect to the role of women, had made use of its new theological insights, and had demonstrated the ability to grow and change.

The thesis of this paper is that the ordination of women to the priesthood is generating a new — and perhaps initially unforeseen — agenda for the church: the call to engage in a radical re-examination of the nature of ministry, lay and ordained. Even as the presence of women priests has resolved some problems for those who were deeply unhappy in a church which barred women from the sacerdotal ministry, there remains in the post-1976 Canadian church a widely-felt, if often unarticulated, uneasiness with the prevailing style and theology of the ordained ministry. That this is so can be seen first and foremost in our rapidly declining membership figures, but it is also manifested within the church structure in the concern of bishops and diocesan staff over the adequacy of the screening process set up by the Advisory Council on Postulants for Ordination, and in the increasing concern of the theological colleges to foster "competence" in ministry.

While for many church people the ordination of women represented simply an opportunity for women to do what men had always done in the same way that men had always done it, others hoped for a more fundamental change in the church's theology and practice of ministry. This latter group believed that the presence of women clergy would supply whatever it was that was lacking in the ministry of the church; that a model of partnership and wholeness would emerge which would include as equals not only men and women, but also young and old, rich and poor, lay and ordained. The hope was that the Anglican ministry would very soon undergo a radical transformation so that it could be seen by all as more nearly incarnating the ministry of Jesus in the contemporary world.

Unfortunately, this has not yet proved to be the case. Furthermore, we believe that it will not come to pass unless those in positions of power within the church engage in a rigorous process of self-criticism and begin to listen attentively to voices which have been largely silent until now: the voices of women, ordained and lay. In their turn, lay and ordained women must remain faithful to their experience as the invisible majority in the church, and become willing to take the risks involved in speaking out in a critical and responsible way. The observations which follow are an attempt to begin this kind of dialogue.

In preparing to write this paper, the authors engaged in considerable reflection upon their own experience as Canadian Anglican lay women. We also met with lay and ordained women in mixed groups in order to talk together about the impact of the ordination of women upon lay ministry. We do not, however, make any claim to speak definitively for all Anglican women, and we freely acknowledge that the scope of this paper is limited both by our own experience and by the relatively brief span of time since women were first ordained in Canada. Our conclusions, then, must be understood as preliminary and tentative. We hope, however, that they will be of some use as a starting point for an on-going discussion of the ministry of the church.

As we sifted through our notes on the meetings referred to above, we began to realize that all of the women who participated in the discussion had some notion of a new direction and shape for the future of Christian ministry in the Anglican context, a vision radically different from ministry as it is practiced and experienced by most Canadian Anglicans today. From these conversations we have distilled two generic models of ministry: one which describes our present experience, and one which represents the hoped-for future. Needless to say, these are broad descriptions and are meant to highlight general trends, not to focus on the work or style of any one person or group. How, then, do we see ministry lived out in the Anglican Church of Canada today?

To begin with, Anglicans far too often identify the word "ministry" with the word "ordination." Given that most ordained people in our tradition are male, we have come to think of ministry as the work done by an ordained man, usually in a parish or congregation.

Clergy who take up teaching or a position in a social service agency are sometimes said to have "left the church," a phrase which reveals a great deal about how we understand ministry.

Second, as Anglicans we must acknowledge that we function within a church structure which is hierarchical, conceptualized vertically and divided into several different orders or classes. The amount of power which one holds in the church today, and the degree to which one's contribution is valued, depend largely upon how close one is to the top of the pyramidal structure and doesn't bear any necessary relationship to fidelity, competence or credibility in ministry. The specific implications of this dominant understanding are at least two-fold.

First, clergy outrank laity in terms of the importance attached to their contribution to the ministry of the church, and also therefore in terms of their power to regulate the life of the community. Second, men are more highly valued by the church and hold much more power within it than do women, at least in part, because until recently the clerical class has not been open at all to women. It is still not open to them in many parts of the Anglican church both in this country and abroad. This has led to a situation in which lay people, and especially lay women, have been permitted, indeed encouraged, to abdicate their role in shaping the church community's present norms as well as its future life.

Another result of the church's hierarchical structuring is that paternalism has abounded among clergy both as individuals and as a class. Most often this attitude has been directed towards women, and has taken the form of a fairly benevolent "There, there, don't you worry about this issue, I know what's best for you." Sometimes, though, it has approached the demonic and has placed women in serious jeopardy, as when women have been told by clergy to go home and passively endure violence at the hands of their husbands because forgiveness of such abuse is part of their Christian duty. In any case, the assumption is commonly made that the cleric has the right to direct the future of another person instead of taking that person seriously enough to allow him/her to make his/her own choices. We can describe this as ministry *to* rather than ministry *with*. The inevitable result is that the one ministered to becomes objectified and disempowered.

It is true that many women, ordained and lay, see no problems in the dominant model of ministry. When permitted by men, these women have willingly adopted it for themselves with few conscious reservations. This imitation of the paternalistic model represents one way in which women have tried to come to terms with their less than equal status in the church, and individual women have "played the game" with considerable success, in the short term at any rate.

Our perception is that the amount of energy required for a woman to buy into this model is tremendous. Coupled with an understandable craving to belong *somewhere* in the church, the necessary outlay of emotional, intellectual and spiritual energy prevents the woman who chooses this path from developing any kind of critical analysis of the way things are for other church women. Her ability to be critical of the status quo is further hampered when she allows herself to be seduced by fatherly male approval, which is sometimes forthcoming from those who pride themselves on their liberalism, and when women assume traditionally male roles and adapt themselves successfully to men's expectations. The great tragedy and danger in this is that such women, some of whom are now clergy, others of whom occupy positions of leadership among the laity, cut themselves off from their own past experience of oppression. Instead of acting as advocates and enablers of other women struggling to be heard, they pose another barrier which women must overcome. Indeed, their presence often increases the difficulties of women who wish to bring a more critical perspective to the attention of the church. Those men and women who do not want to acknowledge the validity of the critique being offered are able to point with relief at the few women — and in particular at the ordained women — who have been allowed to walk the corridors of power, and talk about how far we have come in our understanding of the role of women in the church! If this form of denial of reality (which women and other oppressed groups have named tokenism) is permitted to continue, the Anglican Church of Canada will be no closer to the realization of a truly mutual ministry than it was before the ordination of the first woman in 1976.

Other women, clergy and theological students as well as lay women, have been heard to observe that they are uncomfortable with the paternalistic model of ministry. One problem is that this model does not allow for the particular gifts, strengths, experiences and aspirations of women. More importantly, it perpetuates an oppressive model of leadership and power. Inspired by the example of the secular women's movement, these women have begun to reflect upon their two-thousand-year history of exclusion from positions of power in the church structure. In doing so they have raised serious questions about the fidelity of the prevailing model of ministry to the example of Jesus' own life and work. Realizing that there are serious discrepancies between the two, lay and ordained women in increasing numbers are asking, "Can we in good conscience remain part of a church which limits our participation, denies our experience, refuses to acknowledge the reality of our creation in the image of God, and distorts the message of Jesus' ministry and proclamation of liberation for all people?"

In large numbers, women today are responding to this question with a resounding "No!" For many, this entails a decision to leave the church community behind completely, to dissociate themselves from the sexism of its teaching, worship and common life. For others, however, this "No!" involves a commitment to remain within the church, together with a refusal to accept the church the way it is and a pledge to work for reform.

The vision of ministry nurtured by women committed to acting as catalysts for a new reformation within the church is centred in the mutuality of women and men, clergy and laity, living out God's purpose in the world in an infinite variety of ways. This vision will be realized only when the privileged of the church (i.e., male clergy) are able to see that the present state of the institution is analogous not to the Pauline Body of Christ, but rather to the medieval feudal system in which some wielded great power while others were maintained in child-like dependence "for their own good." In a transformed church, those who have power will understand the distinction between "power over" (one dominates, the other submits) and "power to" (one empowers another to attain a shared goal). They will follow the example of Jesus by consistently rejecting domination in favour of the empowerment model.

In a transformed church, the people of God will understand their mission as a prophetic witness and service to the world through unceasing efforts to transform sinful social structures. They will accept the pursuit of justice as having priority in determining the church's agenda for ministry, and they will not fear the anger of women and other oppressed groups, but rather will understand it as the appropriate Christian response to injustice with the potential to generate creative change.

It goes without saying that the experience of women in the church who are committed to working together for a truly mutual ministry has been fraught with ambiguity in the years since 1976. One woman priest told us a wonderful story about being sought out by a very elderly female guest at a wedding at which the priest had celebrated the Eucharist. This lay woman, a stranger to the priest, told her, "I'm eighty-nine years old. I've been waiting all my life to see this, and now I can die." Surely this woman's comment embodies the tremendous sense of liberation — indeed, of revelation — which the opportunity to participate in the Eucharist with a female celebrant has brought to many Canadian lay women.

Women clergy have also had a significant role in reshaping lay women's self-understanding along more positive and self-affirming lines. For example, one lay woman who had never before seen herself as intellectually able was encouraged by her woman pastor — who had noticed her keen interest in a parish study group — to begin university-level studies in theology. The resulting intellectual stimulation and sense of accomplishment opened a whole new world of possibilities before her.

Finally, lay women have benefited from the pastoral care of women clergy, particularly in relation to issues of sexuality and health. Nurses in hospitals where women clergy visit have spoken about the far deeper understanding of feminine needs and experience which ordained women bring to their pastoral work. Lay women in congregations have expressed an ease in talking about their sexuality which was not possible with male clergy. In other ways, however, the presence of ordained women has not had this positive impact on lay women. Sadly, the relationship between ordained and lay has, at times, been characterized on both sides by mistrust, jealousy, and fear.

The woman priest is sometimes resented because she is perceived to have had chances to succeed which were not available to other women. The question is asked, "Why should she have been able to do that when I couldn't?" At other times, the fear and mistrust is related to the priest's sexuality. She may be a disappointment in that she does not fit the bill as a focus for infatuation on the part of female members of the congregation. Further, some women experience her as posing a threat to their marital relationships — "Is she safe around my husband?" Others may ask, "Is she safe around the (male) rector?"

Still others set impossibly high standards for the priest, and then identify with her to the point where they feel that her failures reflect negatively upon themselves. There is fear that if the priest makes a serious mistake, then the contributions of all women in the congregation will be discounted and their options for involvement and growth in the church decreased accordingly.

Finally, those who hoped that the advent of women clergy would push the church to a radical revisioning of its ministry often become frustrated and angry at women priests who do not appear to be exercising their prophetic ministry, and who fail to struggle to incarnate the dimensions of mutuality and empowerment in their pastoral work. As well as anger, there is a profound sadness, even despair, when women clergy pattern themselves after men in order to achieve ecclesiastical success.

Needless to say, ordained women also have mixed feelings about the church, about the lay people to whom they minister, and about themselves. There is anger that the ordination of women is not accepted everywhere in the church, frustration at the resulting limitations on personal and professional opportunities, a sense of isolation, and, at times, profound loneliness. On the other hand, women clergy also experience excitement at pioneering a new path for women, warm support from those who recognize the ambivalence of the struggle involved in the role, and the rewards of being intimately involved in the lives of others in a caring way.

Further, ordained women who are committed to ministry within a non-hierarchical model state that they find themselves continually called upon to compromise their values in order to survive within the institutional church. While some people, both men and women, have been successful in ministering in non-paternalistic ways which focus on the empowerment of the laity, our present system does not encourage such alternate styles. Those who pursue this model may find themselves frequently at odds with peers and supervisors, for example, with the rector in a rector-curate relationship. It is indeed difficult for women to sustain this kind of critical stance over an extended period. As one priest commented, "I have to push myself all the time to maintain my integrity and faithfulness to the vision of why I wanted to be ordained in the first place, which was to change the church and bring something new to ministry. Sometimes I question whether I'm gaining or losing ground — it requires so much energy."

A profound difficulty in maintaining one's authenticity in the institutional church is a struggle shared by both ordained and lay women in the contemporary Canadian Anglican context. This struggle is perhaps more sharply focused for the ordained woman. She has identified herself more visibly with the hierarchy and is also more vulnerable to its discipline. A corollary of this is that the temptation for her to abandon the vision of a radically reformed ministry is also greater. She therefore requires the on-going support of like-minded women, ordained and lay, to break down her isolation and challenge her to remain faithful to her vision.

This brings us to the question of the ministry of the laity, which is finding a new emphasis in today's church. It is quite comfortable for all of us to think of lay ministry as the Christian intentionality expressed by all church members as they go about their daily work. The church hierarchy is increasingly willing to see lay ministry as encompassing some of the traditional functions of clergy, both in terms of liturgical leadership (reading at public worship, distribution of the elements at Communion) and in terms of pastoral care (parish visiting). Church-sponsored training programs are now available to equip interested lay people to assume these roles.

We contend that there is yet another dimension to lay ministry, a dimension which has surfaced in the years since the ordination of women in 1976. While clergy may have a prophetic function within the community *beyond* the church, we believe that it is the laity who are called to be prophets *within* the church community itself. While many ordained women are publicly critical of the sexism and paternalism still rampant in the church, they must watch what they say and to whom they speak if they expect to retain their positions. It is therefore lay women, not subject in the same way to the authority of the bishop and not accountable to individual congregations, who are truly free to speak out, to expose exploitation and injustice, and to agitate for systemic change within the church. The agenda for the church, and especially for church women, is to raise up and support these prophets in our midst. We do not expect that their voices will be welcomed by the church, but we are convinced that in the long run they will be seen to have enriched and revitalized the Church of God.

V
Economics

Urban People in Poverty: Towards an Alternate Model of Ministry

Stephen Hopkins, Bill Bosworth, Brad Lennon, and David Montgomery

As Christians, our responses to low-income men and women take a number of forms. Individuals give small amounts of cash to those who approach them on the street. Clergy in parishes administer food cupboards and discretionary funds. On a larger scale, we organize soup lines, clothing depots, missions, and hostels. The broader community looks to the church to provide relief in times of social crisis. While these responses vary in their form and scale, they all reflect the same model of ministry. This ministry is characterized by handout charity: a short-term response to the immediate needs of individuals who appear to be in some sort of crisis. The larger projects simply reflect an institutionalization of the quarter given to a "bum" on the street who wants a cup of coffee. Even though these services may be supplemented with counseling, these interviews are often a prelude to or a means test for handouts.

As full-time workers in urban ministries, we are very familiar with this model. To some extent, we each participate in organizing and reorganizing better ways of managing charity. However, as a result of our first-hand involvement (seeing the same people day after day and year after year), we feel angry and frustrated. We have become critical of the charity model. In this article, we want to share our concerns about this, the dominant type of urban ministry, and propose some elements of an alternative approach which we have been using. Our concerns about handout charity are threefold: that it fails to meet the needs of low-income men and women; that it often meets the needs of the giver at the expense of those receiving our handouts; and that it confines the church to an inappropriate social role. Our agenda for the church is a transformation of its ministries to people in poverty.

We must say, at the outset, that we are not sure what the result of this transformation will be. We do not have *the* new model of urban ministry; we are still in the process of discovering this for ourselves. We do, however, have some suggestions about where the process of transforming our ministries should begin. From the perspective of our experience, this transformation will require a reappraisal of the assumptions upon which our urban ministries are organized, a careful examination of the feelings that move us to charity, and a critical consideration of the role of the church in society.

Our fundamental criticism is that charity is based on a number of inaccurate assumptions about the nature of the problem. Handouts can only be an appropriate response if the problem really is a short-term or temporary lack of food, shelter, or clothing. But our experience suggests that these crises recur at such a rate that they are a permanent facet of low-income people's lives and something over which they have little or no control. This recidivism is usually interpreted as a reflection of the personal problems of the individuals involved: those receiving our handouts are perceived to lack employable skills, to be lazy, or to have a medical or mental health condition that bars them from full participation in the economic life of society. Similarly, we attribute poverty to the individual's choice of an alternate ("eccentric") lifestyle.

These assumptions are only partly true. Yes, individuals living on skid row, single parents, and families in poverty *do* have personal problems and these problems would not disappear if the individual's economic security were guaranteed. After all, middle- and upper-income people also experience personal problems. The crucial difference is that they do not land on our doorsteps whenever they are in a crisis. Their economic stability ensures that their medical, psychiatric, legal, marital, and alcoholic problems can be dealt with as such. The financial insecurity of the men and women who use our deacon's cupboards, on the other hand, makes them dependent on us in such a way that we have the luxury of interpreting their lives for them. We can focus on their personal problems and say things like, "You wouldn't be in this situation if you weren't a lazy paranoid schizophrenic with a drinking problem." The poor don't disagree with us because, at that moment, they need our food much more than they need to correct our labels for them. Thus, when we continue to see the same people coming back for another bag of groceries, another "little something to help them through the week," or another night in the hostel, it is easy for us to "blame the victim" by focusing on her or his personal problems.

We perceive many of these problems to be caused or exacerbated by our charity. We have seen young men arrive in the hostel for the first time because of a genuine crisis or emergency, but we have seen the same men grow old, sick, crazy, and pacified as they have become more and more dependent on our charity. We have seen them make many attempts to change their living situation permanently, but we have also seen the same men defeated many times by our society's unwillingness to provide secure and lasting employment, affordable housing, and livable income supplements. Based on these painful experiences, we have come to understand that the problem lies beyond the individual, in the structure of the society and economy that victimizes him or her.

Given this understanding of the nature of the problem, we fail to see how short-term, "charitable" responses to the immediate needs of individuals in crisis can help in the long run. Handouts cannot alter the poverty of poor people. They may relieve temporarily the symptoms of the unequal distribution of wealth in our society, but soup lines, hostels, and clothing depots do not even begin to attack the disease. In fact, our "acts of charity" generally ensure that low-income men and women will simply return for more. By administering such palliatives (Is the patient terminally ill?) we simply patch up an economic situation that is unjust and we sustain the church's complicity in that injustice.

Taken as a whole, the charity model stands for a particular relationship of church and society. By managing handouts, the church fulfills a social role. It performs a function on behalf of the whole society by feeding, clothing, and sheltering men and women in poverty. The church picks up the pieces of a broken world. Because we have experienced the incompleteness of this model, we would suggest that the church reorient itself to healing the causes of the world's brokenness. We believe that, as church, we are called to adopt a critical orientation to the world and its sinfulness, and that this vocation demands that we engage in a prophetic ministry to the social and economic foundations of urban poverty and marginalization. In the long term, only such a prophetic orientation can provide a truly pastoral response to low-income people.

This reorientation from repair to reconstruction is not easy. The charity model is supported by a number of factors which deter us from the critical shift to an alternate paradigm of ministry. At the simplest level, charity is a part of our history. The church has been involved in direct material aid to the victims of poverty for as long as any of us can remember. Low-income men and women ask for handouts and we give them. It is the response we know best and our lack of experience with alternatives prompts us to continue it. Besides, it's the only response that *feels* right: it meets our emotional needs. It has become the "technique" and the basis upon which our institutions of social ministry are organized. It is a key component of the church's place in society as we have understood it as well as an integral part of the theological tradition as we have received it. In order to transform this model of ministry, then, we must understand the power that our history of charity has over us.

On the personal, emotional level, our difficulty in moving beyond handouts can be traced to our ambiguous motivations and feelings: the mixture of compassion, guilt, and fear we experience as we confront others in need. Through our socialization we have learned charity as the best way to deal with these feelings. A failure to respond immediately and concretely leaves us feeling even more miserable as we fear we may have become cold and ruthless, while charity helps us to feel good about ourselves and see ourselves as caring persons. And yet our response, while perhaps born of compassion, may be more a reflection of our own pain and discomfort. It may be our own pain which prompts us to respond with a bag of groceries that will make *us* feel better quickly, but which will sooner or later leave its recipient hungry again. In the face of our fear and guilt related to poverty, we run the risk of retreating from the situation rather than holding onto our compassion through the pain in order to ask ourselves what could better meet the needs of low-income people in the long run. Handouts are often an easy response born of our uneasiness. In this way, our charity is self-serving. With such potent internal rewards available to us, it is not surprising that we find it difficult to give up this model of ministry.

We must change ourselves. At the personal level, the development of an alternative model requires that we become critically aware of the feelings that motivate us to charity. We have learned that, both individually and collectively, we tend to act in accordance with our own emotional needs, to the detriment of those we hope to serve. However, we also know that it is our socialization which prompts us to respond with handouts to the mixture of guilt, compassion, and fear we feel when confronted with people in poverty. There is no necessary relationship between these feelings and our response — it is an accident of our upbringing. Still, those feelings are strong and they demand a response. Therefore, in order to become critical of the way we act on our feelings and to move beyond our self-serving tendencies, we need the support of others. Self-criticism is not something accomplished in isolation, where we can be misled by our needs for easy answers and painless, instant solutions. Rather, the process demands a mutual accountability with others who are struggling for authenticity in ministry. As part of our agenda for the church, then, we would advocate the formation and nurture of support groups for authenticity and integrity in ministry among those involved in social ministry.

The emotional dynamics and self-serving tendencies we have been describing are institutionalized in special urban ministries. As we reflected together on our work experience, we realized that our programs were developed by the givers of charity in accordance with *their* personal needs and perceptions. It is not surprising, therefore, that our soup kitchens, hostels, missions, and clothing depots fail to meet the long-term needs of low-income men and women. We also realized that, because charity-based ministry is focused on an encounter with the individual, our institutions of urban ministry fail to develop the overview of the situation that would enable them to understand how the problem is more social and economic than it is personal and pathological or psychological. This suggests some additional tasks for support groups of those of us who are involved in full-time social ministry: a collaborative struggle to understand our ministry in its social context and to change our behaviour accordingly.

By sharing our work experiences and orienting ourselves to an overview of poverty in its social, political, and economic dimensions, we have come to understand the individual person better and we have found it easier to free ourselves from a preoccupation with short-term solutions. However, a new understanding of the context of ministry requires that we ask different questions of ourselves. For instance, if we ask "Why is there poverty in Canada?" instead of "Why is this person poor?" we will be less likely to focus on the personal problems that seduce us into blaming the victim and we will be more likely to understand the economic forces that create and sustain poverty. Through such a probing with others, we can begin to appreciate how our charity provides only a little symptomatic relief without touching the disease. This reflection has led us to redesign our programs to address long-term needs and to restructure our organizations to include user input in decision-making. We have also begun to cooperate with others in advocating a transformation of the social and economic structures that impede full employment and affordable housing.

This kind of action-reflection is another part of our agenda for the church. Those engaged in full-time social ministry need to organize themselves as "intentional justice communities" to begin to do the kind of self-critical reflection described above. They need to work self-consciously at transforming their work from social service and charity into social justice and prophecy.

In terms of the wider church context, the same emotional dynamics of handout charity are at work. People in parishes come to depend on the rector's discretionary fund and church-sponsored missions as the only means they know of for coping with *their* ambiguous feelings. By donating cans of food to a deacon's cupboard, lay people can assuage whatever guilt they may feel. They can be convinced that "something is being done" and can feel good about having had some part in it. At the same time, the fact that it's being done by somebody else can help them allay their fears by keeping low-income people at arm's length. They are thus kept from experiencing the human costs of poverty and are spared the pain of a direct encounter with the demonic underside of their economic security.

These insights have been very helpful to us in both interpreting and also feeling empathy with the church's reluctance to give up its charitable ministries in favour of a prophetic witness against the inequities of the current structure of the economy. To challenge charity is to challenge the coping mechanism through which we distance ourselves from the darkness, ambiguity, and sin of our economic life together. On another level, to challenge charity is to threaten a number of assumptions about the role of the church in society. The church is seen by others and considers itself the lifeboat of society and (it is tacitly agreed) no one should "rock the boat." The church, therefore, often stands in fundamental and uncritical support of the status quo.

This tendency to accommodation with the dominant forces in society persists. The poor and their powerlessness are not a pastoral priority for the average parish priest. Rather, most Anglicans are well-served by the current economic arrangement and concerned for its preservation. For this reason, handouts are a much more acceptable response to people in poverty than would be activity for a restructuring of the economy to ensure full employment and affordable housing for all. Indeed, patch-up work reflects the prevailing assumption (despite high unemployment) that this economy basically works and is only occasionally or temporarily dysfunctional for a small minority of individuals who suffer some severe personal problems.

Because handouts keep the poor in poverty and keep the givers of charity from discovering the truth about poverty, they function as mechanisms of social control to preserve the current social order. The church's support of charity-based ministries reflects its political option *for* the status quo in Canada. Even when Canadian Anglicans have been moved to critique charity and economics, we have tended to do so at arm's length by focusing on the Third World and the dynamics of international underdevelopment. In a sense, we have chosen to begin learning our lessons in our neighbours' houses rather than at home where the costs of economic justice may be more painfully apparent and where we will be confronted directly.

The crucial issue in making the shift from short-term palliatives to long-term solutions, then, is our fundamental orientation to the current social and economic structures. If we, as church, cannot free ourselves from allegiance to an economy that requires a certain number of men and women to live in poverty without secure jobs and permanent, affordable housing, then it is unlikely that we will ever become free of the band-aid charity which sustains that economy. While this issue of orientation may remain an open question for some individual Christians, there can be no question for the church. If we are to stand with God, then we must stand against the world when it denies full humanity to the children of God. The key to a new model of urban ministry, then, is the church's repentance of its complicity in an economy which creates poverty, and the adoption of a mission of systemic transformation to ensure full employment, affordable housing, and adequate income supplements for all.

Because of the church's social role as the initiator and administrator of charity, the church can become a central actor in this social transformation. For while this social role constrains the church, it also includes many possibilities. The church's decisions about how it will or will not fulfill its social role will have an impact on the whole social order. Furthermore, the church remains an important moral authority in Canada, despite its decline since the Second World War. At some levels of its organization, and on some issues, the church has already assumed a critical stance. Sadly, however, the majority of parish clergy and lay people still have a large investment in the social respectability of their religion which deters them from shedding their accommodation to the status quo. The validity of a prophetic urban ministry is therefore lost on those who provide the donations which sustain our charity. In divesting itself of its complicity in structural sin, the church must set about re-educating itself. To this end, we have three concrete and specific proposals to make as a further development of our agenda for the church.

First, the intentional justice communities mentioned above should seek ways of working collaboratively with parishes to help the clergy and people understand the issue of poverty and to engage them in self-critical reflection on their role in creating and sustaining poverty. We know this will not be an easy relationship to initiate and maintain. To be effective, it would be most desirable if the relationship were to be initiated by the parish, asking those involved in justice ministries to act as a resource for them in deepening their faith and learning a new obedience to the Gospel. This may be a long-range goal that requires the support of bishops and theological educators to help parish clergy understand the need for such reflection.

Second, the church hierarchy needs to recognize and enfranchise those justice communities by giving them a consultative role on diocesan boards and an independent voting status at synods. In so doing, the church's leadership should leave itself radically open to hear what these justice communities have learned and to act courageously on their recommendations.

Third, and most obvious, the church should stop contributing to charity! This is also the most difficult. In the meantime, we may have to rest content with an approach which links our donations to charity with actions oriented to structural change. For instance, people in parishes could be encouraged to write two letters to government for every can of soup they donate to the deacon's cupboard, or to give ten dollars to a non-profit housing project for every quarter they are asked for on the street. But beware! This is a very dangerous half-measure because it allows us to continue meeting our emotional needs in the same way as before and so may do as much to keep us where we are as it does to encourage us to move forward.

The church's re-education must also involve us in a transformation of our ideas. The church's option for accommodation, and its charity, are supported by much of the intellectual and theological tradition as we have received it. The individualism inherent in western philosophy and theology encourages us to consider the person in isolation from her or his social context. Thus we tend to "blame the victim" rather than seek explanations in contextual or holistic categories. Similarly, evil and sin are usually understood in personal (usually moral and often sexual) terms. Only recently have theologians been developing an understanding of sin as a social and structural phenomenon. Given our privatized concept of sin, it is not surprising that redemption is usually limited to the individual sinner in isolation from her or his social context. Accordingly, "love" (agape) is mistranslated "charity" and limited to interpersonal interactions (to the exclusion of the social, political, economic, familial, national, and global facets of human relations).

Our culture's individualistic bias has led us to overlook the rich images of collective salvation found in Scripture. Although this is changing, the deliverance of the people of God from bondage in Egypt and the establishment of the City of God still tend to be displaced by notions of individual election and personal appropriation of salvation. Similarly, the prophetic response to poverty (i.e., a nation of the People of God struggling for justice) is not applied to the Canadian urban scene and biblical exhortations to do works of charity are considered detailed prescriptions for individual behaviour, rather than qualitative descriptions of life in the City of God. A good example is the parable of the Good Samaritan, which is usually interpreted as the example story of charity par excellence. In fact, as Luke tells it, it was a means of illustrating that the neighbour we are called to love is the one who, for political and religious reasons, we hate the most and that self-righteous "religious types" cannot be relied upon to do the will of God.

A final element in our agenda for the church, then, has to do with a careful reconsideration of the ways that the theological tradition continues to inform and sustain our accommodation to the status quo and our short-term, charitable responses to people in urban poverty. Preachers and theological educators need to become involved in the task of a theological reconstruction through which we can understand obedience as justice and salvation as corporate.

Theological educators in particular can contribute greatly to the formation of future clergy who will understand urban poverty as a pastoral priority which demands a prophetic response.

In conclusion, we must learn that we need not be bound by our history. Simply because we have been "doing charity" for as long as we can remember does not mean we should continue doing it until the end of time. A precondition of our shift to a new model is freedom from the old. In this article, we have suggested we give up our inherited techniques and become critical/self-critical instead. We have proposed a sustained, hard look at the actions, feelings, and ideas which maintain the charity model of ministry. We have faith that, through this process, we will discover a new model. We know that this will be a painful process for individuals and groups throughout the church. It is often in response to such pain that we retreat into the inherited techniques of handouts. We take refuge from the brokenness and ambiguity of the world in our soup kitchens, clothing depots, and hostels. Still, we believe that there is a spiritual depth born of this pain that will ultimately lead us beyond our self-serving techniques; that, by taking up the cross of our failure, we will discover the power of the resurrection and transcend the limitations of our past.

Indian Rights for Indian Women

Janet Silman

Section 12(1)(b) of the Indian Act:
> Persons not entitled to be registered
> 12. (1) The following persons are not entitled to be registered, namely
> ... (b) a woman who married a person who is not an Indian ...[1]

Can I ask you a question? How do you make a white woman an Indian, and how do you make an Indian a white woman? I am faced with that situation where, If I married my fiancé now, I am not recognized as an Indian person and I am not recognized as a white person. So what am I? ... Why does the law hold me in that situation where I cannot even make a choice for my child's future?[2]

It seems inconceivable that (as women) our biological constitution should be reason enough for our birthright and heritage to be arbitrarily divested at the moment when we enter into a second union with another child of God.[3]

Jesus' own *mission* was to the marginalized in society: the dispossessed, the poor, women, all those without a voice. He had a passion for *justice*. Hence, seeking justice with those who are most marginalized in our society is a central calling for the Christian church. Mary Two-Axe Early of the Kanawake Reserve near Montreal has referred to non-status Indian women as "the poorest and most despised cultural minority in Canada today ... 'the least members of your society.' "[4] Should we doubt this assessment, we only need contemplate the pejorative connotations of the term "squaw." A

government study done in 1979 concluded that:
> Indian women likely rank among the most severely
> disadvantaged in Canadian society. They are worse off
> economically that both Indian men and Canadian
> women and although they live longer than Indian men,
> their life expectancy does not approach that of Cana-
> dian women generally.[5]

The study also discovered that, "About a third of the Indian deaths (irrespective of sex) are reported as being due to 'accidents, poisoning and violence' in comparison with about 10 percent for the total population."[6] While these grim statistics for status Indians reflect the "double discrimination" *status* women experience as a result of their race *and* sex, *non-status* Indian women bear the weight of triple discrimination.

For the past century the Indian Act has defined who is an Indian, and thus entitled to certain rights and benefits, primarily membership in a band and residency on a reserve. Registration is determined by a *patrilineal* system, i.e., in relation to "a male person who is a direct descendent in the male line of a male person. ..."[7] Upon marriage to a non-status man, an Indian woman born with status loses it, unable to regain it even if she is subsequently widowed or divorced. In contrast, an Indian man bestows his Indian status upon his white wife and their children.[8] Consequently, every Indian woman is dependent on a man — first her father and then her husband — for her identity, rights and status under the Indian Act. Women born and raised on reserves are often later viewed there as strangers and outsiders simply because at one time they were married to men from off the reserve: at best, they are tolerated, and at worst, refused residence. The European patrilineal stamp was imposed upon Indian peoples regardless of their own patterns of inheritance, many of which were matrilineal. This patriarchal colonial system has functioned not only to subjugate Indian women, stifling their independent voice in their home communities; it also has ripped apart Indian peoples by splitting them into "status" and "non-status."[9] The sins of the white fathers are visited upon the present generation.

As early as 1965 Indian women began to raise their voices, calling for an end to the blatant sexual discrimination institutionalized in the Indian Act. Since then the struggle to abolish 12(1)(b) and other offensive sections of the Act has been central in the movement aptly identified as "Indian rights for Indian women." Native women's groups including the Native Women's Association of Canada, Indian Rights for Indian Women,[10] and all but one or two of the many regional organizations have lobbied to amend the Act to have Indian women and their children who have lost their status *reinstated*. Pressure on the federal government to change the discriminatory sections increased during the 1970s: first with legal challenges by Jeanette Lavell and Yvonne Bedard in 1973, and then by Sandra Lovelace of New Brunswick taking her complaint against Canada to the United Nations in 1977. In 1981 the United Nations Human Rights Committee ruled in Lovelace's favour, finding Canada in breach of the International Covenant on Civil and Political Rights. Human rights groups and Indian women's groups applied mounting pressure on the Canadian government, with the United Church of Canada playing a role in this escalation. In 1981 Indian women from New Brunswick approached the United Church Task Force on Changing Roles of Women and Men in Church and Society for support in their campaign. With the assistance of the New Brunswick women the Task Force familiarized itself with the issues and took resolutions and petitions to the annual meetings of the twelve conferences. The resolutions received wide support in many of the conferences where they were moved and addressed by both Indian men and Indian women. "Since the late 1970s promises to amend the Indian Act have been made and broken, the reason given that enough consensus does not exist yet within the Indian community. Even in the 1970s the issue had become "a political football."

While all major Indian organizations, including the Assembly of First Nations (formerly the National Indian Brotherhood), the Native Council of Canada, the Dene, Inuit and Métis, publicly acknowledge that the Indian Act discriminates against women, many of the predominantly male groups argue that other issues are more important. The suspicion has often been voiced that the government is using the "women's issue" to avoid dealing with these more important issues, the principal one being Indian self-government. Many native women's groups note that, while the political football is being kicked, the Indian woman continues to face:

1) the loss of her nationality
2) the loss of her right to reside where she was born
3) the loss of close family ties
4) the loss of her culture and religion
5) the loss of her right to family property and inheritance
6) the loss of her voting rights
7) the loss of health services
8) the loss of educational rights
9) the loss of her right to be buried on Indian land.[12]

Many Indian women have wondered aloud how unimportant these losses would be if they had to be endured by the men. Nevertheless, rather than deal with the issue of reinstatement in isolation, Indian women's groups have been careful to formulate positions which take into account issues they strongly endorse, such as Indian self-government and the enshrinement of aboriginal and treaty rights in the Constitution. As early as 1979 Indian Rights for Indian Women stressed that it fully supported Indian membership and status being enshrined in the Constitution, but it did not want amendments to 12(1)(b) *stalled* by the constitutional renewal process.[13] The Native Women's Association of Canada also clearly views the issue of 12(1)(b) in the context of constitutional rights and self-government. Regarding self-government and reinstatement, its position is that:

> ... Indian governments determine their own member-ship, *but only after all of those so titled have been listed or reinstated on their respective band lists.*[14]

A number of Indian women's groups consider that the responsibility for redressing the legislated injustice against Indian women and their children lies solely with the federal government. It was the federal government which imposed the patriarchal system upon Indian peoples more than one hundred years ago. By making women's status, identity and rights dependent upon men the Indian Act has functioned to disempower, devalue and silence Indian women. In order for them to be ensured the *possibility* of an independent voice in self-government when it comes, these groups contend that Indian women need equality legislated *now*, not later: hence the urgency of their appeal to whoever will listen. Will the church listen?

With one or two exceptions the church has been noticeable only in its absence from the cause of Indian rights for Indian women. A few cases have been reported of church groups "having their hands slapped" for advocating reinstatement: the issues were too complex and why were they imposing their white views of Indians? One Indian woman's response upon hearing this was:

> White people certainly don't agree on everything; I don't know why they expect Indians to! The govern-ment has been saying, "We can't change the Indian Act until you Indians come to a consensus." But if an unjust law is there, they don't wait until all white people come to a consensus: It's unjust and they change it.

As Caroline Ennis of New Brunswick stated so succinctly, justice is justice: it is not simply a "white concept." If we shied away from complex issues as a church we would have an extremely brief agenda. The time has come for native women's rights to be placed on the church's agenda; indeed, be given a high priority by social justice committees and women's groups from the local to national level. This will require a campaign not only to educate ourselves around the issues involved, but also to raise our *own* consciousness regarding racism *and* sexism.

An obvious reason why we have not responded as a church to native women's appeals for support is that we may not have *heard* them. However, if we take seriously our Christian calling to identify in solidarity with those who *by virture of their marginalized status have no voice*, then we have no excuse but to "listen harder" and respond. The complicating factor in native women's issues is not merely the complexity of legalities and conflicting rights: the underlying complication is our *own* confusion regarding the interaction between sexism and racism. The fundamental reason that as a church we have backed away from a tentative response is that we are *unclear* about how racism and sexism function together. Indian women live every day of their lives under the "multiplier effects" of sexism and racism. Just as these two evils do not make life easy, neither are they easy to understand. Consequently, those of us who have been working with issues around sexism need to grapple with how racism functions and compounds the problems of sexism. Those of us committed to fighting racism need to recognize sexism as an injustice which cuts across the lines of race and class. Useful resources have been produced in recent years dealing with these related issues.[15]

Raising our own consciousness and the consciousness of the church regarding racism and sexism is a formidable but essential task for those committed to social justice. We still have many congregations that view mission in terms of sending used clothing to reserves. Consequently, at the local level we need to start with where people are and work from there, for example, getting two or three hours on a presbytery or diocesan agenda (no easy task in itself) for a session on institutional racism.[16] Women's church groups are among the most active at the local level, with the best networks at the regional level. A rich opportunity for cross-cultural exchange and a broadening of horizons awaits those groups which actively *seek out* regional native women's organizations that have been working on equal rights for Indian women. In light of Indian people's past experience of "Christian" paternalism — the sins of the fathers — we as church people may initially meet with reticence and suspicion. However, if we genuinely respect the Indian women we meet, are open and clear about our motives and whatever misgivings we might have, and demonstrate our commitment to the cause and our willingness to learn, my own experience is that our support will be accepted. As white women and men we can learn so much from Indian people — not only about them and their culture, but also about ourselves and Canadian politics and society.

Many native women's groups have been lobbying against the legislated discrimination of 12(1)(b) for years. Consequently, by getting involved in their struggle, we in the church can learn a tremendous amount about how our government and political processes work, and about what is involved in lobbying for social change. As church people we tend to be much better at nurturing good intentions than putting those good intentions into effective action. By working alongside Indian women, we have the opportunity to develop these latter skills. Lobbying and network–building is an expensive business in a country as vast as Canada. Most native women's groups have been plagued with chronic underfunding. What they have been able to accomplish on "shoestring budgets" is amazing, but, as one Indian woman said, "The president of a provincial organization should not have to hitchhike to a meeting (which she did) because there are no funds for her travel!" The president of the Indian Homemakers Association of B.C. described the situation in which native women's groups find themselves:

> We do not appreciate the government taking the position that because there are national Indian organizations they automatically represent the voice of our women. This erroneous position, by the government, is further compounded when these national male-dominated organizations get all the funding and women's organizations such as ours, which deal directly with Indian women, are not funded.[17]

If we believe Indian women should have a voice, an obvious agenda item for us, whether at the local or national level, is in our *budgets*: in other words, we can contribute to their funding, recognizing that the funds we proffer are for justice, not charity.

In supporting native women's organizations, social justice groups need not worry that they are supporting a "single issue" disconnected from wider native concerns. Even those women's groups most closely identified with the struggle for reinstatement are involved in bettering the lot of *all* Indian people — status and non-status, men, women and children — *and* in preserving Indian culture. Their conviction is that the woman embodies the culture and language of any nation and once she is gone, the nation has no chance to survive. There is an Indian saying that the Indian people are like a giant bird — one wing men and the other wing women — unless both wings are strong the bird cannot fly. Consequently, in advocating Indian women's struggle for equal rights, we are not "only" advocating their "individual" rights, we also are upholding the "collective" rights of a people to survive.

For a number of years now the Canadian government has been announcing that it will "soon" amend the sexually discriminatory sections of the Indian Act. Even if and when it does make these changes, *including reinstatement of women and their first-generation children*, continued monitoring of the *implementation* of those amendments will be necessary. Indian women are not so naive as to think that their triply disadvantaged position in Canadian society is going to be overcome with one legislative amendment.

Just as the problem of racism is "a white problem" and sexism is not simply "a women's problem," the problems faced daily by native Indian women are also *our* problems. As a church we had a direct hand in creating them: to avoid "living in sin" countless Indian women married, and thus gave up their status. As women we can see in their legislated status of dependency the clear reflection of our own dependency: as white Canadian women, the law which subjugates them *was meant for us* in the sense that it reflects *not* Indian values but the traditional Euro-Canadian view of "a woman's place." As Christians committed to social justice we are called to be in solidarity with "the poorest and most despised cultural minorities in our midst ... 'the least members of our society.'" When we actually get to know these "least of our society's members" we find that our society is no judge of character. We generally find people with strengths and frailties not unlike our own, people with a wisdom that comes from surviving the worst society has to offer, people with a sense of humour which lightens the bleakest situations. In other words, we discover that we receive much more than we can ever give.

How, then, do you make a white woman an Indian and an Indian woman white? The Indian Act continues to perform this seemingly impossible feat, as it has done for one hundred and fifteen years. By the late 1970s Indian women's groups across Canada had reached a remarkable level of consensus for legislative change, considering the enormous pressures for division. At the same time, these groups had succeeded in mobilizing public support both within Canada and internationally. The momentum appeared strong enough to eliminate sexual discrimination from the Indian Act. However, what then seemed so close has still not occurred. Perhaps the expectation that legislative amendments were imminent functioned to dissipate support, with advocates going on to other issues. Once again Indian women's concerns appear to be a *low* priority on any agenda other than that of Indian women themselves. Once again they are virtually alone in putting forward their cause. By making Indian rights for Indian women a high priority on our *own* agenda, we in the church can stand with them. Surely the birthright and heritage of Indian women and their children are worth our solidarity.

NOTES

1   Indian Act, R.S. 1978, c.I-6.
2   Marion Sheldon, Minutes of Proceedings and Evidence of the Subcommittee on *Indian Women and the Indian Act* (Issue No. 2, Sept. 9, 1982), p.65.
3   Mary Two-Axe Early, Minutes of Proceedings and Evidence of the Subcommittee on *Indian Woman and the Indian Act* (Issue No. 4, Sept. 13, 1982), p.46.
4   Ibid., pp.46,49.

5 Research Branch, P.R.E., Indian and Inuit Affairs Program, *A Demographic Profile of Registered Indian Women*, October 1979, p.31.
6 Ibid., p.28.
7 Indian Act, s.11(1)(c).
8 Even if the white woman who has gained status through marriage is later divorced or widowed she does not lose her Indian status. Consequently, the situation can arise where, should she subsequently live with a white man, her *white* children from that common-law union have Indian status.
9 Altogether there are 325,000 status Indians and approximately a million Métis (of mixed Indian-European ancestry) and non-status Indians in Canada. In the North the Dene and Inuit have managed to overcome this status/non-status split, in part because for historical reasons it did not affect them as much as it did native peoples south of the 60th parallel. The government estimates that 15,000 native women are living today who have lost their status through marriage. Although no statistics are currently available, it is likely that more Indian women have lost their status by marrying *non-status* and *Métis* men than white men. This is important, but often overlooked, because it *counteracts* the accusations that reinstating Indian women and their children would dilute Indian culture, and threaten Indian politics by bringing white men onto reserves.
10 The national organization of Indian Rights for Indian Women is now disbanded due to funding and related problems, but some I.R.I.W. groups are in existence such as Alberta Indian Rights for Indian Women and Quebec Equal Rights for Indian Women.
11 In British Columbia over 90 percent of the delegation signed the petition to the federal government.
12 *Native Indian Women and Section 12(1)(b)*, pamphlet.
13 "Open Letter to the Prime Minister," Edmonton, Oct. 12, 1979 (Prime Minister Clark).
14 Quoted from *Indian Self-Government in Canada: Report of the Special Committee* (House of Commons, Oct. 12 & 20, 1983), p.54.
15 For names and addresses of regional native women's organizations, contact the Native Women's Association of Canada, 195-A Bank St., Ottawa K2P 1W7. There are many resources available on the injustices suffered by Indian women. The film *Somewhere Between* (16 mm, 50 minutes, distributed by Canada Filmakers, 525 West Pender, Suite 1, Vancouver, B.C. V6B 1V5) documents the effects of Canadian government legislation on Indian women. For further information on 12(1)(b) see Kathleen Jamieson (Minister of Supply and Services, 1978), *Indian Women and the Law in Canada: Citizens Minus*, commissioned by the Advisory Council on the Status of Women at the request of Indian Rights for Indian Women, and also the Report of the Subcommittee on *Indian Women and the Indian Act*, Minutes of Proceedings and Evidence of the Standing Committee on Indian Affairs and Northern Development, Issue No. 58, Sept. 20, 1982. (Ask your Member of Parliament for a copy. Issues 1-5 are also available.) Valuable for consciousness-raising are: (1) *The Colour of God's Face* (Racism Kit), Women's Inter-Church Council of Canada, 77 Charles

St. West, Toronto, Ont. M5S 1K5 ($5.00); (2) *Exchange: For Leaders of
Adults* (Vol. VIII, No 2, Winter 1984, on racism), United Church
Division of Mission in Canada, 85 St. Clair Ave. East, Toronto, Ont.
M4T 1M8; and (3) Barb Thomas and Charles Novogrodski, *Combat-
ting Racism in the Workplace: A Course for Workers*, 1983, Cross-
Cultural Communications Centre, 1991 Dufferin St., Toronto, Ont.
M6E 3P9. For a social analysis of the relation between racism and
sexism, see Joe R. Feagin and Clairece Booher Feagin, *Discrimination
American Style: Institutional Racism and Sexism* (Englewood Cliffs:
Prentice-Hall, 1978).

16 Mary Thompson Boyd and Janet Silman, "Breaking the Chains that
Bind: A Workshop on Racism," in *Exchange*, Vol 8, No. 2, Winter,
1984.

17 Rose Charlie, Minutes of Proceedings and Evidence of the Subcommittee on *Indian Women and the Indian Act* (Issue No. 4, Sept. 13,
1982), p.60.

GATT-Fly and the Churches: Changing Public Policy

Brian Ruttan

In 1972, Canadian church representatives went to Santiago, Chile to observe the third United Nations Conference on Trade and Development (UNCTAD). As a result of this experience, it was realized that the churches needed a vehicle to help them participate more effectively in public policy formation in areas such as Canada's trade relations with less developed countries.

During the second half of 1972 and into 1973, the interchurch project GATT-Fly was formed to be this vehicle.[1] It took shape through a series of meetings, seminars and public forums. During the GATT-Fly seminar of February 23-25, 1973, an important insight emerged based on past attempts of churches and other groups to try to revise trade relations between rich and poor countries. The insight was that the churches needed to develop their traditional general moral discussion of economic justice along more strategic lines based on specific issues. As one participant put it,

> A general brief is much less effective than a brief from
> the textile industry asking for a percentage change in a
> certain quota.[2]

The seminar also examined general resolutions put forth by governments of less developed countries in world economic forums such as UNCTAD and the General Agreement on Tariffs and Trade (GATT). These resolutions, while sounding progressive, were ineffective in practice because of their dependence on easily ignored general principles. Trade takes place in particular goods between particular trade partners according to specific contracts and agreements. Therefore, it was thought that progress in more equitable trade relations between rich and poor countries was more likely to come through working for particular changes in given commodities or trade issues.

Based on this insight, GATT-Fly's history has been a constant struggle to move from general moral perceptions of economic justice to particular strategies for change in specific economic areas. In this ongoing struggle, GATT-Fly has developed strategies and opened up new possibilities which propose new agenda for the churches in public policy debate. Generally speaking this agenda is to develop biblical principles of justice in ways which address specific issues of public policy. In other words, the agenda is not only to develop principles of change in public policy but also proposals for changes in particular practices.

I have chosen three examples of GATT-Fly's work in order to show how the group has helped to change the nature of Canadian church participation in public policy formation. The first example is largely strategic: GATT-Fly's participation in the World Food Conference in Rome in 1979. The way in which GATT-Fly participated in the conference gave it and the issues discussed a level of public and parliamentary attention which they would not have otherwise attained.

The second example is primarily a contribution of research and analysis in the 1976-77 northern pipeline debate. The GATT-Fly perspective made a substative contribution to this arena of public policy discussion.

The third example of GATT-Fly's work is the Ah-hah seminar, GATT-Fly's educational vehicle, first used in 1975. The Ah-hah seminar is designed to educate for social transformation. Participants are given the opportunity to clarify their own material interest in basic economic changes and to develop strategies for those changes. At the same time, the Ah-hah seminars enabled GATT-Fly to identify a constituency of people and groups with a conscious material interest in economic changes. Through the Ah-hah seminar, GATT-Fly has established links with groups of working people in various economic sectors: those whom GATT-Fly seeks to serve. GATT-Fly's work in public policy formation then, is in cooperation with those whose powerlessness is related to their need for economic changes. This element may be the most far-reaching in GATT-Fly's contribution to the churches' agenda in public policy formation: the challenge to act in solidarity with those whose need is greatest.

What I want to show through these examples is how GATT-Fly, in developing its own agenda for participation in public policy debate, has been a catalyst for change in the agenda of the churches. This contribution involves new departures in strategy, research and identification of constituency.

The World Food Conference 1974

The actions of the Canadian interchurch delegation to the World

Food Conference in Rome, November 5-16, 1974, were organized and coordinated by GATT-Fly. This initiative developed a new role model for the involvement of non-governmental organizations in international meetings. This model was further developed with GATT-Fly's participation in the seventh Special United Nations General Assembly (SUNGA) in September 1975 and UNCTAD IV in Nairobi, May 1976.

The traditional problems with Canadian Non-Governmental Organizations' (NGO) participation in international conferences have been that delegates have not often been well-prepared for the meetings and were, therefore, very much confined to being passive observers. They were also in need of mechanisms and networks for reporting back to interested constituency. At the same time, Canadian media have not often been ready to provide detailed coverage of such international discussions, so that analysis of Canada's official participation has not often appeared in our newspapers.

The GATT-Fly approach to the World Food Conference aimed to improve past performance in all these areas. GATT-Fly undertook extensive in-depth research of food issues affecting Third World countries and related to Canada. Some of this was done in conjunction with other concerned groups.[3] A Canadian conference on the world food crisis was also convened in 1974 by several NGO groups in preparation for the World Food Conference. From this position of being very well informed, the interchurch delegation was able to engage and influence Canadian official delegates on crucial issues of food production, trade, and aid. Also, by providing a daily communiqué service from the Rome conference to more than twenty cells across Canada, same-day news releases were made available to both national and local media. Through this route, information was made available to concerned opposition and N.D.P. parliamentarians for use in questioning government ministers. Finally, GATT-Fly provided a follow-up reflective publication on the events of the World Food Conference and their long-term significance, particularly in relation to Canadian policy.[4] The collected daily communiqués were subsequently published as an article in *The Canadian Forum*.[5]

The GATT-Fly operation at Rome had considerable impact on official Canadian participation. During the conference, U.S. Secretary of State Henry Kissinger proposed an "Export Planning Group" of grain exporters. In effect, he proposed an international cartel which could exercise political influence through grain markets. The impact of such a cartel would have been potentially far greater than that of OPEC because production of grain for export is concentrated in fewer countries. While less developed and even many developed countries were outraged by this proposal, Canada considered an invitation to join the proposed group. The inter-church group's direct engagement with the Canadian delegation, together with the GATT-Fly network in Canada, brought direct media and parliamentary pressure to bear on the Canadian government on this issue.

The GATT-Fly organized operation at the World Food Conference was a new concentration of effort by NGOs to influence Canadian participation in an international conference. Through research and by being informed in specific areas of conference discussion, by access to national and local media in Canada, and by using the parliamentary process, Non-Governmental Organizations became a far more significant factor in Canadian policy discussions than had previously been the case.

The Northern Pipeline Debate 1977

We turn now to GATT-Fly's research on northern development which is contained most fully in the paper "Paying the Piper" published in June 1977. My concern here is to illustrate what GATT-Fly calls "practical research." It is research which not only offers a unique viewpoint but also aims at policy which is in the interest of ordinary working people. Here GATT-Fly was able to show that the churches' commitment to justice for northern native people was in fact in the common interest of most Canadians. The "Paying the Piper" analysis grew out of the debate over the extraction of natural gas in the Western Arctic and proposals for moving the gas to southern markets in Canada and the U.S. Most of the proposals involved construction of a pipeline south from the natural gas wells of the MacKenzie Delta. Two proposals aimed at construction of a 48-inch pipeline transporting both Canadian gas from the Mackenzie Delta and American gas from Prudhoe Bay, Alaska, to southern markets. The route proposed by the Arctic Gas Consortium travelled along the Mackenzie Valley into northern Alberta. An alternate route proposed by Foothills Pipeline Inc. travelled through the Yukon along the Alaska Highway into northern British Columbia and Alberta: the so-called Alcan route. Each of these proposals carried an estimated cost of about $8 billion. A third alternative was also proposed by Foothills. This involved construction of a 42-inch pipeline along the route of the Mackenzie Valley, transporting Canadian Delta gas only. The projected cost of this alternative was $4.5 billion.

The government of Canada appointed commissions of inquiry into the environmental and social impact of these proposed pipeline routes. The first and more extensive, the Mackenzie Valley Pipeline Inquiry, was commissioned in 1974 under Mr. Justice Thomas Berger. The second inquiry, The Alaska Highway Pipeline Inquiry, was commissioned in 1977 under Mr. Justice Lysyk. The report of the Berger inquiry, *Northern Frontier — Northern Homeland* was published in 1977. This report effectively closed the door on early pipeline construction on the grounds of destructive cultural impact. Mr. Justice Berger concluded that,

> ...under the present conditions, the pipeline, if it were built now, would do enormous damage to the social fabric of the North, would bring only limited economic benefits [to the North] and would stand in the way of a just settlement of native claims.[6]

There remained, however, a general assumption that the demands of a small minority of people in the North were being judged more important than the benefit to the majority of Canadians which would result from pipeline access to northern natural gas. As GATT-Fly points out, Berger himself makes this assumption in the concluding remarks of his report. On the contrary, suggests GATT-Fly,

> We believe that in addition to threatening native peoples with cultural genocide, a pipeline could also become a financial catastrophe with grave consequences for all working people in Canada.[7]

The argument for this conclusion as constructed by GATT-Fly is as follows. Fiscal policies which affect ordinary people — wage controls, high energy prices and cutbacks in education, daycare and health care — are the result of our massive national debt. This debt is directly related to mega-projects for energy and resource extraction, such as Quebec's James Bay hydroelectric scheme and Ontario Hydro's nuclear program. The construction of a northern natural gas pipeline would increase our debt load by at least 25 percent.

GATT-Fly's argument began with a look at Canada's international indebtedness. Canada's debt, the difference between Canada's total foreign liabilities and foreign assets, had escalated "alarmingly" between 1970 and 1976: from $28.4 billion to $48.9 billion. The alarm stemmed from doubts about the ability of our economy to withstand such a debt load. The annual service cost of Canada's foreign debt has to be met by foreign earnings through exports of goods and services and the value of exports has to increase by about $500 million a year in order to cover service costs. However, exports were not increasing relative to imports, and in the years 1975 and 1976 showed a deficit. Such balance of payments deficits further increased Canada's debt load because we had to borrow additional money to service existing debt: $3.3 billion in 1975 and $2.2 billion in 1976.

Canada was the world's largest borrower in 1975 and 1976. Most of this money was borrowed by provincial crown corporations for energy mega-projects. In addition, 50 percent of private sector borrowing on foreign markets was for mining, petroleum, and private utility development. Only 21 percent of private borrowing was for expansion of manufacturing. This kind of huge capital commitment reinforces Canada's role as a supplier of raw materials and significantly reduces opportunities to process more raw materials domestically. Consequently, potential for industrial self-reliance is progressively lost. This growing imbalance in favour of energy and raw material extraction has two major effects. First, resource extraction is highly capital intensive and does not create new jobs in significant numbers. Second, raw material extraction is not an efficient way of balancing the current account and countering the deficit trend in balance of payments.

Historically it has been "assumed that new foreign investment was a preferred way of making up Canada's annual current account deficit." In other words, we have chosen to allow most of our manufacturing, mining and petroleum sectors to be owned by foreigners instead of owing huge sums of money to them. One outcome of massive foreign ownership in the Canadian economy is that through reinvested earnings our level of indebtedness through new direct investment increases dramatically even though little new foreign capital is invested in Canada. As GATT-Fly puts it,

> Reinvested earnings of foreign corporations represent
> a surplus generated by the labour of Canadians that
> remains under the control of the corporate investor,
> contributing to Canada's indebtedness without any
> new investment ever entering the country.[8]

Finally, GATT-Fly pointed out that mega-projects such as the James Bay hydroelectric project and proposed pipelines involve Canadians in borrowing billions of dollars from U.S. sources in order to build facilities primarily designed to deliver power or natural gas to American markets. Canadians incur a huge debt load and accept all the risk involved with little promise of profit or substantial benefit in the forseeable future. In specific terms, GATT-Fly estimated that construction of a pipeline would increase Canada's foreign debt by about $13 billion, or 26 percent over the 1976 level of debt. Further, pipeline construction would increase the price of natural gas significantly since all gas would be priced at Mackenzie Delta levels. Gas prices would double, at least.

The real cost of pipeline construction, however, would be borne indirectly by ordinary working people. GATT-Fly's basic argument is

> ...that present government and corporate leaders are
> unwilling to adopt any policies that are fundamentally
> at variance with the interests of Canada's creditors ...
> [Without International Monetary Fund intervention],

governments are already pursuing policies of benefit to
Canada's creditors and detrimental to working people
in Canada.[9]

With reference to case studies of Argentina, Brazil and Chile where
IMF intervention has been experienced, GATT-Fly shows a connection between right wing coups d'etats in each country and willingness to comply with IMF programs of debt repayment. In each case
the military government has adopted the economic measures recom-
mended by the IMF. These measures serve the interest of their
creditors, with crushing economic consequences for the working
people of these nations. The incentive for these governments is the
availability of new foreign loans.

Typical IMF recommendations are for wage controls and cur-
rency devaluation, severe cutbacks in government spending on
social services, an end to foreign exchange controls (Canada does
not have them), and strong emphasis on production for export.
Canada has implemented programs consistent with these recommendations without any outside IMF pressure. Through these programs the burden of Canada's debt is passed on to the working
people of Canada. These measures offer no solution to debt problems. Their long-term effect in the case of many countries is continual repayment, permanent and, perhaps, increasing indebtedness
and orientation of the entire economic structure toward creditor
interests rather than the interest of the working people of the
country.

While the burden of building a pipeline at public risk would fall on
the ordinary working people of Canada, the benefits would go to the
multinational energy companies who would stand to increase profits
on southern produced gas which would be priced at Delta levels.
Benefits would also come to the banks who stand ready to lend huge
amounts of money at high interest with no risk, since all loans would
be guaranteed by the government of Canada.

The "Paying the Piper" analysis was a breakthrough in perspective for GATT-Fly because it brought home the analysis generally
applied to the situation of economic dependence in less developed
countries. It showed Canada's situation as a clear and dangerous
parallel.

The entry of the churches into the northern development debate
came in support of the Dene Nation of the Mackenzie Valley
through the initiative of the interchurch Project North. The assumption in this debate had been that the interests of all other Canadians
were pitted against those of the Dene. By producing an analysis of
the pipeline debate at the level of its economic feasibility, GATT-Fly
was able to show that the construction of a pipeline would likely be a
huge economic disaster from which it would take years for Canada
to recover. It is important to note that the "Paying the Piper"

analysis was singular in proposing a systematic counterestimate of the cost and economic impact of pipeline to those of the multinational pipeline consortia. Not even the National Energy Board had questioned the optimistic estimates of cost and economic impact used by Arctic Gas and Foothills to sell a pipeline to Canadians.

The Ah-hah Seminars

My third example of GATT-Fly's work is the Ah-hah Seminar.[10] Ah-hah seminars are a significant departure in terms of educational method. The seminars also proved to be an important vehicle for identifying and developing GATT-Fly's primary constituency.

Through this educational vehicle, GATT-Fly discovered the actual people whose need for economic changes was directly related to their powerlessness. By this discovery GATT-Fly transformed the churches' abstract concern for social justice into a working solidarity with powerless people.

In GATT-Fly's beginnings in 1972 and 1973, there were attempts at public education events. These events were efforts to develop a GATT-Fly constituency through education about the economics of development in Third World. At the level of making the church aware of GATT-Fly's existence and to some extent putting new people in touch with the project, these events were useful. On the other hand, the educational events were soon perceived as being at odds with the mandate to do practical research. Each educational event tended to have to cover similar basic territory and therefore did not provide opportunity or impetus to expand or deepen the group's knowledge. Planning and executing the education events consumed much time and energy. As a result, GATT-Fly decided to abandon the general educational events in order to concentrate on research, publishing and, wherever possible, direct political action.

While this decision was fruitful, allowing GATT-Fly to pursue a program of practical research, it also tended to isolate GATT-Fly from a living constituency. The question of constituency was theoretical and ambiguous. Whose interest should GATT-Fly serve? Those of the churches? the poor? the powerless? In other words, it was difficult to do practical research without the sense of responding to real needs of real people. On the other hand, it was recognized that need in political and economic terms is not often immediate to ordinary people, even though they constantly experience the effects of living and working within a particular political economic system.

The GATT-Fly staff members found themselves invited to give lectures to interested groups. Traditional lecture situations feature mostly one-way communication of

> ..."experts" trying to impart knowledge to largely
> passive audiences, with no way of knowing how rele-
> vant the information was to them.[11]

A more "dialogical" process of learning was required so that GATT-Fly could engage in cooperative learning with other groups of people. "Dialogical" means education which does not rely on experts imparting new knowledge, but rather on affirming what participants already know through sharing their life experience. This method was termed the "Ah-hah" seminar, to give the sense of a process through which people discover things about themselves and their life situation which are affirmed intuitively. The keys for the Ah-hah method were found in the work of Paulo Freire, the Brazilian educator, based on his literacy programs with peasants. The dialogical assumption is that all participants are learners and all are also teachers based on their experience and their understanding of their experience. The role of expertise is in management of the dialogical educational process. Finally, the goal of the educational process is empowerment of participants to be agents of social change.

On the one hand the Ah-hah seminar leaders found it difficult to abdicate the role of expert in content as well as process. They tended to have an analysis which they wanted to teach. On the other hand, early Ah-hah seminars, held in the spring of 1975, were made up of church leaders, lay and clerical, who tended to see themselves as consumers of knowledge as well as goods. They had difficulty putting themselves in the economic picture in any integral way other than as consumers. The GATT-Fly leaders often found themselves drawn back into a slightly modified lecture model of education.

Early Ah-hah seminars began with land and tried to build up a picture of the international food system: production and distribution. The picture was constructed using the participants' own experience and GATT-Fly input. The method revolved around drawing a comprehensive picture of the international food system as a way of imaging Canadian relationships with Third World countries. A second stage was to overlay this diagram with strategies for systemic change:

> The picture they've constructed of the economic and
> political system helps the participants identify poten-
> tial allies and makes it easier to determine the possibil-
> ity of common action.[12]

The breakthrough for the Ah-hah seminars came in November 1975 with the discovery of an important relationship between the Ah-hah method and constituency. The occasion was an Ah-hah seminar in St. John's, Newfoundland, with the Newfoundland Fisherman's Union, Oxfam and the Mummers Theatre Troupe. The first part of this seminar followed the established food system model beginning with the land: Who owns it? How is it used? The breakthrough came on the second day when the group decided to make a picture of the

Newfoundland economy focusing on fishing. The GATT-Fly leaders knew little about this area and so had no prejudice about the final
picture to be drawn. The process of the day was genuinely dialogical
because the participants constructed their own picture while the
experts managed the pedagogical process.

This experience led to some conclusions about who the Ah-hah
seminar is for. In a more general sense, the experience of the Ah-hah
seminars between May and November 1975 helped define the primary GATT-Fly constituency. The main criteria for selecting
groups who are able to use the Ah-hah seminar best became that

> ... when the participants have a material interest in
> changing the present economic system and when they
> are members of a group or organization through
> which they can act.[13]

Since persons or groups such as bank managers or businessmen
which benefit from their place in the present economic system have
no "objective" interest in social change, the Ah-hah seminar does
not work for them, or for others when they are present.

On the basis of their experience of trying to carry out education
for social change, GATT-Fly concluded,

> Because the Ah-hah seminar uses the life and work
> experiences of the participants as the content of its
> discussion, it is not suited to educating those who are
> benefiting from the capitalist system.[14]

One rather problematic conclusion here is that most church groups
do not qualify as suitable for Ah-hah method. Most are more
pluralistic than those best served by the Ah-hah method. On the
other hand, GATT-Fly has become a church-based and supported
initiative whose chief work is serving those whose basic life experience has been poverty and/or economic powerlessness.[15] This initiative recovers, in a direct way, a fundamental biblical theme.[16] The
three examples of such groups discussed in *Ah-Hah! A New Approach
to Popular Education* are Toronto area steel workers, the Kayahna
tribal council at Big Trout Lake in northwestern Ontario and Toronto area Latin American immigrants.

Conclusion

The churches have traditionally taken a general moral approach
to public policy discussion. GATT-Fly's early understanding that
such an approach is easy for governments to ignore led to a long-
term effort to work for identifiable changes using more specific
argument and analysis directed at particular issues of economic
justice. The two examples I have chosen illustrate the greater impact
of this approach in public policy debates than the earlier general
moral contributions of the churches. At the very least, GATT-Fly

contributions have been more difficult for official bodies to ignore. GATT-Fly's innovative strategies and important research have allowed church contributions to policy debate to make a new and significant impact.

This impact is difficult to measure. GATT-Fly's arguments have not been translated directly into Canadian public policy. Clearly, on the other hand, GATT-Fly has been regarded very seriously by government and business as the focus of cogent alternatives to status quo policy. Also, from early in its existence, GATT-Fly has held a position of leadership in non-governmental groups concerned with development and issues of global economic justice.

Complementary to this work for changes in public policy, GATT-Fly has develped a style of education designed to empower people to be agents of social transformation within their own sphere of life and work. The Ah-hah seminars have become a means of identifying and nurturing a constituency of agents of socio-economic transformation. This has far-reaching importance for the churches, because it recovers in a specific way a fundamental biblical theme of prayer and action for justice in concert with the poor and powerless.

Through these innovative strategies, important practical research and education for action, GATT-Fly is helping to change the agenda of the churches in public policy formation. This change is from abstract concern to solidarity with the victims of injustice, and from general moral arguments to proposals for specific changes in policy.

NOTES

1 GATT stands for "General Agreement on Tariffs and Trade." This "agreement" is between the richest industrialized nations. GATT has become a symbol of the effective exclusion of the rest of the world from the economic mainstream. The name "GATT-Fly," then, plays on the Socratic "gadfly" in order to indicate the intention of being an irritant to the economic status quo.

2 "Report: GATT-Fly Seminar," February 1973, p. 6.

3 Canada and the Food Issue," [c. 1974]. Prepared in conjunction with the Canadian Council for International Cooperation and the United Nations Association in Canada.

4 "Reflections on the World Food Conference," 1975.

5 January, 1975, issue.

6 Berger, *Northern Frontier-Northern Homeland* (Ministry of Supply and Services, Canada, 1977), Vol. I, p. 200.

7 "Paying the Piper", p. 44.

8 Ibid., p. 19.

9 Ibid., p. 34.

10 The name "Ah-hah" conveys the sense of discovery for the first time: the insight which makes sense of one's experience.

11 *Ah-hah! A New Approach to Popular Education* (Toronto: Between the Lines, 1983), p. 8.

12 Ibid., p. 17.
13 Ibid., p. 17.
14 "Ah-hah!" (in draft manuscript), p. 10.
15 The development of this sense of mission may be seen also in the sugar component of GATT-Fly. Sugar has been a continuing emphasis from GATT-Fly's early days and has recently taken on an independent existence. From 1976 onward, the primary work of the sugar program has been to establish contact and help build solidarity between sugar workers, both field and refinery workers, around the world. This work has been carried out through an International Sugar Workers' Conference in 1977, worker exchanges and the newsletter, *Sugarworld*. This last is designed as a vehicle for workers in different countries and sectors of the industry to be in touch with each others' struggles.
16 "Blessed are you poor, for yours is the kingdom of God" (Luke 6:20, RSV), or the Song of Mary (Luke 1:51-53). Liberation theologians have called this recovery the "preferential option for the poor." For example, see Gustavo Gutierrez, *A Theology of Liberation* (Maryknoll, N.Y.: Orbis Books, 1973), pp. 203-8, "A Spirituality of Liberation."

The Economic Crisis is a Moral Crisis

Lee Cormie

Introduction: Ethical Reflections on the Economic Crisis

On New Year's Day 1983 the Episcopal Commission for Social Affairs of the Canadian Conference of Catholic Bishops published the pastoral letter "Ethical Reflections on the Economic Crisis."[1] The bishops pointed to the widespread symptoms of economic crisis in Canada — plant shutdowns, massive layoffs, anti-union campaigns, cutbacks in government-funded health and social services, for example — and called attention to the connections between the economic crisis in Canada and the crisis in the capitalist world economy. As Christians, we are called to respond, they said, because of the immense suffering this crisis causes in the lives of poor and working people, evident in emotional strain, loss of human dignity, family breakdown, and suicides.

In the midst of this crisis governments and large corporations are developing strategies for economic recovery and a new industrial future. And in these strategies "working people, the unemployed, young people, and those on fixed incomes are increasingly called upon to make the most sacrifice for economic recovery." But, the bishops noted, there are "no clear reasons to believe that working people will ever really benefit from these sacrifices they are called to make." Indeed, it is more reasonable to expect "permanent or structural unemployment and increasing marginalization for a large segment of the population of Canada and other countries." From the point of view of those suffering in the present crisis, the policies of governments and large corporations raise questions that go to the roots of the system.

Specifically, the bishops insisted that the economic crisis is a moral crisis because the strategies for recovery reveal values and sensibilities fundamentally at odds with core Christian values. In particular, these strategies represent the primacy of profits over basic

human needs: we are in the midst of a fundamental restructuring of
the national and international economy in which "capital" is being
"reasserted as the dominant organizing principle of economic life."
Concretely this means that "there is a tendency for people to be
treated as an impersonal force having little or no significance beyond
their economic purpose in the system."

What is required, the bishops insisted, is a basic shift in values:
"The goal of serving the human needs of all people in our society
must take precedence over the maximization of profits and growth,
and priority must be given to the dignity of human labour, not
machines." Their vision of a new society includes the "equitable
distribution of wealth and power among people and regions." But a
vision without strategies to make it real is merely an illusion. The
bishops recognized that the shift in values they call for requires a
fundamentally different economic model that:

> would place emphasis on socially useful forms of pro-
> duction; labour-intensive industries; the use of appro-
> priate forms of technology; self-reliant models of
> economic development; community ownership and
> control of industries; new forms of worker manage-
> ment and ownership; and greater use of renewable
> energy sources in industrial production.

In other words, the bishops' criticism of current corporate and
government development strategies goes to the roots of the system;
they called for fundamental changes in our economic life.

This pastoral letter has stimulated an extraordinarily wide-
ranging national debate, unprecedented in the history of the church
in Canada. So far most of the response to this pastoral letter has
focused on the claims the bishops made in it, the accuracy and
comprehensiveness of their analysis, the moral and economic status
of their vision of an alternative, and the practicality of their proposals for a different strategy. These are important issues, deserving
much further discussion. However, in this short paper I will not
address these issues directly. Rather, I would like to explore some of
the reasons for the unprecedented impact of this statement. In the
following pages I will suggest four reasons for the historical significance of this pastoral letter. In the conclusion, I will offer some
reflections on the challenge which flows from this document to the
church to witness more faithfully to the Spirit in the world and to
serve the cause of justice and peace. For this pastoral letter represents a profound challenge to conversion, for the church as well as
for the world.

The Significance of "Ethical Reflections"

(1) This pastoral letter is a succinct expression of the main themes

in recent Catholic social teachings, evident in papal encyclicals,[2] pastoral letters from regional groups of bishops like the Conference of Latin American Bishops meeting at Medellin[3] and Puebla,[4] documents emanating from the meetings of world synods of bishops, and statements of other national conferences of bishops. The Canadian bishops, then, are speaking from the mainstream of this tradition, bringing to bear in their response to the economic crisis in Canada a growing consensus among Catholics worldwide on a number of crucial issues.

Contemporary Catholic social teaching has developed around five major themes. First, there has been growing clarity about the contribution of the church in the debates and struggles over economic and political issues. As Pope Paul VI insisted, the church offers as its characteristic attribute a global vision of human nature and of human destiny.[7] In this vision of "transcendent humanism," persons are viewed as having, simultaneously, spiritual, psychological, cultural, economic and social needs, and human nature is viewed as essentially social and dynamic. Ethically, this means that development cannot be understood merely in terms of economic growth. In order to be authentic, it must promote the good of the whole person and of every person, the individual and the common good: it must promote "integral human development."

A second major theme in contemporary Catholic social teaching is the growing awareness of the social character of sin. Sin is interpreted as a break with God reflected in ruptures and breaks in our relations to others. Of course, sin is always personal, operative in the hearts of individuals and "mirrored on the level of interpersonal relations in a corresponding egotism, haughtiness, ambition, and envy."[8] And sin can also be social. For when these values are concretized in the policies of corporations, governments and other organizations they become part of the very foundations of social life, producing "injustice, domination, violence at every level, and conflicts between individuals, groups, social classes, and peoples."[9]

A third major theme is liberation. Awareness of profound conflicts in the world has stimulated a rediscovery of the centrality of this theological theme in the Bible. As the bishops said at their world synod in 1971, God is revealed in the Bible as "the liberator of the oppressed and the defender of the poor..."[10] This renewed theological sensitivity has been key in the evolving ethical stance in Catholic social teaching toward poverty and oppression and toward the right of poor and oppressed peoples themselves to struggle for their own integral human development.

A fourth major element in contemporary Catholic social teaching is the "preferential option for the poor." This option for the poor is increasingly being recognized as a theological principle which challenges the church to recognize that the God of the Hebrew and

Christian scriptures was revealed first among the oppressed, the slaves in Egypt, and incarnated in Jesus among the poor and oppressed of first-century Palestine dominated by the Roman empire in collusion with local elites. This renewed biblical insight also challenges us to recognize that the Spirit of God is manifested today among similar groups struggling for justice. In this view, the option for the oppressed is God's option, and therefore must be the option of Christians, too.[11] Ethically, this option means that the needs of the poor should have priority over the wants of the rich in any decision-making process. But it also means that the first task in confronting issues of development is to listen to the poor and unemployed, to get their perspectives on the issues and options, and to include them in the decision-making process.

The fifth major theme, articulated by Pope John Paul II, is "the priority of labour over capital." Ethically, this means that the socially structured division of labour must be evaluated in terms of its impact on human persons, i.e., in terms of whether or not it promotes integral human development. Specifically, this means that labour has priority over capital, the natural resources, technology, plant and equipment, and investment funds which are themselves the "result of the historical heritage of human labour."[12] In other words, the dignity and well-being of individual workers, their families and communities have priority over the needs of capital, i.e., over the needs of investors and corporate managers.

Though the language and method of Protestant social teaching are quite different, the stress on the development of a "just, participatory, and sustainable society" in the statements of various commissions and assemblies of the World Council of Churches reflects the emergence in Protestant churches of a similar set of values and sensibilities concerning development.[13] The focus on justice reflects a concern with the distribution of goods and opportunities for a fully human life in a world where the gap between rich and poor is so obviously growing. The focus on participation reflects a growing awareness that development strategies devised and implemented by elites, no matter how good their intentions, seldom work to the advantage of poor and oppressed people; indeed, they often increase disparities and reinforce passivity and marginalization among the poor majorities. Concern with an environmentally sustainable development policy is generally much more evident in Protestant social teaching than it is in Catholic teaching; however, the Canadian bishops, because of their well-established concern with native peoples and Northern development, reflect an awareness of the devastation of the environment and of the health of workers and local communities which so often results from the usual forms of economic development. Among Protestants, too, there is growing evidence of the "option for the poor" which leads to a fundamentally different analysis of world trends from those which dominate the discussions and policy proposals of the world's elites.[14]

"Ethical Reflections on the Economic Crisis" also reflects the concerns, sensibilities, and principles which the Canadian bishops have previously articulated in their reflections on Northern development,[15] food and hunger,[16] and unemployment.[17] It also reflects the concerns of other Canadian denominations, evident, for example, in the United Church's statement on unemployment.[18]

So the Canadian bishops' statement is in the mainstream of contemporary Christian social teaching ecumenically and in terms of the Catholic tradition, locally in terms of their own and other recent Canadian church teaching, and globally in terms of the teachings of other church bodies.

(2) This statement reflects the actual experience of many groups which have been struggling with issues of social justice. In particular, the statement reflects the experience of many activists in the ecumenical interchurch projects in Canada who are struggling with a variety of justice issues — Project North, The Church Committee on Corporate Responsibility, Project Plowshares, The Interchurch Committee on Human Rights in Latin America, Ten Days for World Development, and GATT-Fly. The positions reflected in this document reflect the distillation of the experience of many committed people deeply involved in efforts to promote justice and peace.

The general thrust of this pastoral letter also reflects an older historical current in Canadian political and ecclesial life — the largely Protestant social gospel movement which emerged in the last decades of the nineteenth century, was revived in the 1930s in the Fellowship for Christian Social Order and the Co-operative Commonwealth Federation, and later influenced the formation of the New Democratic Party in 1961.[19] This many-faceted movement nurtured contact and collaboration among church leaders, workers, farmers, social scientists and political organizers across Canada. It nurtured a critical examination of the economy, and provided a context for many Canadians to redefine their understanding of the functioning of this system. Indeed, many people involved in these movements became convinced that only radical changes leading to a particularly Canadian form of socialism could eliminate the evils of capitalist development as they had witnessed it. In the midst of the current crisis, the bishops' statement has prompted a new appreciation of the lessons learned by many of our forerunners. More and more people are realizing that struggles over economic policies are ultimately moral struggles over different ways of life, and they are discovering the importance of faith and hope in the face of enormous obstacles to fundamental change.[20]

(3) The pastoral letter does more than merely recapitulate recent church teachings. It represents a breakthrough in the efforts of

Christians to identify *concretely* the fundamentally moral dimensions of the policy decisions of governments and corporations and to clarify our responsibilities as Christians for participating in the debates and struggles over economic strategies. Catholics have a long history of insisting that moral concerns should have a place in the development of economic strategies. But historically they have tended to articulate these concerns in terms utterly foreign to the discourse of actual economic analysis and policy-making. In theory church leaders have often criticized capitalist development, but it was difficult to understand the concrete implications of this teaching because the terms were so utterly foreign to contemporary political and economic debates. Early Catholic teaching, in the encyclical Rerum Novarum of Leo XIII, for example, represented, at most, pressure for reform in the context of a militant opposition to radical critics of the system and a fervent blessing of the foundations of capitalism in the private ownership of the means of production. In practice, this often amounted to a de facto endorsement of the separation of morality and economy and a definition of the agenda of the church in terms of moral and religious issues defined in purely personal terms, by and large apart from concern with the economy or the nature of the social system. By the middle decades of the twentieth century, especially in the context of the Cold War, the critical components of this teaching about capitalism were often eclipsed altogether. In the last twenty years, however, both the ways of articulating these issues and the specific judgments themselves have begun to change profoundly.

The bishops of the Commission for Social Affairs have insisted on the immediate relevance of Christian values and sensibilities in economic decision-making, and they have pinpointed their concerns specifically and concretely in terms which are widely used in the debates over economic policy. Moreover, they do not simply criticize policies in certain sectors of the economy or in terms of particular policies of governments and corporations, but they name fundamental issues at stake in the formation of overall development strategy in Canada, and, by implication, throughout the world. In so doing they are able to identify exactly how various policy approaches do in fact involve moral options: the economic crisis is a moral crisis!

So the ability of the bishops to link their discussion of theological and ethical issues directly to their discussion of economic issues leaves little room for confusion about their understanding of current struggles over economic development strategies in the midst of a worldwide economic crisis or about the specific judgments they make in light of the Gospel and recommend to the rest of us. The bishops have been able to speak with a sense of moral urgency and concrete practicality which is rare in church social teaching.

(4) Specifically, "Ethical Reflections on the Economic Crisis" reveals the conviction of the bishops of the Social Affairs Commission and of a growing number of Christians worldwide that, while the capitalist system produces affluence for a few, it also promotes poverty and injustice for the majority of the world's peoples, both within nations and among them in the world system.

According to the social scientific orthodoxy which dominated academic and public policy discussions in the 1950s and 1960s, poverty and repression in the Third World were largely due to the backwardness of the values and institutions of these societies, by the lack of entrepreneurial dedication and unwillingness to foster the free market.[21] Many Third World peoples struggled to "modernize" and "develop" in these terms, using the methods proposed by the so-called experts. And they consistently failed to improve the living conditions of the majorities in their countries; indeed, in some cases the conditions of the bottom 40 percent of the population actually worsened.[22] In the light of these experiences, which were repeated throughout the Third World, it became evident that poverty and the repression which characterize the efforts of so many Third World governments to maintain "order" and "stability" as the prerequisites of "business confidence" and a good climate for foreign investment are intimately linked to the policies of First World governments and corporations and international institutions like the World Bank and the International Monetary Fund which are dominated by representatives from the advanced capitalist countries.

This profound shift in perception concerning the way in which the world capitalist economy simultaneously produces affluence for a few and poverty for the majority has acquired the status of "common sense" among growing numbers of people worldwide.[23] Naive, uncritical acceptance of the capitalist world economy is no longer possible when the experience of the poor majorities of the world is taken seriously. And more and more people share the conclusion that development strategies which promise to benefit the poor majorities require fundamental changes in the world system.[24] Theoretically this critical perception has found expression in the efforts of social scientists throughout the world to analyze unequal development in terms of the functioning of a capitalist world system in which elites in the core nations of the system, in alliance with elites in the peripheries, use their economic, political and military power to promote policies and reproduce institutions and structures in investment, banking, trade, and aid which enhance their privileges and power regardless of the cost of these development strategies to the majority of people.[25]

In the last few years many Christians have come to the same conclusions about the functioning of the world economy, and have increasingly been joining the growing chorus of voices worldwide calling for a new international economic order. This new "common sense" about the world system has clearly shaped Catholic social teaching, in the encyclicals of Pope Paul[26] and elsewhere. The Cana-, dian bishops have been influenced by the same shifting perceptions. Because of their "preferential option for the oppressed" they have accepted the challenge of learning to see the world from the point of view of poor and oppressed people who are the victims of current structures and policies. In so doing they have discovered that many of the patterns of unequal development which can be observed in the world economy can also be observed within Canada, as in the differences between southern Ontario and the Maritimes or the North, and between Canada and the United States.[27] In searching for a framework to understand these realities, the bishops have turned to the same kinds of critical theories which emerged to explain poverty and oppression in the Third World. Moreover, in Canada there is a well-established theoretical tradition, the so-called political-economy school which builds on the earlier work of Canadian theorist Harold Innis and his followers in analyzing uneven development in Canadian history, which the bishops have been able to draw on for clarifying the issues.[28]

This kind of analysis enables the bishops to read the "signs of the times" from the point of view of poor and oppressed people. It enables them to respond concretely as pastors in the context of the current crisis. As they have insisted, "As pastors, our concerns about the economy are not based on any specific political options. Instead they are inspired by the Gospel message of Jesus Christ." In the current context this mandate inspires a radical criticism of the system in which we live.

Revising the Agenda of the Church

The public impact of this document has been significant. Ultimately, though, its significance will probably be determined by its impact on the church. For in the long run the influence of this kind of teaching depends on its impact on Christians and on the priorities of the church as an institution. In helping to specify the nature of sin and evil in the world and to clarify the nature of Christian hope the bishops have contributed to wide-ranging discussions among Christians in which the agenda of the church is being profoundly redefined.

Christians have discovered in the midst of the struggles for justice and liberation that what is at stake in these struggles is, in the words of the submission to the Royal Commission on the Economic Union and Development Prospects for Canada by the Canadian Conference of Catholic Bishops, "What kind of society and people ... we want to become."[29] At root, these are the most basic theological questions about who God is, where God is present in our world, and what fidelity to God requires of us. And these questions are at the very heart of the Christian understanding of the church. As the participants in the Sixth Assembly of the World Council of Churches in Vancouver affirmed, "The Church is thus challenged not only in what it does, but in its very faith and being."[30]

Of course, "Ethical Reflections" and other social teaching documents are themselves the fruits of intense discussion and debate about the nature of the church, symbolized for Catholics especially by Vatican II. Renewed understanding of the mission of the church and renewed understanding of social justice have developed together. And by 1971 the bishops, at their second world synod, were able to affirm that "action on behalf of justice and participation in the transformation of the world fully appear to us as a constitutive dimension of the preaching of the Gospel, or, in other words, of the Church's mission for the redemption of the human race and its liberation from every oppressive situation."[31] But the full implications of this affirmation have only become clear as we have learned to recognize the extent to which the political/economic system in which we live, part of the capitalist world system, represents the incarnation of values fundamentally at odds with core Christian values, promoting forms of individual and community development, more accurately underdevelopment, which are fundamentally antithetical to what, we believe, is the destiny of all the daughters and sons of the Creator.

In this context it is necessary to speak of idolatry. At Puebla the bishops referred to the "great extent to which our nations are dominated by the idol of wealth."[32] And all those gathered ecumenically at Vancouver interpreted "the machine of the prevailing economic order [which] starves millions of people and increases the number of unemployed every year" as "idolatry, stemming from human sin, a product of satanic forces." Therefore, they concluded, "We are in a situation where we must go beyond the normal prophetic and intercessory actions of the churches."[33]

Will the church inspire and challenge us all to make a concrete option for the poor, nationally and internationally? In a society in which class, racial/ethnic, and sexual divisions are so profoundly entrenched, and in a church which so profoundly reflects these divisions, we need to promote new forms of collaboration, communion, and authority which will promote the full development of all people, especially those historically marginalized. Will the institutional church nurture the critical consciousness of the sin and evil that the bishops denounce? We need to meditate on the real experiences of suffering and evil in the world, especially among poor and oppressed peoples, to develop our social analyses of the causes of this suffering, to nurture deeper awareness of the ways we are complicit with this evil, and to find new modes of confession and repentance. Will the church inspire in us a deeper sense of hope for the realm of God which has been promised to all? We need to develop a much more concrete sense of what, as Christians, we can and should hope for in this life, and to promote new spiritualities and forms of asceticisim which embody this hope. Will the church promote the active involvement of Christians in the struggles of poor and oppressed peoples for liberation and justice and peace, nationally and internationally? We need to find more effective ways to organize to promote the values and sensibilities concerning integral human development, and to find new ways of celebrating in our liturgies and prayers our experience of the Spirit in the struggles for new life. In other words, will the church as an institution incarnate the values, sensibilities, and priorities reflected in these teachings? Will we together try to practice what we preach, and in doing so become more fully a sign of the faith and hope that we are called to?

It is important to acknowledge the enormity of the challenge posed by the economic crisis. The issues are so complex, vested interests are so entrenched, ignorance about the issues and options so widespread, and the coalitions favouring strategies promoting full employment and self-reliant national development so fragile. Despair seems to be a reasonable response, and hope for a gentler, more human economy seems so utopian. But this is precisely why the Church has so much to offer in the midst of this crisis. For the issues are ultimately issues of faith and hope, love and solidarity with the poor and suffering, and justice. At its best, Christianity represents the nurturing of communities where dignity and mutuality flourished, often against great historical obstacles. We have a tradition of saying no to naked greed and power. We know that we are called to the fullness of life and to sharing with others in vibrant communities. We know that, in spite of the obstacles, we are called to live in the present an ethic of love and justice. With the help of the bishops and many other committed people, we are learning to recognize again that it is precisely in the midst of the struggles over the future of our society and our world that we grow and fulfill ourselves and meet our God.

NOTES

1   The text of this letter is available from the Canadian Conference of Catholic Bishops, 90 Parent Avenue, Ottawa, Ontario.
2   For a collection of recent documents see Joseph Gremillion, ed., *The Gospel of Peace and Justice* (Maryknoll: Orbis, 1976). For a copy of Pope John Paul II's "Laborem Exercens" and a commentary, see Gregory Baum, *The Priority of Labor* (New York: Paulist, 1982). For analyses of the development of papal social teaching, see: Donal Dorr, *Option for the Poor* (Maryknoll: Orbis, 1983); Arthur F. McGovern,

Marxism: An American Christian Perspective (Maryknoll: Orbis, 1980), esp. chapters 3 & 8; and Christine E. Gudorf, *Catholic Social Teaching on Liberation Themes* (Washington: University Press of America, 1981).

3   For the relevant sections of this document, see Gremillion, pp. 445-76.
4   For text and commentaries, see John Eagleson and Philip Scharper, eds., *Puebla and Beyond* (Maryknoll: Orbis, 1979).
5   See especially "Justice in the World," issued by the Synod of Bishops at their Second General Assembly, in Gremillion, pp. 513-29.
6   See, for example, "Justice and Peace in a New Caribbean," a joint pastoral letter from the Bishops of the Antilles Episcopal Conference, issued on November 21, 1975.
7   See "Populorum Progressio," On The Development of Peoples, para. 13, in Gremillion, p. 391. Cf. also "Gaudium et Spes," Pastoral Constitution on the Church in the Modern World, para. 22, in Gremillion, p. 260.
8   See the Puebla final document, para. 328, in Eagleson and Scharper, p. 161.
9   Ibid., para. 70, in Eagleson and Scharper, p. 132.
10 "Justice in the World," para. 30, in Gremillion, p. 520.
11 See "Octogesima Adveniens," the Eightieth Anniversary of Rerum Novarum, para. 23, in Gremillion, p. 496. Cf. also Puebla, para. 1134-65, in Eagleson and Scharper, pp. 264-67.
12 "On Human Work," para. 12, in Baum, pp. 116-19.
13 See, for example, the official report of the Fifth Assembly of the World Council of Churches in David M. Paton, ed., *Breaking Barriers: Nairobi 1975* (London: SPCK, 1976), esp. the reports from the Sections IV, V, and VI. See also the report from the Sixth Assembly in Vancouver in David Gill, ed., *Gathered for Life* (Geneva: World Council of Churches, 1983). The work of particular commissions of the WCC is especially relevant: see, for example, Jether Pereira Ramalho, ed., *Signs of Hope and Justice* (Geneva: World Council of Churches, 1980); and Leon Howell, *People Are The Subject: Stories of Urban Rural Mission* (Geneva: World Council of Churches, 1980). For commentaries on the development of WCC social teachings, see Paul Bock, *In Search of a Responsible World Society* (Philadelphia: Westminster, 1974); and Richard D. N. Dickinson, *Poor, Yet Making Many Rich* (Geneva: World Council of Churches, 1983).
14 Of course, there are significant differences between World Council teachings and Roman Catholic teachings. In particular, in addition to focusing on the world economy, the World Council has focused especially on the evils of sexism and racism, issues which have been largely neglected in Catholic teaching. These gaps in Catholic social teaching seriously weaken it. For example, it is important to recognize that the problems of development are fundamentally the problems of women, and thus that "any development strategy for the future relations within and between nations must take this core problem into account, not only in the name of justice, but also in the interests of development." See Dickinson, p. 38.

    For an analysis of the differences between Vatican and World

Council social teachings and of some of the obstacles to further collaboration, see Thomas Sieger Derr, *Barriers to Ecumenism: The Holy See and the World Council on Social Questions* (Maryknoll: Orbis, 1983).

15 See "Northern Development: At What Cost?" the Labour Day Message, Administrative Board, Canadian Catholic Conference, 1975.

16 See "Sharing Daily Bread," the Labour Day Message, Administrative Board, Canadian Catholic Conference, 1974.

17 See "Unemployment: The Human Costs," Administrative Board, Canadian Conference of Catholic Bishops, 1979.

18 See "The Control of the Canadian Economy and the Human Problem of Unemployment: A Christian Perspective," The Working Unit of Social Issues and Justice of the Division of Mission in Canada, 1979.

19 For analyses of this movement see: Richard Allen, *The Social Passion: Religion and Social Reform in Canada, 1913-1928* (Toronto: University of Toronto, 1971); Roger Hutchinson, *The Fellowship for a Christian Social Order* (Th.D. Thesis, Toronto School of Theology, 1975); Richard Allen, ed., *The Social Gospel in Canada* (Ottawa: National Museums of Canada, 1975). For an analysis of Catholic involvement in the social gospel movement, see Gregory Baum, *Catholics and Canadian Socialism* (Toronto: James Lorimer, 1980). For some examples of current attempts to revitalize political theology in Canada, see Benjamin G. Smillie, ed., *Political Theology in the Canadian Context* (Waterloo: Canadian Corporation for Studies in Religion, 1982).

20 One expression of the revitalization of these currents in Canadian history was the conference sponsored in Ottawa by the Canadian Centre for Policy Alternatives on January 27, 1983, which brought together bishops, professional economists, union leaders, community organizers and church workers. Most participants supported the thrust of the document and acknowledged that its publication was a major event. For example, Dennis McDermott, president of the Canadian Labour Congress (CLC), said that labour backs their "principled and valid assertion that economics and morality cannot be separated." He said that the CLC had already begun to use the New Year statement as a basis for arguing with Finance Minister Marc Lalonde. And he indicated interest in exploring the possibility of some alliances. See the report of the conference, "Canadian Economists Endorse Bishops' Statement" in *Catholic New Times*, February 13, 1983, p. 8.

21 For a very influential example of this kind of analysis, see W.W. Rostow, *The Stages of Economic Growth* (Cambridge: Cambridge University Press, 1960).

22 See the analysis published by the Sao Paulo Justice and Peace Commission, *Sao Paulo: Growth and Poverty* (London: Bowerdean Press, 1978).

23 Cf. James H. Weaver, Kenneth P. Jameson, and Richard N. Blue, "A Critical Analysis of Approaches to Growth and Equity," in Charles K. Wilber, ed., *The Political Economy of Development and Underdevelopment* (New York: Random House, 1979), p. 421: "... there is a growing feeling among the intellectual elite in the developed and underdeveloped countries that the traditional approach is simply not working, especially in terms of helping the poor."

24 For an influential statement of an alternative "basic needs" strategy, see International Labour Office, *Employment, Growth and Basic Needs: A One-World Problem* (New York: Praeger, 1977). For a critical analysis of the basic needs approach to development, with special reference to development experiences in Africa, see Richard Sandbrook, *The Politics of Basic Needs* (Toronto: University of Toronto Press, 1982), esp. pp. 1-32, 228-46.

Whatever their rhetoric, First World leaders during this period, and up to the present, continue to analyze the development problems of Third World countries in traditional economic terms, insisting that the existing international institutions and rules of trade are adequate, that there do not need to be major changes in the current system, and that Third World nations should not have a greater voice in decision-making about this system. For analyses of various aspects of these negotiations, see Gerald K. Helleiner, ed., *For Good or Evil: Economic Theory and North-South Negotiations* (Toronto: University of Toronto Press, 1982). For an analysis of the Canadian government's foreign aid policies, see Robert Carty and Virginia Smith, *Perpetuating Poverty* (Toronto: Between the Lines, 1981).

25 For an example of criticism of orthodox developmentalist theory, see Andre Gunder Frank, "Sociology of Development and Underdevelopment of Sociology," in James D. Cockroft, Andre Gunder Frank, and Dale L. Johnson, *Dependence and Underdevelopment* (Garden City, NY: Doubleday, 1972), pp. 321-98. For examples of critical analysis of the current crisis of the capitalist world system, and reflections on the differences among them, see Samir Amin, Giovanni Arrighi, Andre Gunder Frank, and Immanuel Wallerstein, *Dynamics of Global Crisis* (New York: Monthly Review Press, 1982).

26 "On the Development of Peoples," March 26, 1967, para. 8, in Gremillion, pp. 389-90.

27 See especially the pastoral letter of the Atlantic Episcopal Assembly, "To Establish a Kingdom of Justice," June 6, 1979, which expresses clear awareness of the similar patterns of uneven development in Canada and the Third World.

28 Christopher Lind notes the dependence on this perspective by the bishops and analyzes some of the issues at stake in it; see Christopher Lind, "Ethics, Economics and Canada's Catholic Bishops," *Canadian Journal of Political and Social Theory* 7 (3) (1983), pp. 150-66. For a bibliography of writings which reflect this perspective, see Wallace Clement and Daniel Drache, *A Practical Guide to Canadian Political Economy* (Toronto: James Lorimer, 1978).

29 Cf. "Ethical Reflections on the Future of Canada's Socio-Economic Order," a brief to the Royal Commission on the Economic Union and Development Prospects for Canada, submitted by the Canadian Conference of Catholic Bishops, December 12, 1983.

30 *Gathered for Life*, para. 6.1, in Gill, p. 84.

31 "Justice in the World," para. 6, in Gremillion, p. 514.

32 Puebla, para. 494, in Eagleson and Scharper, p. 193.

33 *Gathered for Life*, paras. 5.2-5.3, in Gill, p. 84.

The Church and the Free Market Economy: The Need for a Critique

Ronald Preston

In North America, as in Europe, the church exists in countries whose economies are based on the concept of the free market, modified to a greater or lesser extent by social welfare considerations. That economy has developed amid, and is directly and indirectly related to, values which have grown out of western civilization with its roots in Judaeo-Christian and Greek thought. It is an economy experiencing rapid change of a long-term structural character. One urgent agenda for the church is therefore not to accept the values and structures of this economy without reflection, but to take a cool look at it and subject it to an appraisal and critique.

The churches have made more progress in the last decades in becoming well informed about what is going on in economic life than ever before in modern history. This has been largely due to the work of the "Church and Society" side of the World Council of Churches, and to Boards of Social Responsibility and the like of various denominations. Previously the churches were alert to the need for private and voluntary action, and developed a large variety of educational and social service activities, much of the latter of which we could call "ambulance work." This will always be necessary, but it is limited. It deals with disasters, but not with their causes and prevention.

Such activity was often accompanied by a very out-of-date and amateurish understanding of what was happening. In the last fifty years or so the churches have made much more effort to understand their own times, to isolate the significant issues, to examine tendencies, and not to be archaic. To get beyond ambulance work means taking social, economic and political issues seriously; and how the church can best handle them is much discussed.

In arriving at such an analysis relevant experience and expertise has to be drawn on. I have frequently grumbled at economic amateurishness in church circles, but it is necessary to point out that there are inescapable problems in handling expert evidence. It is all the more important to be aware of these problems because we cannot do without the advice. Five points occur to me in this connection.

1. Experts differ. There are schools of thought in almost any area of study. This is true of the natural sciences, and more so of the social sciences. It is an old joke that if you get three economists together there will be four opinions.
2. Experts often have unexamined presuppositions, which may not be logically necessary to their discipline but are commonly found in it, and need theological scrutiny. (Theology itself, of course, must submit itself to scrutiny: I am not advocating theological imperialism.)
3. Experts often speak beyond their expertise without realizing that they are doing so.
4. Experts may have their own personal or corporate, intellectual or economic, vested interests, of which they may or may not be aware.
5. Every discipline has "cranks" on its fringe. Occasionally they are subsequently vindicated, though the presumption is that they will not be. It is very hard to know what weight, if any, to give them.

We cannot do without the experts, but the issues involved in our theme are too important to be left to the experts, and there is no escape from the effort to sift what the expert says. The church has a difficult but inescapable task in this matter, requiring disciplined, sustained and corporate effort.

I turn now to make seven points in connection with a critique of the free market economy. These points arise out of an attempt to draw on both economic and theological considerations.

1. The economist has one value associated with his or her discipline, an ideal of efficiency in maximizing the use of resources which are relatively scarce compared with all the different things that could be produced with them. Waste is the economic vice. The economist is bound to be impressed with the enormous economic growth since the end of the Second World War and indeed with the enormous increase of productivity produced by the Industrial Revolution. So was Karl Marx. He thought that it was necessary for capitalism to fulfill its historic mission of solving the problem of production, superseding the division of labour which he regarded as alienating human beings from their work, so that a socialist, and then a communist, society could be founded on the basis of this abundance. That is why there is nothing in classical Marxist theory on how to run a communist economy. It is assumed there will be no problem of the

allocation of scarce resources. Ironically, the communist takeover first came in an economically backward country, Russia. The vast progress of the Russian economy has been largely due to the power of an irremovable government to impose on the population a forced rate of savings which no free electorate would tolerate. It has had to learn problems of resource management painfully, and the result so far is not an inspiring model for others.

The economist has to admit that his or her value is only one among others. If the pursuit of economic efficiency is carried to an extreme it will result in inhumanity. The economist will then hope that the economic cost of these other considerations will be faced by the community and not fudged, as is often the case.

2. God does not want human misery. God does not want people to be short-lived, hungry, ill-housed, ignorant and miserable. Also, there is no Christian virtue in either physical or mental toil as such. I am old enough to remember Monday washing day with its dolly tub and other hard physical labour. I am sure we can baptize the washing machine. However, what the Christian gospel says is concerned with all human beings, not just with some relatively affluent persons and countries. It especially requires us to be sensitive to the needs of the poor, indeed of all society's rejected, of whom the poor are most numerous. If removing hard and miserable conditions from people in the west is to be approved by Christians, it applies as much to the inhabitants of Bangladesh, to mention one of the poorest countries in the world. Indeed, the traditional Christian defense of private property, that of St. Thomas Aquinas, though very inadequate to the modern situation, requires its possession by all. The gospel also warns us against the danger of riches, because they are the greatest means of escape from trust in God. Our heart is where our treasure is. Those warnings were given in a society where there were great inequalities of wealth and poverty. So there are today, nationally and globally. The warning to the affluent remains, with great force, a point to which I shall return.

3. The very dynamism of the western economy has meant it has been rough in its development. In its early stages in England, 500 of the new factories were burnt down by arson in the years 1811-15 because of the dislocation of workers such as the handloom weavers, whose home industry had been displaced. The western economy has also worked on the principle of "to him that hath shall be given," by which competitive success in the market becomes cumulative. It produces great inequalities of income, compounded by inheritance. And wealth means economic power, that is to say, the power to attract relatively scarce means of production to the production of luxuries when the economically less successful lack the power to attract them to the production of necessities. Re-distributive taxation and inheritance policies modify this, but not as much as is often

supposed. In Britain, for instance, the chief result in the last thirty years has been to re-distribute the wealth of the top one percent among the top five percent of the population.

Moreover, the economy did not develop smoothly, but in the classic swing of the ten-year trade cycle of boom and slump, until after the First World War. Since then we have had the massive depression of 1929 onwards, and now the present one, in which long-term structural changes in manufacture are also included. These downward turns have catastrophic effects on those displaced. And yet there is a persistent tendency to attribute most poverty to personal defects. The nineteenth century spent much time in discriminating between the "deserving" and the "undeserving" poor; this distinction was demolished by the Minority Report of the U.K. Poor Law Commission of 1909, written by Sydney and Beatrice Webb (no one remembers the Majority Report). The institutions of the welfare state which have been gradually constructed since then are an embodiment of the conclusions of that report. There has been something of a backlash against this in the last few years, unfortunately often supported by "born again" Christians.

The upshot is that a lot of relative poverty remains in the affluent society. In 1903 Edward Caird, the Master of Balliol College, Oxford, who so influenced William Temple, urged his two student friends R.H. Tawney and William Beveridge to go to the East End of London "to discover why with so much wealth there is also so much poverty in London." In 1979 Professor Peter Townsend, in his exhaustive study *Poverty in the United Kingdom*, concluded that the poor numbered 14 million, on the definition of poverty as "lacking the resources to obtain the types of diet, participate in the activities, and have the living conditions and amenities which are customary or at least widely approved in the societies to which they belong."[1] This is, of course, higher than a bare subsistence standard; but a relatively affluent society can hardly have the face to restrict the term "poor" to those who have no more than minimum survival resources.

4. This successful post-war economy is running into severe problems.

(i) Its very success is producing increasing rigidities which make it harder and harder for governments to manage the economy, something that all governments have now to do, whether they lean ideologically or not towards "getting government off the people's back." The affluence of the present is relatively new to the middle-aged and over, even if the young take it for granted. People enjoy it, want it to continue, and do not want to be disturbed by technical and social change. Professional people do their best to put themselves and their profession in an invulnerable position, and wage earners try to preserve their existing jobs and existing differentials. Medical folk and miners have used their power the most fiercely in these ways. Electorates also want incompatible things — full employment, stable prices and free collective bargaining. The economist at least has a negative role in pointing out that they are incompatible, and that the political and economic task is to arrive at the best mixture of the three in given circumstances. There are also signs that the electorate appreciates good social services but at the same·time is unwilling to pay for them, and responds to a call to cut taxes. Many higher paid wage-earners voted for Mrs. Thatcher on these grounds in both the 1979 and 1983 elections in Britain. Moreover, clinging to the status quo makes the rich countries particularly rigid in hampering the import of manufactured goods from the Third World, a process which is essential if we are to get beyond aid to trade with them, in the effort to lift them from the poverty floor.

(ii) We are beginning to reach the limits of private consumption. The privileges made possible by the financial rewards which have been the entrepreneurial incentive to the production of goods and services have been dependent on their relative scarcity, otherwise they lose their attraction or are eroded. The more who can afford to live in suburbia, the more extended and less attractive suburbia becomes; the more motor cars, the more traffic jams; the more and longer holidays with pay, the more the holiday spots in danger of destruction. In the words of a recent English economist, who died regrettably young, "If everyone stands on tiptoe no one sees any better."[2] The incentives I have mentioned worked well in the early and more buccaneering days of the market economy; not so now. More collective consumption is needed.

(iii) Most workers have hitherto earned their living in routine dead-end jobs, usually physical, but sometimes mental. We are now seeing the rapid disappearance of such jobs. Yet half our future population of working age is involved; all the less academically and technically able. Advanced industrial societies move from a manufacturing to a service economy. That is to say, that fewer are needed to sustain the manufacturing base, which is highly productive but narrower, and the movement is towards service industries, like tourism or education, and personal social services (just as in the early stages of industrialization people moved from agriculture to industry because of the new higher productivity in agriculture). But are we willing to pay for the personal services, or do we cling to individual consumption? Can we say to middle-aged, redundant, relatively unskilled workers that they have nothing to contribute that society is willing to pay for? Can we say the same to the unemployed school-leaver of the same type, that he or she will never have a paid job? More leisure is one thing, being paid to be idle because society says you have nothing to contribute that it values is quite another. Not only is it cruel, it is untrue. Apart from a small number who are unemployable, the rest have personal qualities which could be used and which are needed in services to the young, the disabled, the elderly, and to the community in general which would greatly increase the quality of life for all. But we must be ready to pay. If we do not, we are storing up the potential for serious social disorder.

(iv) The ecological "limits to growth" argument has been greatly exaggerated, but cannot be entirely dismissed. We have been in danger of polluting the environment beyond the capacity of nature to recover, and are not free from that danger. Perpetual vigilance will be necessary. Also energy is fundamental, and the rich nations are squandering it on a dangerous scale, and are engaged in dangerous ways of replacing it. I refer, of course, to nuclear energy. This is too technical an issue to develop now; the point I want to make is that the market is not a good instrument for settling this issue. It discounts the future at about ten percent per annum, and this effectively means that it does not look more than fifteen years ahead, not long enough to deal with energy questions such as the disposal of long-term radioactive waste. What basis there is for moral and rational decision making on this question is not clear, and this requires urgent attention.

(v) The present economy of the rich world depends on communal human values which are an inheritance of centuries of teaching in the past. It has not only taken these values for granted, but it has done a good deal to undermine them by its uncritical individualism. As a result, they are rapidly weakening.[3] I am thinking of the virtues which have been exemplified at their best in a number of well-known Quaker industrial families.

Where is there to be found a source of moral renewal? What of the churches? Bryan Wilson, the Oxford sociologist of religion who has taken a special interest in religious sects, at one time thought that they would be a source of "disinterested good will" in society (he had written off "established" churches); but in a later book he has taken a more pessimistic view of them so that, since he does not like modern society, his gloom is unalloyed.[4] It is connected with a view of secularization which holds that in a society such as we are discussing, mainstream religion is effectively on the way out. I do not share this view for reasons which cannot be gone into now, but the point remains that the economy of the rich world is in need of a moral undergirding, something which it shows little sign of realizing.

5. There is a danger that the rich world might resolve its domestic problems by becoming wealthy, white (for the most part), Christian or post-Christian (for the most part) ghetto, in the midst of a "two-thirds" world of poverty. The rich world is powerful. It can, if it puts its mind to it, be independent of the Third World. It can devise substitutes. Oil is almost the only present exception, and that need not be for long. The Third World has very few weapons to use against the rich world. Yet it does seem clear that the rich rarely

listen to the poor unless the poor put pressure on them; this is even
more true of rich nations than of individuals. I find this one of the
most worrying factors. I recently heard an economist (and a Christian) who is enthusiastic about the benefits of a market economy say,
"It is absurd to go on trying to make one set of people feel guilty
because they are prosperous, while at the same time trying to make
the same set of people help you make another lot prosperous too". It
does not seem at all absurd to me. In fact, I think that it is what we
should do. Granted that it is not easy to help the Third World wisely,
that there are dangers of paternalism and of foolish mistakes, that
Third World governments need wiser and more just policies, it is not
convincing to say to the Third World that the best way the rich world
can help is by continuing to become richer along the path it is already
taking, and that the benefits will trickle down by the general growth
of the world economy. Nor, if I am right in what I have written, is it
in the best interests of the rich world itself.

6. This brings me to a prayer which often appears in collections of
prayers, at the end of which are the words, "Save Lord, by love, by
prudence and by fear." The thought is that human beings are so
recalcitrant that the Lord needs to use all the three motives at his
command if they are not to destroy themselves in their sin and folly.
Let us briefly consider the three. (i) Love. This is, of course, the
supreme Christian virtue, and the Christian life can be called a
"school of charity (love)." Christians often sentimentalize and triv-
ialize love, but nevertheless the increase of love in the world is the
acid test of worship of God through Jesus Christ in the power of the
Holy Spirit, which is at the heart of the Christian church. Moreover,
all human beings know something of what love is, but their love to
the neighbour is fitful and limited. Their own rights and wants loom
larger than their neighbour's needs. Their understanding of love
needs deepening and widening. An increase of love in the affluent
world is much needed. (ii) Prudence. Bishop Butler, one of the
greatest English moral philosophers, has a subtle argument to show
that the conduct dictated by benevolence and by "cool self-love" is
in the end the same. Whether this is always the case is not essential
for my purposes. To the extent that this can plausibly be shown to be
the case, can there be pressure put upon the affluent world. This is
the line taken by the Brandt Reports *North-South: A Programme for
Survival* (1980) and *Common Crisis North-South: Co-operation for
World Recovery* (1983).[5] The Brandt Reports, which are primarily
addressed to the wealthy world, try to make their recommendations
in terms of mutual interest. How convincing is it? The trouble is that
the benefits do not accrue necessarily or usually to the group which
makes the sacrifices, especially in the short term; and the gainers in
one country are consumers in general, whilst the losers are particular
groups of employers and employees who have a much more power-

ful lobby than do consumers. This brings us back once more to whether our rich societies have developed institutions which prevent the process of technical and economic change pressing too harshly on particular individuals and groups. But the more we can strengthen the "mutual interest" argument the better, as a means to move the affluent nations. (iii) Fear. "The fear of the Lord is the beginning of wisdom" is a frequent Old Testament maxim. What of our fear? I have already mentioned the danger of social disorder within affluent societies. Is there a fear of international disruption if mainly whites concentrate on increasing their own affluence, indifferent to the squalor in the mainly coloured two-thirds world? Insofar as a convincing case can be made that there is, it is a third way of seeking to move the affluent to constructive action.

7. Many on the political left have not faced up to the usefulness of the free market as a human institution provided it is set in a firm institutional framework of wider government social and political policies. It is a bad master, especially when it is ideologically blown up into an entire philosophy of life.[6] This has happened in the past and is having something of a revival now. It is possible to distinguish to some extent between policies and institutions on the one hand, and ideologies with which they are usually associated on the other. Pope John XXIII did this in his encyclical *Pacem in Terris* (1963) with respect to Marxism, though without explicitly mentioning it. He asked artlessly whether anyone could deny (knowing that his immediate predecessors had done so) that certain overall philosophies incompatible with the Christian faith might still not have certain economic, social and political ends which accord with right reason, interpret the lawful aspirations of human persons, and be deserving of approval. Similarly with a predominantly market economy, we should make use of the institution of the market, within limits, and at the same time query the over-all philosophy associated with it. That philosophy is best called one of "possessive individualism." It holds that people will only cooperate with one another so long as their self-interest requires it. The aim of each is to be as independent of others as possible, and not "beholden" to anyone. I think this philosophy is false and unchristian. The Christian understanding of society is that men and women should live in a community of giving and receiving, at different times giving more or receiving more according to their situation, and that social institutions should be such as to encourage this community. It is a direct challenge to the philosophy of most of the rich world, and one which the Christian churches in them should put with some vigour.

NOTES

1 See Peter Townsend, *Poverty in the United Kingdom* (Berkeley: University of California Press, 1979).

2 See Fred Hirsch, *The Social Limits to Growth* (Cambridge: Harvard University Press, 1977).

3 This is much too big a theme to be treated here. I have dealt with it more fully in *Religion and the Persistence of Capitalism* (London: SCM Press, 1979) and *Church and Society in the Late Twentieth Century: the Economic and Political Task* (SCM Press, 1983).

4 See Bryan Wilson, *Contemporary Transformations of Religion* (London: Oxford University Press, 1976).

5 Both studies have been published by M.I.T. Press, Cambridge, Mass.

6 I have developed these points more fully in the books mentioned above.

VI
War and Peace

·

Peacemaking in the Twentieth Century: The Role of the Churches

Ernest E. Best

Nowhere has the profound ambiguity in human history been more apparent than in the struggle of humankind for peace with justice throughout the twentieth century. On the one hand, there has never been a time when humans have been more acutely conscious of the blessings of peace, nor longed for it more. While we have had visions of world peace and harmony for millennia, in this century, for the first time, we have believed that it was possible to create political institutions to maintain peace without major outbreaks of violence on a universal basis. On the other hand, humankind has been tortured by violence in this century on a totalitarian scale, outdoing the travesties of any other age. The inhumanity of this century exceeds the power of both words and the imagination to adequately describe. Such is our plight Anno Domini 1984 as the sword of Damocles in the form of nuclear extinction hangs by a hair above our heads. The metaphor, we know, is not overdrawn.

I

A brief summary of how we have gotten where we are from the beginnings of the century may help us to understand why we are here. It may help us to assess the current "two track" policy which is simply a new edition of Clausewitz's dictum, "If you want peace prepare for war." As early as 1898 Czar Nicolas II, concerned at the arms buildup in Europe and especially over the increase in the degree of violence available through the discovery of dynamite, called a Council of Nations to discuss universal disarmament. Through the first decade of the century a number of peace delegations moved between Germany and England, at the time the principal antagonists. Prominent among these delegations were exchanges between church people, including in 1908, a young Paul Tillich. Unfortunately, there were strong countermovements on both sides. The result was the tragedy of World War I which made the world, we know now, neither safe nor democratic.

Though the result of World War I was the punitive Treaty of Versailles which was to have a fateful relationship to the emergence of nazism in Germany, the totalitarian dimensions of the war itself did produce a stronger public awareness of the tragedy of modern warfare and its ineffectiveness as a political instrument for the securing of either peace or justice. While there was some proportional disarmament between the wars, the failure of the League of Nations was sealed by the persistence of national autonomy and of national self-interest. In actual fact, "pacifism," a serious commitment to the search for alternatives to warfare and for alternatives to violence in every area of life, was neither understood nor supported by significant numbers between the wars, as some would have us believe. Nevertheless, a substantial peace movement did develop within the Protestant churches between the wars and by 1932 the United Church of Canada proclaimed through its General Council that Christians could not, in good conscience, support modern warfare. This position was supported primarily by biblical interpretation of the life and death of Jesus, though the witness of the historic peace churches (Society of Friends, Mennonites, etc.), of Thoreau, of Tolstoy, of Schweitzer, and the example of Gandhi were also influential. A number of church leaders, both men and women, in Europe and North America became committed to non-violent resistance as the best expression of the Christian faith in concrete action and as a response both to violence of an interpersonal and structural kind. A few were martyred during World War II and some, such as André and Magda Trocmé, as part of the French underground, were able to transform their situations in such a way as to save many refugees from death while at the same time remaining faithful to their commitment to non-violence.

This, however, is to anticipate the now familiar theological debates that took place during the thirties over whether Christians could, in good conscience, support participation in modern warfare. Reinhold Niebuhr argued that modern totalitarian political systems, backed by military might, were beyond redemption and thus reluctantly Christians had to use whatever means were necessary in order to overcome them. War sometimes was the lesser of two evils because violence was an irradicable part of human history and would always be so. Pacifists claimed that Niebuhr's stance in *Moral Man and Immoral Society* was essentially amoral since it made too strong a distinction between personal face-to-face relationships and the nature of social structures, as though persons did not after all make and shape structures, and thus were personally and collectively responsible both for the good and evil in them. Though it would take more than single individuals to change them, only transformed persons singly and collectively would be likely to do so. Both sides in the debate saw in Hitler and nazism the very epitome of evil. The difference was over the way in which evil was to be met and overcome in history, both in the short and in the long run.

Of course, there was another whole dimension to the struggle of those days which should not be forgotten because it helps to illuminate what is going on today in the struggle for peace with justice. It is sometimes forgotten that during the thirties many in Europe and North America were more opposed to Russia and the Russian form of communism than they were to emergent German nazism. The latter appeared to them less threatening to capitalism. This was one of the major reasons why resistance to Hitler did not begin sooner. At the same time a split occurred among democratic socialists over whether the movement should reluctantly reject a certain commitment to pacifism in the face of the Nazi threat. Many Christian pacifist leaders in both Europe and North America, people such as Muriel Lester, Dorothy Day, A.J. Muste, Nevin Sayre, Norman Thomas and J.S. Woodsworth, saw pacifism as implying democratic socialism as the way to peace with justice. In my judgment, these comments apply as much to Canada as to the United States, the only difference being that in Canada the pacifist community was so small as to be almost unheard of, save for the lonely voices of J.S. Woodsworth and Stanley Knowles and a few beleaguered but outstanding clergy such as Harold Toye and James Finlay. "Christian Realism" easily won the day.

II

Any realistic account of the struggle for peace with justice in the twentieth century must, of course, be divided into two. The first part must deal, as we have done, with the pre-atomic, pre-nuclear age and the second with the post-atomic, post-nuclear age. I speak as one who lived for five years in the aftermath of the bomb that fell on Nagasaki, trying to be of some use in that critical situation. In my judgment, anyone who fails to realize that the quantitative change in the nature of warfare since 1945 has changed its qualitative nature is surely living in a fool's paradise. The need to eradicate warfare has become a necessity of the first order if humankind is to continue to exist in any civilized way. Surely it is the realization of this fact that accounts for the massive numbers in the present peace movement. Whether their influence and numbers are sufficient to bring about a new order, however, is the critical question.

The early proposals for the outlawing of atomic weapons by both the U.S. and the U.S.S.R., it can be demonstrated, were not meant to be taken seriously, for both had unacceptable terms attached to them. It was the era of the Cold War. One of its tragic implications was the gradual immobilization in many ways, though by no means in every one, of the United Nations; another was the continuing reign of international anarchy. By 1960 the U.S. downgraded its activity in the United Nations because there was no longer a guaranteed majority on its side in the Assembly. That majority had previously contained the influence of the U.S.S.R. However, the Cuban Missile Crisis of 1962 gave chilling evidence of how close the human community could come to a nuclear holocaust. On the good side, its upshot was the Nuclear Test Ban Treaty of 1963 and a cooling of direct confrontation between the U.S. and the U.S.S.R. At the level of the superpowers there was increased dependence upon the doctrine of deterrence (Mutual Assured Destruction, M.A.D.). It has been noted, however, that this doctrine, based essentially upon fear, not trust, is basically irrational. On the one hand, the theory does not work if the powers are not really prepared to use their weaponry, and, on the other, the security it ostensibly guarantees is that, in fact, no power would ever use them. The growing contemporary peace movement is testimony not only to the fallacy of this doctrine but also to increased talk among military and political leaders especially, but not only, in the United States, of the possible use of such weapons and the possibility of "winning" a nuclear war. The inauguration of the Reagan regime in Washington, with its deep hostility to the Russians, appears to have returned us to the Cold War of the 1950s, but with a nuclear arsenal on both sides now capable of destroying human life on earth as we know it.

In the background of all this, however, is that other factor which we noted was already present in the thirties. It is the question of social justice. As I have said, in the thirties we saw those who were hostile to Russia not only because of her totalitarian political structures, the vicious nature of which must be recognized by all persons of goodwill, but because she represented a threat to the profit system of private, if not "free," enterprise. The underlying question is whether any non-cooperative economic system can ever guarantee freedom, justice, and peace for those millions who continue to live in abject poverty in so many parts of the globe. Many of these are violently put to death each day through economic deprivation. They cannot be expected to sit idly by indefinitely and allow this to happen to them and to their loved ones. Indeed, the majority of them will, and do, react violently to their plight. In so doing their plight may well provide the spark which will become the occasion for the undoing of us all.

It was this state of affairs that Gandhi and Martin Luther King saw so clearly. They knew, on the one hand, that there could be no peace without justice. They knew, on the other, that only a transformed human spirit could do anything of a lasting kind about these issues. Gandhi and King also knew the reality of unjust social structures but they were convinced, like the Old Testament prophets, that only those who had creative alternative visions and were personally committed to them were likely to change them.

The biblical record comes alive when we allow it to speak to us in terms of prophetic challenge. We cannot allow it again to be dismissed as some utopian idealism. Its universalism makes us all children of one Creator, mutually loved and therefore essentially interdependent. Jesus' announcement of the nature of his own ministry compels his followers to oppose all systems that mean privilege for some at the expense of others. It calls us to constantly struggle for justice for those both far and near, whatever their colour, their religion, their age or their sex. It certainly calls us to oppose those blasphemous systems which plan nuclear annihilation in the vain search for a security that cannot be had so long as we and our exploitative systems remain unchanged.

We do not lack for such visions. In so many ways at the end of the twentieth century we have the potential political machinery for effecting them. It is primarily the hope and therefore the will that is lacking.

This suggests the role of the churches in the contemporary crisis and we may thank God that there are so many, especially in the leadership of the World Council of Churches, not the least of whom has been the present primate of the Anglican Church of Canada, who are aware of it. Do we really believe as Christians that the Creator wants the creation destroyed? That God intends every person's hand to be turned against another? That there are no alternatives to destruction? Are we convinced that with all the talents we have been given as a human race we are utterly incapable of living together in peace? That we cannot create those structures that will enable us to live in reasonable security?

To put it this negatively is to show how preposterous the suggestions are. As professed followers of the One who said, "I am come to give life and to give it abundantly," we are committed to the opposite path and we are committed to it not just for ourselves and our loved ones but for all human beings everywhere. To paraphrase A.J. Muste, "God's justice will not let us off because God's love will not let us go."

Space does not permit me to make more than a few brief, general suggestions as to the positive course towards peacemaking which I believe prophetic Christians should take in the immediate future. I make them, nonetheless.

First, the content of this piece suggests the vision in the light of which I believe we must be changed. The basic task of the churches is to continue to transform our attitudes from ones that rely upon violence to ones of sensitivity and concern for others based upon that love through which we know ourselves to be loved. We are called to trust in that strong loving God who wills the best for us and for all others. Because our trust is there we continue to hope, even when on other grounds we could not hope. The greatest obstacle to be moved in our present impasse is our continued willingness to believe in ways of relating to others that have failed in the past and which will betray our future. We do not believe in some "unchanging human nature." We believe in a nature that is always open to the transforming power of the divine Spirit.

Second, the churches should continue to speak truth with power as the leadership in the World Council of Churches and the Catholic Council of Bishops in the U.S.A. have been striving to do. The last thing we should do is to give in to the persistent attacks against the efforts of the churches to influence governments in the struggle for peace with justice.

On the political front, this means a fresh commitment beyond the national to the international community and to international structures that will lead to serious disarmament, not mathematical gamesmanship. Economically it means a renewed dedication to the transformation of present aid and trade arrangements that will be actually useful to those in greatest need. We do not begin from scratch. Many of the necessary agencies are already in place. They, like us, need to be renewed and transformed.

Finally, the international peace movement, which takes its cue from neither of the "superpowers," has already demonstrated that, though it may be ignored for a time, it makes a difference over time and will make a difference for as long as there is time. Those who have taken to the streets have not done so in vain. Many of our political leaders are calling today for renewed relations between the Soviets and the U.S.A., not only because the Reagan doctrine of threat and counterthreat has proven a dangerous failure, but because millions took to the streets, and because those few "saints" of civil disobedience dared to be faithful to us all.

Peace and War

James G. Endicott

There are many different ways of discussing the problem of peace and war.[1] There can be a general analysis of recorded history which is a constant record of wars. There can be psychological and sociological discussions on "human nature" and "nature red in tooth and claw" and arguments about the "territorial imperative." The possibilities of theological speculation and argument about why we have wars and how peace can come about are many and ingenious. So also are the possibilities of imaginative, utopian, hopeful and wishful thinking. Christians often avoid coming face-to-face with the harsh realities of economics and politics by the simple formula, "Peace depends on changing the human heart," and hoping and praying for the Second Coming of Christ.

On the basis of my long experience in missionary work in China, in the Chinese Revolution and in the World Council of Peace, I have come to the following conclusion: In addition to our Christian concern for evangelism and for justice and the Kingdom of God as taught by Jesus, it is now necessary to study seriously the *Communist Manifesto*, some basic writings of Lenin such as *The State and Revolution* and *Imperialism, the Highest Stage of Capitalism* as well as some of Mao Zedong's explanations of the Chinese Revolution. This relatively new knowledge is as necessary as was the new knowledge given by Copernicus and Galileo, Newton, Darwin and Einstein. Without it a sincere Christian who wants peace and justice may become confused and lost in the struggles of the day. Let me illustrate this with some reflections on my own experience.

I went as an eighteen-year-old soldier to the First World War. We were persuaded (or brainwashed) by state, school and church into believing that it was a "war to end war" and to "make the world safe for democracy." It included noble principles, such as the sanctity of treaties and the "rights of small nations." We had no understanding of the realities of economics and politics on which the struggle was based, and consequently were taken completely by surprise when the October Revolution came in the Soviet Union. We were easily persuaded by horror stories that what had happened was evil, godless and sure to fail.

There were, of course, other voices, but they were drowned out in the chorus of denunciation, especially by the testimony of Russian aristocratic exiles. My father, who became the second moderator of the United Church of Canada, once said to Joseph Atkinson, the editor of the *Toronto Star*, "What the Russians are trying to do, I see no reason why any Christian should not approve, and if they fail, I hope they will try again."

However one assesses the revolution in the Soviet Union, those of us who went to war to make the world safe for democracy and the rights of small nations were hoaxed and betrayed. We made the world safe for a quick restoration of the same old order which had produced the war. U.S. President Harding called it a return to "normalcy."

National rivalries, big corporation rivalries and reckless stock-market gambling became the main characteristics of the time. All this ended with the great stock market crash of 1929 and the ensuing depression, the rise of fascism under Hitler in Germany, Mussolini in Italy and Franco in Spain, and the expansionist militarism in Japan. These developments made the Second World War inevitable.

One of the chief excuses these people gave for their repression, terrorism and militarization was anti-communism. What had happened in the Soviet Union since 1917 was frightening the capitalist world. It is amusing now to examine the double-barrelled style of propaganda: "Everything in Socialist Russia is such an inefficient mess and failure that it has become a great threat and danger to us." But it is also true that communist parties, bent on getting control and promoting a socialist alternative to capitalism were gaining strength in many countries, especially in Germany, France, Italy and China.

This is one of the explanations of why western capitalism, in general, supported the various dictators. It is recorded in captured German documents that Lord Halifax, supposedly a deeply religious man, said to Hitler on November 19, 1937, "By destroying Communism in his country the Führer barred its road into Western Europe and Germany, [and,] therefore, might rightly be regarded as a bulwark of the west against Bolshevism." As long as Hitler was killing communists, socialists, trade unionists and anyone who wanted to change the free enterprise system, he was regarded as a useful bulwark of the west.

The same was true, to a considerable extent, of how the west with its League of Nations regarded the Japanese aggression against China which began in 1931. Ten years later, in private conversations at the Rotary Club in Hongkong, I was urging support for China's resistance to Japan. The head of the Hongkong Shanghai Banking Corporation answered me in these words: "After all, old boy, the Japanese are eradicating the menace of Bolshevism in Asia for us." He later died in a Japanese prisoner-of-war camp.

The end result of "making the world safe for democracy" was a Second World War of unprecedented and difficult-to-imagine ferocity; a destruction which undermined the psychological, social and economic foundations of the old order. Two consequences of that period stand out as being largely responsible for our present situation in which we find ourselves at the brink of war again.

The Soviet Union suffered enormously: 1,700 of its cities and 70,000 of its villages destroyed totally or partially, 20 million of its people killed and two-thirds of its industrial capacity lost. All this was done by invaders from the West who had passed through the countries of Eastern Europe and were sometimes actively aided by the them, e.g., the Hungarians under Admiral Horthy and the Rumanian Iron Guard. But the Soviet Union ended the war with a huge and experienced army.

The Soviet Union was therefore determined to make sure of her territorial integrity. She took back that part which the Germans had taken in the First World War by the Brest-Litovsk treaty: it consisted of one-third of her crop lands, almost half of her industrial capacity and 62 million of her people. In the second place she insisted on setting up near her borders either friendly governments or governments she could control — Finland, Poland, East Germany, Czechoslovakia, Hungary and Bulgaria.

In contrast to the Soviet Union, the United States ended the war immensely rich, industrially powerful, having suffered no serious destruction except Pearl Harbour, and, above all, in possession of atomic bombs successfully tried out on Hiroshima and Nagasaki. Moreover, they believed that they had a long-term monopoly on these weapons. They went in for a high-speed, large-scale nuclear arms development. Under John Foster Dulles and later Henry Kissinger, the U.S. developed doctrines of roll-back, containment, nuclear blackmail, and, if necessary, the use of nuclear war.[2] U.S. policy was based on the principle that communism must be eliminated or destroyed, held that there must be powerful mobile forces able to quickly crush revolutionary changes and that this policy would only be credible if the United States was determined and prepared, if necessary, to use nuclear war. John Foster Dulles nailed his colours to the mast with the infamous phrase, "massive retaliation at times and places of our own choosing."

In his book *America and the World Revolution* (1962), Arnold J. Toynbee, possibly the pre-eminent historian of his generation, summed up the position of the United as the leader of the forces of order in the following terms:

America is today the leader of a world-wide anti-revolutionary movement in defence of vested interests. She now stands for what Rome stood for. Rome consistently supported the rich against the poor, in all foreign communities that fell under her sway; and, since the poor, so far, have always and everywhere been far more numerous than the rich, Rome's policy made for inequality, for injustice, and for the least happiness of the greatest number. America's decision to adopt Rome's role has been deliberate, if I gauged it right.[3]

It is beyond the scope of this essay to give a detailed analysis of the rise of anti-communist hysteria and the Cold War which prepared the way for the dangerous situation which now prevails in the world. By 1948, however, it was obvious to an increasing number of people that the framework of private ownership of technology and the means of life was not necessarily the only or the best organizing principle for a worthwhile, healthy society. If there was a workable alternative to the private enterprise system, then knowledge of two world wars, some major revolutions and a bottomless economic depression was enough, in the phrase of E.H. Carr, "to convince all but the blind and incurable that the forces of individualism have somehow lost their relevance in the contemporary world."[4]

The forces of individualism, however, as represented by the western industrialized nations and above all by the United States, mobilized for a strong counterattack against revolutionary movements. Even though their own experts told the Washington government that it was useless and hopeless, the U.S. government continued to pour huge sums of money and large amounts of military supplies to the disintegrating forces of the Kuomintang in China.

American policy in Japan was reversed and replaced by one aimed at turning Japan into a modern center of power capable of offsetting a strong, united revolutionary China. British Foreign Secretary Ernest Bevin served notice that his government intended to "stamp out" communist-inspired revolutions wherever they appeared in the Empire. Truman announced the policy in 1947 known as the "Truman Doctrine" which would place American economic power, diplomacy and even her armed forces at the services of a world-wide crusade to stop the spread of communism. Right-wing dictatorships were set in Greece and Turkey, and within three years U.S. troops were fighting in Korea. William L. Shirer, in *The Trend in World Affairs*, commented that 1948 "was the year of the cold war between Russia and the United States, between East and West, between communism and capitalism . . . and the best that could be said of it was that [it] did not develop into a hot war, a shooting war."[5]

A recent book made possible by the Freedom of Information Act, *Containment: Documents on American Policy and Strategy 1945-1950*, by Thomas H. Etzold and J.L. Gaddis,[6] shows that the U.S. government had come to the conclusion that the U.S. would have to make herself strong enough to use force, including, as a last resort, possible use of atomic bombs to frustrate Soviet designs and that there could be no lasting solution "unless and until a change occurs in the nature of the Soviet system." All the forces of the "Free World" were to be mobilized to contain the Soviet Union and force her to change.

With the advantage of hindsight we now know that the Soviet Union was fully informed about all this as well as the prediction that war was quite likely by April 1949. Their informants included Kim Philby and Donald Maclean.

It was at this point that I came into the peace movement. I was an amateur, without the comprehensive knowledge that is now available, but I sensed the genuine dangers and felt that to counter the very real danger of war, the demand for peaceful coexistence between differing social systems and the abolition of nuclear weapons was well-timed, useful and necessary.

Under the leadership of Fredrich Joliot-Curie, a French atomic scientist, a world congress held in Wroclaw, (Breslau), Poland, brought together several hundred widely representative intellectuals from socialist and non-socialist countries. In this discussion, disagreements about the source of the war danger were not lacking and the issues of imperialism and racism were hotly debated, but ultimately an optimistic view prevailed, based on the idea that war is not a natural catastrophe like a flood or an earthquake: it is created by people and people can prevent it. In the past people had been the passive object of warring rulers; the new peace movement conceived of itself as an all-inclusive movement of people all over the world and from all walks of life who would organize themselves to take the cause of defending peace into their own hands. Perhaps, as we look back, it will be the crystallization of ideas about the possibility of the peaceful coexistence of differing social systems and about the urgency to combat the threat of nuclear war which will prove to be the most enduring and meaningful legacy of the world of 1948.

Now the world situation has not only changed but has become much more complicated. If there ever was a communist monolith, as U.S. Cold War propaganda claimed, it ended with the break between China and the U.S.S.R. in the 1960s and the new Chinese analysis of the Three Worlds. In the First World, according to the Chinese, there are two superpowers contending for world control. A group of middle powers, including Canada, form the Second World, and everyone else is in the Third World, of which China is a part. China's peace program demands the total abolition of nuclear wea-

pons brought about by a world conference of all nations, big and
small, all treated as equals. China fully supports the agenda for peace
as set forth by the Special Session of the United Nations, May 1,
1974. It is too long to print here. It demands a new international
economic order, in which the poor and underdeveloped countries
would benefit the most. That would be justice. If anyone wants
peace, let them accept the demands of the overwhelming majority at
the United Nations and help to bring about such a new international
order.

It is rather ridiculous to suppose that the human mind can devise
ways of putting people on the moon and yet has to leave the question
of war and peace to the mysterious "ways of Providence" or the
fatalism of original sin. Even if they do not have eyes to see or ears to
hear, as Jesus noted of his generation, they are a part of our long
evolutionary march from primitive to economic to social humanity.

War has been a natural and inevitable accompaniment of that
long struggle. It will remain so until a qualitative change has taken
place in matters of justice and cooperation and until the control of
natural resources and production is aimed at benefitting all in a spirit
of mutual sharing.

Dr. Joseph Needham has stated this truth clearly and eloquently:

> We have no reason to suppose that our present condi-
> tion of civilization is the last masterpiece of universal
> organization, the highest form of order of which
> Nature is capable. I believe there are many grounds for
> seeing in collectivism, of the kind of which we could
> approve, a form of organization as much above the
> outlook of middle class nations as their form of order
> is superior to that of primitive tribes. I think it would
> hardly be going too far to say that, so clear is the
> continuity between inorganic, biological and social
> order, the transition from economic individualism to
> the common ownership by humanity of the world's
> productive resources will be a step similar in nature to
> the transition from lifeless proteins to the living cell, or
> from primitive savagery to the first community. From
> this point of view, the future state of social justice is
> seen not as a fantastic Utopia, not a desperate hope,
> but as a form of organization with the full force and
> authority of evolution behind it.[7]

There seem to be good reasons for Christians to view that future
state of social justice as having behind it the full force of the moral
insights of the Jewish prophets as well as the teachings of Jesus
about our relation to the Kingdom of God. But we will become
hopelessly confused about how to achieve that justice if we fail to
take a scientific approach.

After 1848, a new and different way of thinking about and analyzing economic and political matters came into the world with the works of Marx and Engels. It came in time to give an analysis of the Paris Commune which resulted from the Franco-Prussian War of 1870. The idea of a different social order, based on cooperation and controlled by the working class, spread and developed organizations and parties to promote it. By the middle of the twentieth century, the majority of Christians in the west felt threatened by a force which was considered monolithic and threatened to control the world in the interests of an atheistic philosophy of dialectical and historical materialism and a centrally planned economy of production and distribution.

Christians prayed regularly for peace. They nourished in their hearts the biblical dreams and visions of peace as expressed, for example, in Isaiah 2:4, "and he shall judge among the nations and shall rebuke many people; and they shall beat their swords into ploughshares and their spears into pruning hooks; nation shall not lift up sword against nation, neither shall they learn war any more."

We can be inspired by these biblical visions and we can dream and pray about them, but unless we come to grips with the harsh and difficult necessities of change and repentance from wrong, selfish and evil ways, we are part of the problem, not part of the solution. We must realize that as long as there are powerful states and organizations which want to occupy markets, plunder natural resources and promote non-unionized cheap sweated labour, there will be arms races and wars, no matter what prayers and pious speeches are made for peace and disarmament.

Today the ideological issue is becoming increasingly clear, even in the smoke of battle in Central America and the Middle East, Southern Asia and Southern Africa. The recent meeting of the World Council of Churches in Vancouver, and the type of attacks made on it made that fact quite clear. If we take time to listen to the television evangelists, the 700 Club and some of the Reaganites, we get the impression that God is an American patriot who ordained free enterprise and that most of the evil in the world is due to atheism and communism and that, therefore, America's military might is the guarantee of peace.

In response to this a Jesuit priest has raised an important question. "If, as the Bible makes clear, God is Justice and Love, who are the contemporary atheists? Those who wear the label but fight for a civilization based on equality and love (Marx, Freud, Camus?) or those who believe in God as an idol, who blesses and protects their power and possessions in a world divided between rich and poor?"[7]

If we want peace in the long term, we must have justice. If we want peace in the short term, though, we must remove the menace of nuclear destruction. Albert Einstein's warning, "The atom bomb has changed everything except our way of thinking," was interpreted in two ways. By ordinary people of commonsense and by most atomic scientists it meant, "humankind must get rid of nuclear weapons or nuclear weapons will get rid of humankind." By the U.S. Pentagon and the State Department it was interpreted to mean a secret all-powerful weapon which would compel Soviet retreat and ultimate surrender and the crushing of all people's movements for social change. The Soviet Union quite naturally responded by quickly developing a matching nuclear strength. Under the administration of President Reagan, the U.S. has made massive increases in the military budget and a first-strike theory lies behind the development of the "Cruise" the "Pershing" and the MX missiles. The U.S. is also extending the arms race into space.

The Christian church, Catholic and Protestant, is now responding in an increasingly effective way to oppose the acceptance of nuclear war, to challenge the morality of nuclear weapons and to demand a new era of economic and social justice which can give a foundation for peace. There are many organizations and movements now active. There is useful work for peace to be done by anyone who wants to help. We all have to remind ourselves that this is the agenda for the church today:

Don't just stand there, do something!

NOTES

1   Some of the ideas and quotations in this essay are borrowed from an as yet unpublished manuscript by Dr. Stephen Endicott, *The World of 1948*.

2   See Henry Kissinger, *Nuclear Weapons and Foreign Policy* (New York: Harper, 1957).

3   *America and the World Revolution* (London: Oxford University Press, 1962), p. 92.

4   E.H. Carr, *The Soviet Impact on the Western World* (London: Macmillan, 1947), p. 114.

5   Stephen Endicott, *The World of 1948*.

6   New York: Columbia University Press, 1978.

7   Quoted in Stephen Endicott, *James G. Endicott: Rebel out of China* (Toronto: University of Toronto Press, 1980), p. 357.

8   See Antonio Perez-Esclarin, *Atheism and Liberation* (Maryknoll, N.Y.: Orbis Books, 1978).

War and Peace: A Japanese Perspective

Reiko Shimada

To remember the past is to commit oneself to the future.
To remember Hiroshima is to abhor nuclear war.
To remember what the people of this city suffered is to renew our faith in humanity, in their capacity to do what is good, in their freedom to choose what is right, in their determination to turn disaster into a new beginning. In the face of the calamity made by human beings that every war is, one must affirm and reaffirm again and again, that the waging of war is not inevitable or unchangeable.

> — Appeal for Peace by Pope John Paul II in February, 1981, at Hiroshima Memorial Peace Park

The YWCA in Japan has been conducting field trips to Hiroshima every summer since 1970, for adult members first and then for junior and senior high school students. The YWCA is now emphasizing the anti-nuclear movement, having come to have a deep interest in the nuclear question. We believe that Japan has the responsibility to assimilate and distribute information and knowledge about the atomic bomb and nuclear power, to increase the awareness of all people of this peril. At the same time we have to communicate the war experience to younger generations. The field trip to Hiroshima has been our attempt to know more about Hiroshima ourselves and to pass on the experience to our children and young members. In the beginning, the danger of nuclear weapons was the main concern, from the standpoint of the peace issue, but we gradually began to take up the danger of nuclear power plants and then moved into the "nuclear power society" as a whole in this age.

In the nuclear bombing of Hiroshima, the lives of 200,000 people were snuffed out. Terrific heat, wind pressure and radiation took their toll. Both steel and tile were melted by 3000 to 4000 degrees centigrade of heat at the site of the explosion. The people who were close to the epicentre evaporated within a moment. The wind pressure was 20 to 23 tons per square meter. Concrete buildings were blown away like stacks of cards by winds caused by the blast. The most dreadful radiation destroyed not only the skin surfaces but cells and internal organs. Within weeks tens of thousands of suffering people died. Furthermore, the neutrons in the radiation turn materials into radioactive particles. This is called residual or induced radioactivity. It continues to attack the mind and body of the person for prolonged periods of time.

Many victims of the A-bomb who survived the hell of this world and whom we met in Hiroshima told us that their experiences could never be communicated to other people who were not there. They challenged us by their deep sense of guilt — asking why they were still alive, what was the meaning of life and how could they live as human beings? Their sense of guilt came from their experiences of escaping the fire and destruction, but failing to save neighbours: the man who shouted "Save me, save me, please" under the broken building, a dying woman who begged a cup of water, a child who was crying in the arms of a dead mother. People were deprived of a dignified human death. Survivors, too, have been hindered from living human lives by the A-bomb. After keeping a long silence, they started telling the story of the Hiroshima tragedy as living witnesses. They do not want ever to make vain the lives of the hundreds of thousands lost in Hiroshima. They now think it is their turn to appeal to the people of the world, "No more Hiroshimas," and to work for the cause of world peace and human dignity.

Toshi Maruki, the painter who is one of the victims of the A-bomb, draws the tragedy of Hiroshima with her husband. When she had almost died from the aftereffects of radiation, she made up her mind to expose the hell of this world in her paintings. She drew "Ghosts," "Fire," "Water," "Girls and Boys," and others on behalf of the 200,000 who died at Hiroshima. She confessed that she began to draw the pictures from hatred of a people who dropped such a cruel bomb on the Japanese people. However, she knew that 23 American soldiers imprisoned in Hiroshima, including three American women, also died by their own country's bomb. The most shocking fact of this story was that they were all beaten to death by a mad crowd of citizens before dying from the radiation. She saw the horrible picture of human beings — and she knew that she herself had the possibility of becoming one of that mad crowd. She could not continue drawing anymore from hatred, but she finished "The Tragedy of 23 American Soldiers" as an expression of her prayer for peace. She was also shocked by the story of the Korean people, and it inspired her to complete another work, "Crows." Many Koreans who were forced to come to Japan during the War were killed in the factories or on construction sites in Hiroshima and Nagasaki and discriminated against even after death. Their bodies were neglected and left to the depredation of flocks of crows. Her next work was "Nanking," which condemned the Japanese invasion of China and the massacre of tens of thousands of Chinese. The act of exposing Hiroshima led her bit by bit to the depths of human life and the eternal questions of war and peace. She and her husband built an A-bomb Art Museum in a small city far from the noise and pollution of metropolitan Tokyo. Now they live in an old farmhouse, working their natural and organic farm for self-support. Her latest work is "Minamata," the name of a small fishing village on Kyushu island, a symbol of the tragedy of the mercury poisoning by the chemical waste from industry.

The suffering of people who died in the red-hot hell of the A-bomb explosion is expressed in the moan, "Give me water." The seven rivers which run through the city of Hiroshima were filled with thousands of bodies — those of people who jumped into the rivers for water. Many victims died soon after they had a cup of water, so relatives of the dying refused to give a cup of water, fearing its effect.

When we had a small conference for peace with YWCA Asian friends at Hiroshima, using the appeal, "No more Hiroshimas" as a foundation for world peace, our eyes were opened to the fact that August 6th, the day of the dropping of the A-bomb on Hiroshima, was the "victory day" freeing Asian people from Japanese military invasion. We were told the story of how the husband of one of the Asian friends who came from Malaysia was paralyzed and badly disabled by the torture of Japanese soldiers. He groaned for a cup of water on the pole on which he hung. Soldiers threw away the water just at the moment his lips touched the edge of the cup. She also challenged us, telling us that Asian people feared the "Second Coming of Japan," that is, the economic invasion of Asia. We acknowledged with Asian friends that the nuclear question was deeply connected with the suffering of Asian people everywhere during World War II and the suffering of victims like the Minamata mercury patients, due to modern industrial technology and the economic structure of the present society. People now ask, "Give us back clean water, air and sunshine," not only in Japan but also in the developing Asian countries. The same groan, "Give me water," from the hell of Hiroshima is also heard in the torture of Asian people by Japanese invaders and again in the suffering of present and future generations who are losing nature, clean water, and clean air.

"Nuclear power" is the visible peak of modern civilization's advancement in technology and science. In Japan today, people seek a richer and more comfortable life at the expense of natural resources, the surroundings, and the lives of other people in the developing countries. In addition, to answer the greed of the consumer society, we build nuclear energy plants which cause the destruction of the environment and the ecosystem. People in the YWCA Movement who have been involved in the anti-nuclear movement have gradually noticed that they have to examine their way of life and try to change their lifestyle.

A wives' group noticed that chemicals, additives, and fertilizers used in daily food were very dangerous to health, especially for children. Recently Japanese children have been suffering from teeth and bone troubles and have less muscle strength. The women were shocked at the statistic that the top cause of death in children was cancer. The group started a movement to get good and natural foods, encouraging a few farmers and manufacturers who were producing natural foods, organizing a natural food market once a month in the YWCA hall for the public, and publicizing the issue through a teach-in about polluted foods, agriculture in Japan, the energy crisis, nuclear energy, the danger of cosmetics, pollution and the environment, etc.

In this initiative, they discovered the reason why they can eat bananas which are very cheap and beautiful. Farmers in the Philippines had their land taken away by multinational corporations and were now exploited as seasonal workers, suffering from too much insecticide on the huge plantations — all to make beautiful bananas, 90 percent of which were imported by Japan.

The movement to question the quality of life and to change our lifestyle has been rising everywhere in Japan. It is a radical challenge to the highly developed industrialized consumer society.

The atomic bomb explosions over Hiroshima and Nagasaki on August 6 and 9, 1945, marked the beginning of a new era of war and peace in the present world. These bombs demonstrated the devastating might of nuclear power and its effects for the first time in history. The people of the world need to be informed about what really happened at the time of the explosions and thereafter, so that they can understand the nature and significance of this new era. The nuclear energy which was brought to being by human hands is a demonic power which seems beyond the control of human knowledge. We have to seek a way for the human race to survive the "nuclear age."

We now face the possibility of the total destruction of the human race because of the expanding nuclear arms race and the escalation of destructive power. The total strength of present nuclear arsenals is regarded as equivalent to about one million Hiroshima bombs. The United States and Soviet Union missile systems are always ready to fire. Moreover, the dangerous possibility of a nuclear war has greatly increased in Europe as well as in Asia because of the strategy of the limited nuclear war. In President Kennedy's words, "The danger of atomic annihilation hangs, like a sword of Damocles, with a tiny thread, over every man, woman, and child, and it could be cut at any moment, by chance, error, or by act of insanity."

The destruction of the environment caused by nuclear experiments and nuclear energy plants will, it is thought, affect humankind for hundreds and thousands of years. The issue here is our responsibility towards future generations. More than 250 nuclear energy plants are in operation in 22 countries as the expansion of atoms for "peaceful use" continues. At least 100 tons of the resulting plutonium are left without adequate care, creating the possibility of the production of nuclear weapons from this product of nuclear energy production. The construction of nuclear energy plants is often closely related to schemes of nuclear arms in each country.

Because of the concentration of nuclear power in the hands of a few powerful people, the extreme danger of nuclear energy means that systems of control over the lives of citizens are tightened and people deprived of more and more of their freedom. Because the economic and social control that is exercised by nuclear giants tends to pursue profit relentlessly without limits, it invites more oppressive measures and expands the structures of discrimination. The race by the superpowers and advanced countries to export arms to developing countries is causing the starvation of many people. Some $700 billion is spent for military purposes each year while millions of people are starving to death.

Christians have a responsibility for making peace. We believe nature, as well as humanity, has been created by God, and that we are entrusted to manage all natural resources responsibly, not only for our own self-interest in this generation, but also for those who come after us. We also acknowledge that the love of God for us, God's creatures, gives immense value and dignity to the life of every person. If we are to respond to this love of God, we must seek to protect the integrity of nature and defend the lives and dignity of all people. In this spirit, one of the most urgent current issues in which we Christians should be involved is the matter of nuclear power, both in its military use as a weapon of mass destruction and in its peaceful use as a source of energy. We human beings cannot coexist with nuclear power.

The peace movement is becoming a giant wave in Europe, America, and Asia. People are extending their hands and banding together across the boundaries that separate East and West. Voices for peace, coming from the grassroots people in the marginalized areas of the world, have been raised more and more wherever oppression has become dominant. Today more people believe that their small actions for peace can become a cornerstone for peacemaking and have realized the importance of solidarity among people for uniting their power together for peace. We have to commit ourselves to the world peace movement and give effect to our determination to save succeeding generations from the scourge of war and destruction of our earth.

The Web of Violence and the Christian Response

Donald Grayston

No alert Canadian can deny that Canada is a violent country. As soon as the subject comes up, of course, someone says, "Yes, but not as violent as the United States." But this is small comfort. In other areas of social and cultural life, the lag between the time that something hits or takes off in the United States and in Canada is between five and ten years. In any case, both the United States and Canada are affected by currents of violence and kinds of violence which arise in other nations. Violence, in fact, is a cosmic reality: as close as the local policeman killed on duty, as far away as Afghanistan or El Salvador. We fear it; we fear its increase; we wonder how human beings got this way; and in our better moments, we wonder how we can respond, as Christians and as Canadians.

In this brief chapter, I want to tackle two concerns. First, where *does* violence come from, in Christian perspective, and what response can we make to it? Second, what can local Christian communities do to apply this response, in the Spirit, to the violence we perceive around us and within us? What place, in other words, should our response to violence occupy on the agenda of the local missional community, the congregation?

Violence in Biblical Perspective

The first question was the focus of a whole day's discussion at the General Synod of the Anglican Church of Canada held in Fredericton, New Brunswick, in June 1983. Although the issue was dealt with there in relation to Anglican structures, it concerns all Canadian Christians, indeed all Christians of good will and human concern.

The angle of approach to the issue was this: Is there a connection between the nuclear violence which threatens the entire globe and the violence which so many women and children experience in our society at the hands of men? Those of us who were planning and presenting the issue believed that there was a direct and dangerous connection; and so we asked the delegates to that synod to consider these two aspects of violence together.

A recent article by American theologian Rosemary Ruether, written out of her American context, makes the connection very clear. She asserts a

> continuity between male violence toward women in the home or in the streets, and war. For many men, violence in Vietnam was serious and important, whereas violence against women was merely private and trivial. Feminists argued that both were expressions of the same mentality of patriarchy [authoritarian rule by "the fathers," i.e., by men]. The socialization of women to be victims and men to be aggressors is the training ground for the culminating expression of male violence in warfare, they said.[1]

What she means is that men who have experienced and practised violence against the women and children of their own families will have no rational or emotional objection to war, and may even have enthusiasm for it. This does not mean that they will consciously make this connection in their own minds. The fact that they are accustomed to violence on the domestic level simply prepares them to accept the decisions of their governments to engage in violence on an international level.

Many experts in this field believe that the crux of the problem of domestic assault is found in a *combination* of two factors: the transmission from generation to generation (on this, see my discussion of Genesis 1-4, below) of a tendency to violence nurtured through the experience of male children of the violent behaviour of their fathers in the home; and a rigid adherence by these children-become-insecure-men to so-called traditional sex roles, many aspects of which simply do not work in our time. Thus a man who has witnessed violence by his father against his mother (or experienced it against himself), and who also holds a rigid view of the relation of husband and wife, will often feel justified in using force to maintain his position. In former days, when many married couples lived in extended families, or near their parents at least, the influence of other family members acted as a check on this behaviour. Now, however, with most families living in single-family quarters, and with the ever-increasing mobility which often places thousands of miles between generations, many women in nuclear families experience personal isolation and vulnerability.

According to recent studies, assault on wives or female partners constitutes 76 percent of family violence, and is responsible for 20 percent of all homicides in Canada.[2] Of these victims the vast majority are women murdered by their spouses or common-law partners, most often in their kitchens or bedrooms. The view which many Canadians have inherited about the "sanctity" of the home (the "Englishman's-home-is-his-castle" viewpoint) has often been used to prevent "interference," i.e., to prevent friends and others outside the nuclear family coming to the assistance of battered women and children.

Turning to the issue of nuclear violence (actual in what is happening to South Pacific islanders whose homes and food sources have been devastated by French and American nuclear testing; potential in relation to the 50,000 nuclear warheads presently in place), we find that the same unredeemed attitudes which threaten women and children in their homes are threatening all of us who live on this fragile earth, our island home in God's universe. At present, Canada's membership in NATO is understood by our government as committing us to the immoral readiness, under given circumstances, to cooperate with our allies in the incineration of millions of children, women and men in the Soviet bloc; to risk the destruction of the ozone layer, and with it the death of the animals and birds; to risk the end of human civilization as we have known it; in the meantime to raise a generation of children many of whom (as revealed in school surveys) do not expect to live into adulthood: and all this in the name of "national security." The parallel with the "sanctity of the home" viewpoint is obvious. Like "national security" understood as at present, "domestic security" can brook no interference. But a caution here: national security as a political goal is perfectly legitimate, as is domestic freedom from unwarranted interference. But both become gods, become idols, when there are no limits to what we will do in their name.

With the two major issues of violence identified and far too briefly qualified, fundamental theological questions can now be asked. Why are we linking these microviolent and macroviolent realities? Is this a helpful link, or are we trying to mix apples and oranges? What is our biblical anthropology (view of humanity) of violence? Is there something in human nature which inevitably moves us to violence, or is it our culture which has corrupted us? Is it, in brief, nature or nurture? And where can we find a comprehensive answer to the question asked by James the Apostle, "What causes wars, and what causes fightings among you?" (James 4.1).

For me there is profound meaning in the biblical story of creation and fall. This story (really a complex of stories) locates the beginning of violence in a fundamental dislocation between humankind and God which is *at the same time* disruption between the sexes. In Genesis 2, often overlooked, we have a brief glimpse of original innocence, of woman and man both made (as we learn from Genesis 1) in God's image, and living together in tranquillity. Then in Genesis 3 we find both of them disobeying God and disrupting their own relationship in so doing. This alienation is followed quickly by the account of the first murder, in Genesis 4, and later in that chapter by the readiness of Cain's descendant, Lamech, to work mass destruction on his enemies. By the time of Lamech, in fact, the nature-nurture question has already become a chicken-and-egg question. On our part, we simply have to recognize that violence ever since has had both a personal and a social aspect.

These ancient and powerful accounts of marital recrimination and sibling rivalry are stories through which our spiritual ancestors accounted for the violence they experienced. They portray a cosmic breakdown of the trust-relationship in which men and women were intended to live with God, a relation of communion and the sharing of power. From these stories emerges an image of violence as a continuum of alienation passing back and forth through the human heart. On that continuum domestic and nuclear violence then differ basically in the scope of the damage they may cause. In other words, violence is one terrible reality, a mystery of evil in which the dislocation of the sexes holds a critical place. Adam is estranged from Eve, and Eve from Adam.

God's eternal response to this mystery of evil was made, we believe, in the restoration of humanity's relationship with God through Christ, New Adam (I Corinthians 15.22, 45), in whom there is neither male nor female *as opposing entities* (Galatians 3.28). Yet a gap remains between the kingdom that has already come through Christ, and the kindom for the coming of which we continue to pray. Thus, in terms of sexual stereotypes, for example, we continue to oppose masculine and feminine, forgetting that their unity has been restored in Christ. We say that women are more in touch with their need to express feelings, and so we ignore this capacity in men. We say that more men are ready to act assertively, in their own strength, to meet life-needs, and so we ignore this capacity in women. We have to take all our images of femininity and masculinity, in fact, to make up one whole person. If then the church was birthing and raising such whole persons, adults combining in themselves the gentleness and strength of Jesus, and if such adults took leadership among us, would not war begin to wither away? Are not the women of the peace camp at Greenham Common in England pointing to this connection between our damaged sexual identity and nuclear violence when they cry, "Take the toys away from the boys!"?

The synod responded to the presentations and discussion by passing resolutions 45 (on domestic violence), 46 (requesting a theological statement on the equality of men and women) and 11 (on war and peace, with a focus on nuclear concerns), together with resolutions on such specific issues as chemical and biological warfare.[3]

Violence and the Agenda of the Local Church

Resolutions passed by national churches, of course, lead only to despair and depression unless they are acted on locally. How then can these resolutions become vehicles of hope and empowerment in the life of the local church, and what might the proper place of the issues they concern be on the local church's agenda?

The whole matter, it seems to me, comes down to a question of spirituality. What kind of person is capable of acting on the scriptural mandate for justice and peacemaking? What kind of wisdom beyond the conventional (James 3.16-18) is *normative* among us? In Jesus, strong and gentle, assertive and caring, whole in his masculinity and femininity, sure and deft in his response to violence (Matthew 21.12-13, 26.47-53; John 8.2-11) we see someone filled with the Spirit we need, we see the *person* of our salvation, our wholeness. The agenda before the church today, then, is how to enter in practical ways into his gentleness and his strength.

This brings us to the question of spiritual formation in the local congregation. How are our members — children, youth, adults — formed into mature Christians able to deal with violence in all its aspects? I envisage a number of contexts in which this can take place: new member classes, baptism preparation, confirmation classes, marriage preparation, parish study programs, ministry teams, home Bible-study groups, parish governing boards or councils, and so on. In all of these contexts I see two essential elements: (1) Bible study of a kind which leads forward into (2) action-reflection leading back into further Bible study. In Bible study we hold up the person of Jesus as the lens through which we examine the rest of scripture. Himself the personal Word, he governs our approach to the scriptural Word. The passages mentioned above provide a good place to start; Philippians 2.5-11 is also a critically important passage; and probably the wars of the Old Testament need to be reconsidered by most of us.[4] In action (involvement in peacemaking groups within and beyond the parish; invovement in teams and groups dealing with domestic violence in our local communities) we will test out the insights of our study of scripture. In common reflection on that action with others engaged in the same ministry, we can share the failures and successes we have experienced, and return with them for refreshment to the living waters of the Word.

More specifically, however, let us consider what opportunities for spiritual formation are offered by particular moments in the faith-life cycle.

Consider in the first instance the way we welcome new members into our congregations. Given the current social situation, should we not have "intake" procedures of an intentional kind in place of the ways we currently just let people "come to church" in the rather pathetic hope that they will become "active in the parish"? The apostolic church recognized that certain renunciations were needed by the Gentiles as they entered the Christian community (Acts 15). Is not something similar needed today, when new members may so easily bring with them unredeemed attitudes towards both sexuality and violence? In rough outline, these steps seem appropriate:

(1) identification of those who wish to "join" the church, either through appearing at worship or asking for baptism for a child;

(2) classes for these persons, including at least one residential weekend, during which attitudes to sexuality and to violence would be explored, and the nature of the church as a community of love and peacemaking made clear;

(3) personal sessions of a quasi-confessional or confessional kind, with a trained lay person or priest as appropriate, in which identified negative attitudes could be renounced, at least in principle; and

(4) a public, non-sacramental welcoming of these persons into the life of the congregation in an act of worship which would also make clear the community's commitment to justice and peace.[5]

A second such opportunity is Christian Initiation (sacramental, that is, in contrast to the congregational initiation described above). Parents (of child-candidates for baptism) who had not previously been members of the congregation would have been introduced to the process of spiritual formation by the approaches described in the last paragraph, approaches which assume that baptism of children does not take place until their parents have been integrated or re-integrated into the congregation. They would then join with other parents who were already members of the congregation, with adult candidates for baptism, and with personal and parish sponsors, in baptism preparation sessions. Contemporary baptismal liturgies contain specific promises of commitment to peace and justice, and so provide excellent kick-off points for discussion of the spirituality and the practicalities of ministry. These sessions naturally need to be dovetailed with whatever preparation the congregation offers to adults making a first profession of faith (in the Anglican tradition, confirmation, which is now increasingly seen as public, personal and adult profession of faith in Christ). Adult profession/confirmation gives the local church the opportunity to present this public celebration of maturity in Christ as a commitment to a ministry in which a concern for sexual wholeness and for issues of violence find a prominent place. These classes or sessions also give the parish a chance to work on these issues with those who have grown up in the church as well as with those just coming in.

A third such opportunity is marriage preparation. Although I have been active in this ministry for ten years, it was not until I was personally involved in preparing for the 1983 General Synod presentation that I realized the urgency of the need to raise the issue of domestic violence with *every couple* coming to the parish for the blessing of their marriage. In encountering individual cases of family violence, I had thought of them as individual situations, and had not related them to the wider social reality. Thus, for an adequate and church-wide response to this issue, we have to ask how clergy can be introduced to the broader picture, and helped to become competent and comfortable in raising the issue with the couples coming to them to be married. We must further ask what needs to happen in terms of theological education and denominational requirements for ordination to make this competence a norm among new clergy. Marriage preparation programs, preferably lay-led, must also include an opportunity for couples to confront the issue in a peer setting. With input from both pastor and program, a couple's chance of recognizing the importance of the issue is much increased, and with that recognition their chance of avoiding violence in their marriage.

In other parish contexts, study programs need to be offered which will provide opportunities for church members to struggle with some hard questions, among them the following. What implications does the connection between our damaged sexual identity and violence have for the spiritual formation and re-formation/healing of children, youth and adults in our parishes? What, specifically, are we doing to provide positive linkages of sexuality and faith for our children and teens? How are we helping persons of all ages in our congregation to deal with their fears of nuclear annihilation? How are we helping people to activate their personal power as power-with rather than power-over?[6] Have we adhered to a theology that in effect blames Eve more than Adam for the fall, that therefore downplays women's equal reception of the divine image, and that therefore in a subtle way justifies domestic violence? Are there, in the life of our congregation, structures or customs that reinforce the inequality of women? Conversely, are there things we could do which would enhance the equal participation of women and men in our parish life? An honest facing of these questions can lead us to both repentance and renewal: repentance of the tacit ways in which we have condoned both violence against women and the increasing threat of nuclear violence; and renewal of the educational, sacramental, legislative and minstering structures of our community life in a spirit of inclusiveness, equality, reconciliation and commitment to peace-and-justice ministry as normative for Christians.

I stress that I am not saying that the whole answer to the nuclear question depends on a resolution of the sexual question, nor that the ministry of reconciliation entrusted to the church can be completely carried out on the local level. But in the long run, we will know we are moving in the right direction when at any level Adam and Eve come together again in Christ, and when redemption replaces fall as our primary image both of the woman-man relationship and the God-world relationship. When men recover their capacity for intimacy and gentleness and women their capacity for assertiveness and strength, and when such women and men take leadership within and among the nations, we will be on our way to Shalom, to the city of God's peace.

NOTES

1 "Feminism and Peace," *Christian Century*, C, No. 25 (August 31-September 7, 1983) p. 774.
2 *Wife Assault in Canada*, obtainable from Support Services for Assaulted Women, 427 Bloor Street West, Toronto, Ont. M5S 1X7.
3 Complete texts of these resolutions, together with comparable statements of the Lutheran, Presbyterian, Roman Catholic and United Churches of Canada, and the Canadian Council of Churches, are obtained from Project Ploughshares, Conrad Grebel College, Waterloo, Ont. N2L 3G6.
4 On this, a most helpful book for group leaders is Millard Lind, *Yahweh is a Warrior* (Kitchener, Ontario: Herald Press, 1980).
5 For more on this, see A. T. Eastman, *The Baptizing Community* (New York: Seabury, 1982).
6 On these last two questions, see Joanna Rogers Macy, *Despair and Personal Power in the Nuclear Age* (Philadelphia: New Society Publishers, 1983).

Appendix

Marjorie and Cyril Powles:
A Critical Biographical Sketch

Terry Brown

Marjorie Agnes Watson, elder of two daughters of Agnes McKnight and Mark Harrison Watson, was born on July 28, 1913 in Saskatoon, Saskatchewan. Both her parents were part of the Canadian-American prairie culture of the early twentieth century that paid little attention to the international boundary. Her mother was born in Kirkwall, Ontario (near Galt), but came to live with her aunt in North Dakota where she worked in a private land titles office. Marjorie's father, whose own family had come from England and Quebec, was born and grew up on a farm in Minnesota. He met Marjorie's mother in North Dakota where he was collecting accounts for a coal and lumber firm. They were married in Kirkwall and returned to Minnesota where Marjorie's father continued to work in the coal and lumber business. Shortly before Marjorie's birth, the family moved to Saskatoon, where her father was employed by the Winnipeg Paint and Glass Company. Soon after Marjorie's birth, the family moved to Winnipeg where her father first continued to work for the same company, then left to establish his own wholesale lumber business, the Watson Lumber Company.

Marjorie was educated in the public schools of Winnipeg where, according to her sister Florence, she was an excellent student and a leader amongst her friends. The family home was frequently full of company — friends and family from the country, visiting lumbermen and many others. Marjorie's mother was active in the church, neighbourhood and American Women's Club; the home's social life was somewhat oriented towards the States. The family lived in the West End of Winnipeg in an Anglo-Saxon area about a mile and a half from downtown. Marjorie's mother came from a Presbyterian background, her father from a Methodist one; the family worshiped at the Home Street Presbyterian (later United) Church, where Marjorie taught Sunday school, led a Canadian Girls in Training group and was active in the Mission Group.

Both Marjorie's parents influenced her early interest in social justice. She recalls her mother's refusal to blackball a prospective Jewish member of the American Women's Club and the controversy which followed. She remembers her father's stories of growing up poor in Minnesota. The family's associations cut across religious and cultural barriers. Her father had Jewish and Francophone business associates and his own mother was brought up in a Roman Catholic family.

Marjorie began attending the University of Manitoba at the age of 16, moving on after two years to Wesley College (now the University of Winnipeg) where she majored in English. For several summers she worked with James Shaver at All People's Mission which, shaped by J. S. Woodsworth, ministered to large numbers of new immigrants in the North End of Winnipeg. This work provided a broader exposure to life outside West End Winnipeg. Watson family politics were Liberal; Marjorie openly argued against her father and his opposition to the socialist Co-operative Commonwealth Federation. While at university, Marjorie also became involved with the Student Christian Movement. She graduated from Wesley College with a B.A. in 1934, in the middle of the depression.

As the degree was of little use in finding a job, Marjorie enrolled in a short business course in shorthand and typing at the Angus Business College and was employed by her father as his secretary. The business, which depended on commissions earned from selling railroad cars of lumber, was badly affected by the depression but survived. Marjorie continued to be active in a graduate group of the SCM and All People's Mission. Her interest in ministry grew and she began to make plans to attend Covenant College (the United Church training college in Toronto, now a part of the Centre for Christian Studies). However, her father suffered a heart attack and Marjorie chose to stay in Winnipeg a couple more years, running the business for him. Her efficiency and business acumen were recognized and her father would have been happy for her to take over the firm. Finally in 1942 she moved to Toronto where she attended Covenant College for a year, also taking courses at Emmanuel College. Upon graduation she moved to Montreal where she served as SCM Secretary at McGill University from 1943 to 1946, while continuing to take theology courses at Divinity Hall. In 1945 her assistant was a young Anglican priest, Cyril Powles.

Cyril Hamilton Powles, eldest of the three sons and three daughters of Percival Samuel Carson Powles and Beatrice Ruth Mount, was born on September 1, 1918, in the mountain resort of Karuizawa, Japan, in the summer home of the Canadian bishop of Mid-Japan, Heber J. Hamilton. His parents had arrived a few years earlier as Missionary Society of the Church of England in Canada (MSCC) missionaries in the Canadian-affiliated Diocese of Mid-

Japan and had just completed their Japanese language training. Cyril's father was of Montreal working-class stock, who were proud of having in Canada for the first time owned land; before coming to Japan he had served a short incumbency at St. Cuthbert's, Montreal, and had decidedly Evangelical leanings. Before coming to Japan, Cyril's mother had been Latin teacher and vice-principal of West-mount High School in greater Montreal. Soon after Cyril's birth, the family moved to their new permanent mission station, the small city of Takada near the west coast of Japan south of Niigata.

The part of rural Japan in which Cyril grew up was very isolated and as yet little touched by the West. The situation of the people included poverty, malnutrition and disease, particularly tuberculosis and beriberi. Cyril's father travelled up and down the coast with a Japanese co-worker, ministering to small devoted congregations and conducting preaching missions, first with tents and drums, later with magic lantern shows. In an early report of the MSCC activities he gave an account of street preaching in Takada:

> Street preaching of a steady, systematic nature has claimed our evenings during the past year.... A favourite place for preaching is in front of the hot bath, for the people can sit in the bath and listen, and when they come out they are feeling good, and will stay on and listen attentively. I think I know almost every bath in town now, and they are not a few.[1]

The view of mission was a traditional Evangelical one, that measured success by the number of converts. Cyril's father's prematurely white hair and blue eyes excited amazement. He preached in Japanese, after having first had the sermons corrected by his Japanese tutor. As his ministry in Japan progressed, he became more concerned with the physical misery of the people and organized the building of a tuberculosis sanitorium by the diocese.

The home in which Cyril grew up was also very open: visitors included church people, neighbours, other missionaries and Japanese interested in the West. The household always included young Japanese women, sent by their families as part of their education, who performed domestic duties for their keep. Cyril's mother, who oversaw the household, took great personal interest in them. According to household routine, the young women cleaned the house before breakfast; after a formal breakfast, the whole house-hold said family prayers in Japanese, after which the day's work began. Again, after dinner in the evening, the whole household gathered for family prayers. Cyril's mother also organized the women's auxiliary (*Fujin Kai*), sought to make personal contacts in the community and taught piano. She also taught the Powles children at home.

Cyril grew up in a bilingual setting, playing with the children of the Japanese family who rented the porter's lodge of the army officer's residence that the Powles home once had been. Both Cyril's parents were fascinated with Japanese culture. They studied the Japanese tea ceremony, talked with Buddhist priests, and Cyril's mother helped arrange marriages for the young women under her charge. In the end they gave their children a strong double identity, so that when they realized they could not be Japanese, they had something to fall back on. The family was also on good terms with neighbouring Roman Catholic and Methodist missionaries.

The family took a year-long furlough to Canada once every five years. In 1933 Cyril returned to Montreal with his next youngest brother, Bill, to attend high school at Westmount High School, living with an eccentric great uncle and aunt. After graduating from Westmount, they moved into Montreal Diocesan Theological College where they lived while attending McGill University from which Cyril graduated in 1940 with a major in classics. (At McGill, Cyril helped found the McGill Choral Society, the first coeducational group on the McGill campus.) In the meantime, the whole Powles family had come back to Montreal for their regular furlough in 1939. After a year, with war on the horizon, Cyril's father, who had a major financial responsibility for the Diocese of Mid-Japan, returned alone to Japan to clear up finances and sell diocesan property because of the imminence of war. He returned to Canada just before Pearl Harbor.

After graduating from McGill, Cyril enrolled in Montreal Diocesan College. From childhood he had talked of becoming a priest, so the move was not unexpected. He also continued to be active in the McGill SCM where he worked with Marjorie. (They first met at SCM anniversary celebrations in 1941.) The SCM experience, especially the exposure to radical Christianity and participation in student works camps, was formative for both Cyril and Marjorie. In 1943 Cyril graduated from Montreal Diocesan, was made a deacon and appointed curate of St. Matthew's, Hampstead, Montreal; he was ordained a priest a year later. In 1944 Cyril, along with his father, became a founding member of the Anglican Fellowship for Social Action, a group of laity and clergy in the Diocese of Montreal (and later, Nova Scotia) committed to social justice both in the Anglican Church and society at large. AFSA protested the anti-labour policy of the Duplessis government and advocated in Montreal diocesan synods a basic stipend for clergy and other social justice issues, to the annoyance of the Bishop of Montreal and the Anglican financial establishment. In the spring of 1945 Cyril left St. Matthew's to become Dean of Residence at Montreal Diocesan College.

In the spring of 1945 the Anglican Church of Canada's national office in Toronto also hired Cyril for six months to survey opportunities for ministry to Japanese-Canadians who had been detained in government relocation camps in western Canada during the war. He travelled across Canada, visiting the camps and seeking groups in eastern Canada (churches, YMCA, YWCA, SCM, etc.) who would sponsor Japanese leaving the camps. He also tried to make the churches more aware of the problem. Marjorie served on the Relocation Committee on Montreal.

The work with Japanese-Canadians made much more real for Cyril the possibility of returning to Japan. As his and Marjorie's relationship deepened, the possibility of their both going to Japan emerged. Because she had worked with West Indians in Montreal, Marjorie had been approached by the World Student Christian Federation to go to Jamaica to help found an SCM group there. However, in the end she chose Cyril and Japan. She wanted to go somewhere outside Canada and was happy to choose Japan, particularly because she would be going with someone, rather than alone. Marjorie and Cyril became engaged in January, 1946. Soon after, Marjorie joined AFSA.

Cyril and Marjorie were married at All Saints Church, Winnipeg, on June 29, 1946. At the time it was unthinkable that the wife of a young Anglican priest could remain in the United Church, so Marjorie was confirmed in the Anglican Church. They returned to Montreal Diocesan College where Cyril now became the first married Dean of Residence. In the year that followed, they began preparing for their move to Japan. Cyril's parents had already returned to Japan. (During the War, Cyril's father had served as priest-in-charge of the Hebrew Mission and as chaplain of St. Andrew's Mission, a social service institution for immigrants, both in Montreal. In 1948, after his return to Japan, he was elected Suffragan Bishop in Mid-Japan.)

In looking at Cyril's and Marjorie's years in Japan it is clear that, although both were officially designated as missionaries, in the eyes of many in both the Canadian and Japanese churches, Cyril was the missionary to Japan, Marjorie was his wife. The church's patriarchal character, Cyril's superior language ability and theological training and the semi-cultic mystique around the Powles family in the Dioceses of Mid-Japan all contributed to making Cyril's and Marjorie's ministry to Japan a somewhat patriarchal one, at least initially.

Before leaving for Japan, Marjorie and Cyril spent the 1947-48 school year at Harvard, where, financed by the MSCC, both studied Japanese language and culture. There, too, they became friends with F. Hastings Smyth, Superior of the Cambridge-based Anglo-Catholic Marxist religious community, the Society of the Catholic Commonwealth, a group which both joined in 1948 and which became an important part of their ministry to Japan. (Both had met Smyth previously when he was a speaker at the AFSA summer conferences in Arundel, Quebec. Smyth, however, came to regard

AFSA as insufficiently radical politically and insufficiently Catholic theologically. With the formation of a SCC cell in Montreal in the spring of 1948, AFSA forced its members to choose between the two groups. Those who chose the SCC were expelled from AFSA. In joining the SCC the Powles were forced out of AFSA) Along with the SCM, the SCC was a formative influence on Cyril's and Marjorie's thinking.

Both Cyril and Marjorie were also involved in work with Japanese youth, running summer work camps in Nojiri and establishing a Japanese cell of the SCC. Cyril also became involved with the peace movement in Japan. When the British exploded their first atomic bomb on Christmas Island in 1956, Cyril worked with other missionaries to organize a petition, circulated among British-connected Cyril's anonymous writings on the Japanese Church in the *Anglican Outlook* would anger his own father.

In 1949, Marjorie, Cyril and their newly-born son, John, moved to Japan, to the same isolated area of the Diocese of Mid-Japan in which Cyril had spent his childhood. Japan was still suffering great difficulty from the war: poverty, malnutrition, starvation, primitive living conditions and social unrest were all common. Japan was still occupied by the U.S. Army, political activity (especially on the left) was restricted and overseas mail was censored. The population was demoralized and the situation in the church unsettled. There were bad feelings between those who had cooperated with and those who had opposed the Japanese government during the war.

In the three parishes in which they first served (the last of which was the pro-cathedral in Nagoya), Cyril and Marjorie continued much of the work of Cyril's parents, though with the strengthening of Japanese leadership in the diocese, their work in parishes became more problematic. In the fifties both of them began struggling with the question of just what was the role of western missionaries in the Japanese Church. Cyril was under considerable pressure to allow himself to be elected a bishop, but both he and Marjorie resisted. Cyril took on more and more of the advisory and administrative duties of his father; he took an active role in the revision of the Japanese liturgy (following SCC principles) and eventually became the senior Anglican missionary, responsible for Canadian Anglican missionaries working in Japan. Marjorie taught English in both church and government schools. In 1952 they adopted Peter, an Anglo-Japanese child, as their second son.

Both Cyril and Marjorie were also involved in work with Japanese youth, running summer work camps in Nojiri and establishing a Japanese cell of the SCC.Cyril also became involved with the peace movement in Japan. When the British exploded their first atomic bomb on Christmas Island in 1956, Cyril worked with other missionaries to organize a petition, circulated among British-connected nationals, protesting the test to the British government. This came to the attention of Japanese peace groups and Cyril was nominated to the executive of *Gen-sui Kyō*, the umbrella Japanese peace organization.

Many of these activities increased the pressure on Cyril and Marjorie to stay in Japan and upon Cyril to move up to the episcopate. Yet, as any westerner who lives in Japan discovers, the Japanese attitude towards westerners who try to identify with Japanese culture is ambivalent. On the one hand, Japanese culture in all its subtlety and complexity is very ethnocentric: it is virtually impossible for non-Japanese (including mixed-race Japanese and Koreans and Chinese born in Japan) to be accepted as Japanese. No matter how well they knew the language and culture, there was no chance of Cyril's and Marjorie's ever being accepted as Japanese. On the other hand, the Japanese church felt (and, indeed, still feels) deep appreciation for western missionaries such as the Powles who have made the sacrifice of learning Japanese and living many many years in Japan — an appreciation sometimes developing into an unhealthy dependence and submissiveness. The Powles had to deal with very ambivalent attitudes of Japanese towards themselves as western missionaries in Japan — sharp criticism mixed with submission. The submission was often particularly linked with loyalty to Cyril's father, further frustrating their efforts to introduce new ideas into the Japanese church.

In 1958 Cyril was appointed Professor of Church History at Central Theological College, Tokyo, the principal institution for training *Nippon Seikokai* (the Anglican Church in Japan) clergy. (Cyril had spent 1953-54 at Trinity College, Toronto, where he gained a S.T.B., writing a thesis on "The Relation of Penitence to Oblation in the Eucharistic Offertory." In 1959-60 he finished his M.A. at Harvard while Marjorie took courses at Harvard Divinity School.) The move to Tokyo represented a shift in the Powles' view of the role of the western missionary in Japan — a shift from working in a position that any Japanese priest could hold, to working in a highly specialized one in which a westerner might have special expertise. Both Marjorie and Cyril were much happier in Tokyo. Cyril's duties were much more clearly defined. Many visitors passed through, both from other parts of Japan and overseas, and the Powles home became a hotel. Their lifestyle also improved — for the first time in Japan, they had a flush toilet.

It should be emphasized that although the church tended to see Cyril as the missionary and Marjorie as his wife, Cyril and Marjorie envisioned their ministry as a partnership. There was constant dialogue going on (as now!) between Marjorie and Cyril on political, theological, ecclesiastical and other issues. Sometimes the disagreement was quite sharp. (Marjorie with her analytic mind and United

Church background was quicker to appreciate the theological developments of the sixties than Cyril.) Although Marjorie was forced to
stay in the background because of the expectations of Japanese
culture, her forceful critique of Cyril's thought (or more correctly,
their dialogue) greatly shaped Cyril's ministry. She also led discussion groups on Christianity, social issues and theology for various
women's groups. During these years, both Cyril and Marjorie were
particularly critical of the developing "economic miracle" of post-
war capitalist Japan, fearing the resurgence of militarism. They
sought to instill in students and co-workers a critical attitude
towards capitalism, competitiveness, militarism, and a positive view
of Marxist analysis and the economic dimensions of Christianity.

With the move to the theological college in Tokyo, the problem of
the role of western missionaries in Japan did not go away. The
Powles' ambivalence about their ministry in Japan increased. The
sixties saw calls for a moratorium on western missionaries in non-
western countries and critiques of the inherently imperialistic character of Christian mission from many parts of the church. Cyril put
forward his own view in a paper given in Japanese at a Conference
on the Foreign Missionary sponsored by the National Council of the
Nippon Seikokai in 1966. He remarked,

> The day of the missionary in Japan is long past and the
> Church in this country ought to stop calling missionar-
> ies from abroad. It is bad for the Church and it is bad
> for the missionaries who have been called. After nearly
> twenty years of working as a missionary in Japan I am
> more clearly convinced of this than ever before, and I
> intend from now on to work for the abolition of the
> missionary system.[2]

This view was also Marjorie's; indeed, it was she who consistently
sensed the impermanence of their life in Japan and first saw the
inevitability of their departure. This insight was initially very painful
for Cyril, because of his attachment to Japanese people and the
Japanese church, but in his and Marjorie's *Japan Christian Quarterly*
articles in the sixties, one sees them working out their theological
justification for leaving Japan.

These articles were quite controversial, bringing forth some very
hostile responses from other western missionaries in Japan and from
Japanese Christians. The articles challenged traditional views of
mission and the church. For example, in a 1968 article Marjorie and
Cyril asked, "What then is to be the new face of the Church?" They
answered,

> The borders between Christendom and heathendom,
> even between church and society, will have to be abol-
> ished. The proof-text will not so much be "Go ye" as
> "God so loved the *world*." Proselytizing is a non-

Christian activity (Matthew 23:15). Wherever people
are seen as concerned for the neighbor, even if, as in the
parable of the Good Samaritan, those people happen
to be "non-Christians," there must we be prepared to
see Christ at work.

In this relation, perhaps we ought to rethink our
ideas about church statistics and the vexed question of
lapsed members (*besseki-sha*). Might it be that the
organized church in Japan has been called to act as a
kind of school to train people in the achievement of
autonomous personality? May it be that we need not
regret the "apostasy" of people like Tōsen Shimazaki
or Masamune Hakucho, but rather give thanks that
they were helped in their experience as church
members to attain the kind of *shutaisei* which allowed
them to stand out against the smothering effect of
traditional society? In that case then, the well-known
fact that the churches lose almost as many members
each year as they gain might be regarded as being at
least the partial fulfillment of their mission, rather than
as a failure.[3]

In a final *Japan Christian Quarterly* article before leaving Japan,
Cyril put forward his and Marjorie's final reflections. He wrote that
he felt it was no longer necessary to work "for the abolition of the
classical missionary system" because "its era has already ended and
there is nothing we can do about it except recognize the fact. But
there is some value in recognizing reality. Only sick people live in a
dream world."[4]

The decision to leave Japan was hastened by two years in Vancouver where Cyril completed his doctorate in history at the University of British Columbia and Marjorie taught English to new
Canadians at the Vancouver Vocational Institute. (Cyril's thesis,
"Victorian Missionaries in Japan: The Shiba Sect," was on the early
Canadian Anglican missionary to Japan, Archdeacon A.C. Shaw.
The thesis met resistance from conservative academics who doubted
that such a thing as Japanese history existed.) The student revolution
was underway at UBC and Marjorie and Cyril supported it. The
time in Vancouver initiated a period of "loosening" for Cyril; he
finally began to wear non-clerical dress extensively. The time away
from Japan made for increased objectivity about the situation there.
When they returned to Japan in 1968, Cyril continued at Central
Theological College. The experience at UBC was helpful in another
way. The CTC students had their own revolution and went on strike.
The College was closed down for a year and Cyril was given the job
of helping to reorganize it.

In 1970 Marjorie and Cyril left Japan permanently for Toronto, where Cyril took a one-year appointment as Visiting Professor of Church History at Trinity College. During the second year, Trinity made the appointment permanent. Japanese Christians who were interested in the international scene were deeply saddened by their departure, seeing themselves as abandoned to sink into the minutiae of Japanese culture. However, by this time Cyril and Marjorie had made very clear their fear that their continued presence in the *Nippon Seikokai* would be harmful to the life of the church. The time of making the decision to leave was very stressful, especially for Cyril; he suffered serious attacks of asthma. The attacks lessened and eventually disappeared with the return to Canada.

Perhaps because of the many trips back and forth to Canada over the previous twenty years and the intensely urban quality of life in Tokyo, Marjorie and Cyril had little difficulty readjusting to life in Toronto. After several weeks of exploring Toronto's Anglican parishes, they settled on Holy Trinity Church in downtown Toronto as their parish church. (Under Jim Fisk, who was then rector, the parish had acquired a reputation for radicalism and rebelliousness centred around the Eucharist.) Marjorie began working with the Centre for Christian Studies and became involved in literacy work. At Trinity College Cyril specialized in Third World Christianity and Christian Social Thought, developing a model for learning in which students not only listened to lectures but, through involvement with Third World and social justice coalitions, participated in the subject matter as well. Eventually Cyril was cross-appointed to the Departments of History, Religious Studies and East Asian Studies in the University of Toronto. He also continued his post-doctoral research on the Emperor System in Japan.

Both Cyril and Marjorie continued to be involved in a large number of Third World and social justice organizations and coalitions such as the Canada-China Program, Hiroshima-Nagasaki Relived, the Ecumenical Forum and the Centre for Christian Studies. Cyril has also worked with the Canadian Urban Training program and the Downtown Church Workers Association while Marjorie has worked with the Canadian Council of Churches and the national board of the SCM.

In 1978 Cyril was elected bishop of Tohoku, one of the poorest and most isolated dioceses of the *Nippon Seikokai*, a position which he refused. In 1979 Cyril and Marjorie travelled to China, spending much time with K.H. Ting and his wife Guo Siu May, whom they knew well from Montreal SCM days. The next year Marjorie returned to China, as an invited delegate, on an extensive Canadian Council of Churches tour. They have also been enthusiastic visitors to Cuba and supporters of the revolution there.

In 1980 and 1983 Marjorie was elected to the Ministry Committee of General Synod of the Anglican Church of Canada and has been responsible for formulating a church position on professional lay ministry. She has also worked actively with the Women's Unit of the Anglican Church of Canada. Both she and Cyril were early supporters of the ordination of women (Marjorie wrote an article advocating it in 1953) and have been influenced in recent years by the Christian feminist critique of the patriarchal character of the church and much of Christian belief. Both have sought to support women theological students at Trinity College and the Toronto School of Theology in their struggle against sexism in the church.

In this short sketch of Marjorie and Cyril I have concentrated on issues rather than personalities since that has been their own approach. Indeed, because of their concern with social justice, they have been able to befriend the marginalized and rejected, offering support and acceptance to those whom others have rejected. They have been successful in this ministry because they have experienced marginalization themselves, first as *gaijin* (foreigners) in Japan, then as returned missionaries, strangers in their own land. Yet, in spite of the alienation they feel in Canada, their life here (as in Japan) has been one of hospitality, good humour, joy, openness and warmth. They clearly enjoy life — whether friends, family, food and wine, travel, the summer cottage or the Eucharist at Holy Trinity. Consistently they have brought others — particularly the outsider and the powerless — into their joy and into the work of bringing about a just church and a just world.

NOTES

1   W.E. Taylor, *Our Church at Work: Canada and Overseas*, 3rd edition, (Toronto: Missionary Society of the Church of England in Canada, [c. 1920]), p.119.
2   Cyril Powles, "The Church and the World," *Japan Christian Quarterly*, July 1966, p.215.
3   Marjorie and Cyril Powles, "The End of an Era: Further Thoughts on the Church and Mission," *JCQ*, Winter, 1968, p.41.
4   Cyril Powles, "Some Final Thought on the End of an Era," *JCQ*, Summer, 1970, p.197.

List of Contributors

Gregory Baum teaches in the Department of Religious Studies, St. Michael's College, University of Toronto.

Ernest E. Best teaches in the Department of Religious Studies, Victoria College, University of Toronto.

Bill Bosworth is Director of Homes First, a project of the Fred Victor Mission in Toronto providing housing for single displaced persons.

Pauline Bradbrook is a graduate student in New Testament at Trinity College, Toronto School of Theology.

Terry Brown is a doctoral candidate in Church History at Trinity College, Toronto School of Theology, and formerly taught at Bishop Patteson Theological Centre, Solomon Islands, on behalf of the Anglican Church of Canada.

Arturo Chacón is a missionary in Chile on behalf of the United Church of Canada.

Lee Cormie teaches in the Faculty of Theology, St. Michael's College, Toronto School of Theology.

Mary Rose D'Angelo teaches New Testament at St. Thomas Seminary, Denver.

James G. Endicott is editor of the *Canadian Far Eastern Newsletter* and the subject of a recent biography, *James G. Endicott: Rebel out of China*, University of Toronto Press, 1980.

Donald Grayston is rector of All Saints Anglican Church, Burnaby, B.C. and the author of *Thomas Merton: The Development of a Spiritual Theologian*, Edwin Mellen Press, 1984.

Stephen Hopkins is Programme Consultant in Training and Education in the Anglican Diocese of Toronto and formerly staff to the Coordinating Committee of the Single Displaced Persons Project, Toronto.

John F. Howes teaches Japanese history in the Department of Asian Studies, University of British Columbia, Vancouver.

Donna Hunter is General Secretary of the Women's Inter-Church Council of Canada, Toronto.

Roger Hutchinson teaches in the Department of Religious Studies, Victoria College, University of Toronto.

Joy Kogawa is a Canadian poet and the author of the award-winning novel *Obasan*.

Brad Lennon is rector of All Saints Anglican Church, Toronto.

Christopher Lind is a doctoral candidate in theology and social ethics at Trinity College, Toronto School of Theology.

David Montgomery is Supervisor of the Men's Hostel, Fred Victor Mission, Toronto.

Yuzo Ota teaches in the Department of History, McGill University, Montreal.

Willard G. Oxtoby teaches in the Department of Religious Studies, Trinity College, University of Toronto.

Virginia A. Peacock is a priest at St. Michael and All Angels Anglican Church, Toronto, and a doctoral candidate in theology and ethics, St. Michael's College, Toronto School of Theology.

Ronald Preston is Emeritus Professor of Social and Pastoral Theology, University of Manchester.

John Rowe works as a maintenance electrician in a brewery in the East End of London where from 1956 to 1984 he was a worker-priest.

Jeanne Rowles is Consultant of Women's Concerns and Director of Social Action Ministries, Anglican Church of Canada.

Brian Ruttan is a priest at Grace Church (Anglican), St. Catharines, Ont., and a doctoral candidate in theology and ethics at St. Michael's College, Toronto School of Theology.

Reiko Shimada is General Secretary of the Nagoya, Japan, YWCA.

Janet Silman is a doctoral candidate in theology and ethics at Emmanuel College, Toronto School of Theology.

John Takeda is Principal of Central Theological College, Tokyo.

Don Thompson is Director of Academics, Centre for Christian Studies, Toronto.

Elizabeth Wensley is a chaplain at Humber Memorial Hospital, Toronto.

Raymond L. Whitehead is Director of the Doctor of Ministry programme of the Toronto School of Theology.

Rhea M. Whitehead is Asia and Pacific Secretary for the United Church of Canada.